Collaborative Writing as Inquiry

Collaborative Writing as Inquiry

Edited by

Jane Speedy and Jonathan Wyatt

**CAMBRIDGE
SCHOLARS**

P U B L I S H I N G

Collaborative Writing as Inquiry,
Edited by Jane Speedy and Jonathan Wyatt

This book first published 2014

Cambridge Scholars Publishing

12 Back Chapman Street, Newcastle upon Tyne, NE6 2XX, UK

British Library Cataloguing in Publication Data
A catalogue record for this book is available from the British Library

ISBN (10): 1-4438-5540-5, ISBN (13): 978-1-4438-5540-2

TABLE OF CONTENTS

Epilogue

INTRODUCTION

What this book is about

This is a new and overdue contribution to the recently burgeoning literature of writing as a branch of qualitative inquiry (Richardson, 2000; Richardson & St. Pierre, 2005; etc.). Much has been written about writing as inquiry, not least by Laurel Richardson who originally coined the phrase 'writing as inquiry'; collaborative writing as inquiry, however, the intersection between participatory/democratic inquiry methods and creative and arts-based writing approaches remains an under-published and under-researched, yet vibrant and emergent inquiry space. Where publications in this field do exist they tend to be collaboratively written books that adhere to a particular approach (e.g. Davies & Gannon, 2006; Gale et al., 2012; Clandinin et al., 2007) or lack a literary and arts-informed practice and/or self-consciously transparent interest in process.

This book has been generated by the myriad collaborative writing groups that have emerged from the interdisciplinary research centre for narrative inquiry (NIC) within the Graduate School of Education, University of Bristol. The NIC has an international reputation for, and interest in, both writing as a form of inquiry and, specifically, collaborative and participatory research methods. This book places a diversity of approaches to collaborative writing alongside each other and explores these methods and the spaces between them as critical arts-based inquiry practices within the social sciences. It is not intended or written as any kind of a handbook, more of a scrapbook, containing summative and rich prologues to each section, and substantive chapters (some adapted from work previously published in international peer-reviewed journals), fragments and snippets of 'writing in progress' as well as more extensive excursions into a range of approaches to writing collaboratively, including: collective biography; call and response (to people, to landscapes and to 'what happens' in the writing spaces); 'take three words'; poetic writing; writing in scholarly communities and/or on retreat and writing between various twos and threes in a range of ways). This book seeks to illuminate but also to investigate and interrogate these emergent spaces, particularly as a critical gesture towards the individualised, market-driven agendas and neo-liberal practices of the contemporary academy.

How we wrote this book

The various chapters in the book were constructed by different collaborative writing groups associated with NIC between 2005 and 2013 and comprise much of what is unique and distinctive about that centre's particular, and particularly European, contribution to the expansion of the social/narrative imaginary; to qualitative inquiry methods and about what it means to 'inquire'. The majority of these writers were either University staff or students associated with NIC, with the exception of Susanne Gannon, one of the authors of Chapter 23 'Inquiring into Red/ Red Inquiring', a visiting fellow from the University of Western Sydney to NIC during 2012, and Tami Spry, one of the authors of 'Collaborative Writing in Real Time': a visiting professor to the centre during 2011. NIC has benefitted greatly from the time and energy given by visiting scholars to the centre: we have also benefitted during the time we were producing this book, from generous long or short-term visits by Cathy Riessman (Boston College University); Jean Clandinin (University of Alberta); Elyse Pineau (Southern Illinois University, Carbondale) and Bronwyn Davies (Melbourne University) all of whom, particularly Cathy Riessman and Bronwyn Davies, our visiting Benjamin Meaker professors, have contributed directly to the spirit of narrative, collaborative inquiry and to the particular commitments to writing as a form of scholarship that NIC engenders.

Some of these contributions such as 'Friend and Foe' (Chapter 20) and 'Remembering and Forgetting with Sue' (Chapter 15) were written by longstanding communities of scholars who had been writing together for a decade or more; other work was produced by 'one off' groups who came together in the moment, brought together by a particular interest or through the energy created around a particular visiting professor, such as 'Between the Four' (Chapter 18).

Once most of these chapters had been produced the process of collaboratively gathering and bringing together these texts into an interrelated body of work began. A group of nine scholars: Laurinda Brown, Christine Bell, Nell Bridges, Ken Gale, Mike Gallant, Ying-Lin Hung, Ann Rippin, Artemi Sakellariadis and Jane Speedy, went away together on a long weekend's writing retreat at the Ammerdown Centre—a retreat centre in rural Somerset, just outside Bath, nestled amidst wild flower meadows, next-door to a Georgian stately home—a worthy setting for a Jane Austen novel, never mind a collaborative writing retreat[1]. At that first weekend retreat in 2010, we planned which pieces of our existing writing were going into this book and wrote some of the pieces that we saw as missing, including material for 'Retreating out of our Selves' (Chapter 2) and 'Collaborative Writing from our Bodies' (Chapter 16). After that retreat we gave ourselves a year to fulfil various book producing tasks and then planned another retreat in order to compile the various section prologues. However, in November 2011, Jane Speedy, the research centre coordinator, suffered a massive stroke, which brought a number of our centre's projects, including this publishing project, to rather an abrupt halt. After Jane came out of hospital in 2012, we began to grapple with this venture again and in the early summer of 2013 we finally organised our second 'editing and collating' writing retreat at Ammerdown with another, overlapping, group of six scholarly collaborative writers: Davina Kirkpatrick, Sue Porter, Artemi Sakellariadis, Jane Speedy, Jonathan Wyatt and Tessa Wyatt. This second group set themselves the two tasks of integrating a more recently produced group of collaboratively written texts into the book and writing prologues to all the sections of this book, together with the epilogue.

How we conceptualise and position our work

This book represents collaborative writing as inquiry by both exploring and modelling the process of working collaboratively and presenting examples of collaborative work. This is reflected in the joint authorship and the editorship of texts.

The authors of this book represent a multiplicity of different voices in terms of identities, but also of cognitive disciplines, training, positionality, and theoretical and philosophical allegiances. Disciplines and professional practices represented, for example, include counselling and therapy, the creative and performative arts, education, business and management, social work and policy, psychology and medicine. The book goes beyond the espoused interdisciplinarity of much academic work, where the various disciplines are represented, each informing an area of inquiry. This book comprises a collaboratively produced series of texts in which the writing comes from embodied authors, each situated in a disciplinary area but contributing to a fully integrated end 'product', a

---

[1] Ammerdown features throughout this book, appearing as context, landscape, space, background—or, better, collaborator—for and in much of this writing.

text in which no disciplinary claim for ownership can be made for any one part. The texts are all situated within the overarching genre of narrative inquiry, giving attention particularly to the juxtapositions of time, space and relationships that Clandinin et al. (2007) would describe as the 'commonplaces' of narrative inquiry, and including different notions of mythical, autobiographical, fictional time and the reflective uses of hindsight as illustrated by Freeman (1998, 2010). Much of this writing sits comfortably within poststructuralist/feminist systems of thought, although humanist philosophers and researcher activists such as Buber (1970) and Marshall & Reason (2007) are also cited by some. Deleuzian concepts, particularly in relation to nomadic writing and rhizomatic research methods (Deleuze & Guattari, 1988), are the main underpinning of the chapters by Wyatt and Gale and their ideas are scattered throughout these chapters, as are references to Derrida (1992, 1994, 2003) and Cixous's foundational work on writing, difference and experimentation in liminal spaces. With Cixous (1986, 1993) we recognise the embodied, and sexual, nature of language itself, whilst (also with her) recognising the inadequacy of this. Kristeva's (1984) work on poetic language weaves its way throughout this collection and in particular her work on abjection and the powers of horror we ascribe to our bodies (1984) has also been important in texts exploring the embodied nature of writing. All of which brings us to the huge, often unacknowledged influence on this kind of research of African American womanist/feminist experimental writing into (for instance) the inadequacies of using the master's tools (language) to dismantle the master's house (Lorde, 1984) and to develop a poetics of the people (Jordan, 1995).

Possibly the most influential works on these writings, in qualitative research terms, have been Laurel Richardson and Elizabeth St Pierre's texts on writing as a method of inquiry (e.g. Richardson, 1990, 1997, 1999, 2000, 2002; Richardson & St Pierre, 2005) and St Pierre (1997) and Lather's (1997) work on experimental and nomadic writing practices. The influence of much twentieth and twenty-first century experimental literature from other arts-informed fields can be equally traced in these texts (such as the stories of Angela Carter (1979/2006) and Paul Auster (2002) and the poetry and essays of Alice Walker and Margaret Atwood).

Richardson's insistence on writing as an emergent research method is entirely consonant with the experience of collaborative writing in this group of authors, where writing was shared and sense-making emerged in the collective reading. As the participants wrote in response both to each other's writing and to subsequent reflective conversations about the written text, the inquiry cycle was completed. This cycling between the interior world of the writer and the exterior social world of both the group and the wider environment mirrors the co-operative inquiry approach of Marshall (2007) and Reason and collaborators (see Reason & Bradbury, 2007).

There is also a strongly feminist strand to the theoretical framework for collaborative ways of working within this volume. Several of the groups of writers have, for example, been heavily influenced by the work of feminist memory workers such as the pioneering German scholar Frigga Haug. Haug and her collaborators combined autobiographical approaches with political analysis to critique processes of female sexualisation (Haug, 1987). Others took up this tradition, the most influential being Bronwyn Davies and Susanne Gannon and their collaborators, who have developed a genre of 'collective biography' that can be traced through their feminist work on constructions of girl and womanhood in Australia (Davies & Gannon, 2006).

An important element in this book has been notions of space and place. Several of the examples of collaborative writing are clearly 'emplaced', reflecting the physical locations in which they were produced. Space and place has become a 'hot' topic in much recent social sciences writing, and this is reflected in the text through the influence of Doreen Massey's work with her emphasis on space as "a simultaneity of stories so far" (Massey, 2005, p.9) and place as constituted by an element of 'throwntogetherness' (ibid, p.140), a term which also goes some way to capture the experience of being immersed in a group with a collective pool of lifeworlds and the narratives which compose them. In a similar vein, the influence of Tim Ingold (2007) can also be traced in this book with his conceptualisation of place as a series of enmeshments and entanglements, as lines and threads coming together to constitute our emplacement. The connection between Ingold's metaphor and the lines on our pages that make up our writing is hard to resist.

Our final Ammerdown gathering

The editing and collating group gathered at Ammerdown for a weekend in June 2013. We wrote, between us, on our first evening together:

'Ammerdown' is a newly-formed Dropbox folder that Jane just made, with chairs of various kinds and a flecked brown-ish carpet and a load of electronic gadgets and six bodies, all of which are now inside a rectangular golden electronic folder thing.

We're immersing ourselves in a book, with chapters and parts and titles and thousands of words that I don't feel I know yet. Though what does it mean to know? We're feeling our way in together, fingers on keys, after talking about it for 20 minutes. It feels—I feel—a responsibility, being in this folder within a folder of a book, surrounded by other folders of others' work, waiting to know how and what to write in order to stitch some together and then it all.

Maybe not stitch it together; maybe it's waving at each text, or flying between them with thread; or word baristas sprinkling chocolate powder on some and cinnamon on others.

Coming together, sharing a space, organising
writing, drinking, eating, chatting and doing,
Partaking, thinking, typing, snapshots of events
past and present, in this room, this building and elsewhere
People, in this group, others who were here before, drawing together, finding, exploring texts
Drawing threads together, energy, technology, Dropbox
Weaving a path, structure, typing, exploring holes, pulling at the fabric, stitching together.
Book in six sections:
What are we doing here?
Do I know?
As ever feeling a bit adrift, but quite relaxed. I like being here with the five of you, the six of us.
Us, I like that, us.
Comfortable and stimulating,
like coffee ice cream, with bitter grains to grind between my back teeth,
with a gentle curving bite.
Here to mix and lift, like dough. To turn and fold the chapters, finding ways in, building signposts for those who come to the book. Here to help the raising, spacing the dense texture of enfolded texts written between friends, comrades, colleagues.

Here to make meaning for ourselves, in service of other's meaning making. Lift, twist, expose the grain, open to the air, then crush down again to mix some more.

Here to enact the we-ness of the enterprise, carrying the trust of those absent, the hopes, the fears, the excitement. Making interleaves, like tissue between pages, absorbing the juice of the writing and adding form to dense text.

We are the bookmark, notes scribbled on a page to aid memory by condensing sense...

I keep wanting to suggest getting out the black ink... I suppose I always want to take it back to an embodied making process. Feel more at ease and comfortable with a process I can label drawing rather than writing.

Eek I am here and I'm now 48 and I suppose that means I'm part of the collaborative writing group. Did I not realize I was part of this maybe not, because I'm surprised and delighted to be here and welcomed and part of this wonderful company?

The sound of fingers on keys... and a stopping time is announced and joked about and a need in me to keep on writing not edit... just let the words flow out and be enthused and healthily challenged by the collective focus of fingers on keys, thoughts forming, words forming sentences on screens falling into word documents and then a Dropbox folder to be shared and added to.

I love this, no procrastination just common purpose and energetic intensity and starting... the refrain of a song plays around my head: "food in my belly, a license for my telly and nothing's gonna get me down..."[2]

Ah yes, being in Ammerdown being fed and cared for... is that an integral part of this process, I wonder?

We all found our way here eventually. To Ammerdown, I mean. From Cornwall, Wales, Bristol or Oxford, via Radstock, Midsomer Norton or possibly even Timbuktu, we all eventually got here. We gather together, once more. And as we ask ourselves what we are doing here and what we expect to do over the weekend, I find myself wondering if we are about to have a journey through texts in a manner not too dissimilar to our journeys on country roads this afternoon. Travelling alone or in pairs, revisiting routes that we've taken before or discovering new ones, exploring the familiar and the novel, steering towards a familiar sense of collective arrival.

Here we are doing the grown-up, joined-up, difficult, get-it-all-to-hang-together bits to do with writing. Not the arty-farty let-it-all-hang-down-over-the-sides-of-the-page kind of writing that we leave for the grown-ups to weave into something that makes sense. In collaborative writing groups we often write into some kind of space, but then somebody has to sweep up the space and gather the writing together into a piece of cloth. In Stuart Kelly's interview with the dying novelist Iain Banks in last Saturday's Guardian review[3], Banks said that the trouble with writing

---

[2] Nutini, P. (2009) Pencil full of lead. London: Atlantic Records
[3] http://www.theguardian.com/books/2013/jun/15/iain-banks-the-final-interview

fiction was that it had to make sense, not like real life: real life could be absolutely outrageous, but novelists couldn't get away with that kind of stuff. So what is collaborative writing? Fiction or real life? And why are they different? What if we ended up making some outrageous kind of sense?

There are six of us, probably the right kind of number... any less and we might feel we'd cheated on the collaboration factor; any more and we'd simply be too many. Six is a good number and even I can do all the dividings and multiplyings to do with sixes.

Davina Kirkpatrick, Sue Porter, Artemi Sakellariadis, Jane Speedy,
Jonathan Wyatt and Tessa Wyatt

June 2013

PART I

BEGINNINGS

CHAPTER ONE

PROLOGUE TO PART I

DAVINA KIRKPATRICK, SUE PORTER, ARTEMI SAKELLARIADIS, JANE SPEEDY, JONATHAN WYATT AND TESSA WYATT

Beginning with our beginnings feels oddly perverse. We have just written, or at least placed together, the pieces that will make up the epilogue, so going now to the beginning somehow feels very conventional of us. We do not do conventional very well in this community of scholars, not because we set out to shun convention, but rather because we choose not to feel constrained by it.

Conventional is not a keyword in our lexicon, but we do like and honour the making of our own conventions and rituals.

There are three chapters in this section as well as this prologue: Ken Gale interrogating the simplicity of the notion of virtual 'call and response' writing; Mike Gallant weaving together the zig-zagged, face to face 'call and response' writing that began the weekend retreat at Ammerdown when this book was first planned; and the riff off Laurel Richardson's 'take three words' technique for 'anybody who can string three words together' (http://www.icqi.org/home/workshops/), which a group of us took and played with on the social media site 'Twitter'.

An invisible thread of interconnection between all these beginnings was the mixture of live yeast (in the shape of people who had accumulated experience in the various practices and ways of coming together in collaborative writing communities) and other ingredients for the dough (in the shape of people new to this genre). For the spirit of collaboration to rise there needed to be enough live, wild yeast (a yeast accumulated over the years) in the mix—alongside other fresh new ideas and contributions. All the groups in this book had slightly different ways of working and slightly different beginnings or methods of beginning to meet, write and interconnect, but all had strong commitments (often borne from a politics of experience such as a feminist stance) to non-hierarchical ways of working. All the writings produced by these communities of scholars were forged through methodologies of the heart (Pelias, 2004), whereby spaces were explicitly left for readers to imagine themselves into and between the lives of the writers.

In some groups, mostly face-to-face communities, there was a shared convention to begin with 'chat' about the chosen topic and then to proceed to written text by consensus at a chosen time. Thus, a substantial aspect of the beginnings of these groups is lost to writing in the ephemeral context of 'chat' that nobody thought worth recording at the time. In online communities a certain amount of email chat has also been lost in the ether, but on the whole their workings out, as well as their answers to the questions, both appear in the texts in this section.

This is one of the real ethical dilemmas and pitfalls that people encounter as they talk about their research methodologies—leaving out a lot of what happens, or seems obvious to the cognoscenti, is something that often occurs when people report their research to others. Researchers of everyday life processes, like these collaborative writers, are in the business of 'exoticising everyday life' by making the familiar unfamiliar as much to themselves as others (Myerhoff, 1980). Many research texts involving group and community processes choose to leave out the messy bits, the rows people had, and gloss over difficulties and sticky times[1]—all of which is essential background knowledge for anybody starting a collaborative writing community.

All the writing groups contributing to this book, for instance, had at least one community member trained and experienced in facilitating therapeutic communities and groups: not a necessary requirement, but a key constituent of the yeast nonetheless.

The three chapters in this section are positioned very differently from each other in terms of context. Gallant's chapter talks about a way of beginning to work together as a face-to-face group, to zig-zag around the group in our calls and responses to each other's writing, whereas the other two chapters are describing groups of people working together digitally at some geographical distance. It is not inconceivable that an online group could decide on a zig-zag order of call and response writing before starting to work together, just as the group taking three words to twitter agreed an order of writing; but this kind of structuring of the process would rather undermine the middle-of-the-night spontaneity involved in writing across

---

[1] See http://writeinquiry.org/the-toolbox/starting-out/beginning-to-write/

time boundaries and continents described by Gale et al. (2012). Were we to continue with an 'ideas for beginning groups' list, borrowing from Gallant, we could mention taking 'take three words' off Twitter, or trying out the kinds of interventions into each other's writing that Gannon suggests in 'Inquiring into Red' (see Chapter 23) or writing into social dreaming spaces, as suggested by Speedy in the epilogue to this volume (see Chapter 24). However, this would reduce this volume to a 'collaborative writer's handbook' and each constituent chapter to a shopping list of suggestions, rather than the series of exemplars of collaborative writing that we have sought to set out before other arts-informed researchers and writers.

This book is designed not only to introduce our readers to the practices of collaborative writing, but also to problematise and theorise those practices, within the context of writing as both an everyday and an extraordinary social inquiry space. Our intention is to extend the arts-based imaginary towards social and collaborative forms of inquiry, whilst simultaneously expanding the aesthetics and poetics of social and human inquiry. These are big claims for a small book, but they are claims informed by both our experience and our ethical know-how (Varela, 1999).

CHAPTER TWO

RETREATING OUT OF OURSELVES: SHARING AND SPILLING THE LIFEBLOOD OF COLLABORATIVE WRITING

MIKE GALLANT, LAURINDA BROWN, CHRISTINE BELL, NELL BRIDGES, KEN GALE, YING-LIN HUNG, ANN RIPPIN, ARTEMI SAKELLARIADIS AND JANE SPEEDY

In autumn 2010, a group of nine academics, writers, educators and therapists came together to write collaboratively for a long weekend: a retreat in which to ponder their personal experiences of this form, to ask the apparently simple question 'what is this thing we call collaborative writing?' For some it was a continuation of the Bristol Collaborative Writing Group (BCWG), while for others it was simply a group of respected colleagues, associates and friends gathering to take up an opportunity to write together. If there were a shared plan, it was to explore the field of collaborative writing through collaborative writing; to push our pens together and create some record of what this process can be, to celebrate its nurturing, its developmental outcomes, and to work out some way of disseminating this joy to others who might be interested. With Derrida (2003), we are unhappy creating boundaries between differing forms of writing, regarding aesthetic forms such as writing itself as the essential performance or act, and being unable to dissociate thinking, teaching, and writing. This chapter is layered with individual writings from our residential weekend sutured by strands of reflexive and metaphorical musings.

We began the project by purposefully presenting, in spoken form, a short piece of individual writing about our experience of collaborative writing. We chose to present this specifically to one person in the room, though in the presence of us all. This presence was as crucial as was the individuality of the 'present' we read to our one chosen colleague. Having received our 'present' we chose to whom we would address our own written words. Then, with a particular focus on the individual writing addressed to us personally, we wrote again—in whatever form and in whatever direction we had been moved to create. In lacing together the zig-zag call and response of nine inquirers we were able to draw from the wellspring of what Park (2005) refers to as the Riparian Zone: a metaphorical riverside plain often flooded by murky life-giving waters that leave a landscape of intense fecundity.

This zig-zag writing[1] uses pinking shears that minimise fraying at the edges of connection, paradoxically cutting and protecting the delicate contact boundary between the secure material of woven warp and weft, and the uncertain drifting space where the cloth has left traces of past patterns; patterns of thought and of practice, of grand narrative and academia. We stitch our bespoke wardrobe with shared words, tailored, safely held (and sometimes hidden) as our own and yet simultaneously belonging to others:

I have already filled a sheet of paper by listening to you all. Relationships. The miracle of falling in love. Writing together. Side by side. Shoulder to shoulder. Sliding between the two. Bouncing off each other's work. The quality of the relationships. The interconnectedness of the writing. The interconnectedness of the people. The writing together, in the face of inordinate calls on our time. Scratching pens together, in the face of tiredness. Side by side with tiredness, shoulder to shoulder with other pressures, with a work/life balance in which each—the work and the life—pull you, yank you, in opposite directions, leaving a space in the middle for the writing to emerge between the two. A parting of the seas (so Moses has descended from the shelves and is in this writing too[2]) parting of the seas, creating the space, enabling the writing to blossom. "Hood up" writing or "hood down"[3] writing, we all become leech-like—drawing

---

[1] See Guttorm et al. (2012) for a description and theorizing of a variation of this zig-zag writing method.
[2] This is a reference to the predominantly religious and spiritual content of the library in which we met.
[3] See Chapter 7: we had identified a metaphor of hiding our radical and critical writing from the closed circuit cameras of academia in a similar way that young people might deploy the hoods of their clothing to escape identification on the street. This metaphor had the strength of uncertainty about it, in that there was at

from others—and allow others to draw from us. Sliding beneath the radar, being badly behaved, and being inordinately fond of it. The writing also, occasionally, being badly behaved. It may hang in space for a while before it lands and connects. Or, if this is anything to go by, before the seas reconnect and swallow the writing up for good until, in time, it evaporates into the cloud of the unknown.

For the record, this was the writing that came off my pen when I was too exhausted to even think of saying "I am too tired to write". I remember my last morsel of alertness registering that I am writing this for us, not for publication.

We have been practising a methodology of the heart since before Ron Pelias named it so. We have developed our very own ways of being/ becoming-talking-writing-connecting. We have valued the collective, put our values into action and oh, if Artemi at Ammerdown may be allowed a Deleuzian term, we have dared to deterritorialise academia's stronghold: scholarly writing.

Artemi S

I am focusing here not so much on establishing facts concerning collaborative writing, but rather searching to create understanding through what Mair (2012, p.184), in his final work, described as Enchantment "arising from the marriage of feeling and imagination". Our shared experiences certainly reflect an embodiment of feeling (see Chapter 16) and a heartful (cf. Ellis, 1999) creativity, freely and transparently given by each to each other. This presence we experience, a sense of gift-giving and receiving, may be that which leads to what others (see also Chapter 19) have named "Gerald", a group experience of relational depth (Mearns & Cooper, 2005), as Geller (2012) has proposed. She suggests that four aspects go to make up this presence that leads to the shared, and therapeutic, experience of relational depth: "being grounded in one's self, being immersed in the moment with the other(s), being connected to a larger sense of expansion...', and 'being with and for the...' other (Geller, 2012, p.178). This description seems to resonate with our experience of synchronous collaborative writing practice. Individual simultaneous

the time of our gathering a political move from the British Conservative party leadership asking that the public "Hug a Hoodie"—a move to shift the entrenched socio-political assumptions about a class of younger people typified as wearing hooded garments and assumed to be involved in anti-social behaviour—and to bring them back into (Conservative) mainstream culture.

experiences of 'flow' (Csikszentmihalyi, 1992) in this environment
contribute to the overall sense of this enchanting experience:

*As I listened to Ann yesterday I was aware of picking up words and
running with them, almost taking them like a thief. Taking them,
squirreling them away, burying them in the pages of my notebook, then
later, digging them up and out and in so doing regurgitating them in some
strange, half-digested way, using my own take, my own line of escape,
almost selfishly translating them with the venomous sting of my own bile.*

*Today I have found myself listening and writing in flow. I have loved
listening to the ring of 'shoulder to shoulder' talk, feeling energised by the
talk of 'edginess', smiling fast at the pregnant indistinctiveness of the
spaces in between, the happy curiosities emerging out of being lost in
intensities. Mike, finding himself jumping sideways into the writing; Sue
finding herself saying things she couldn't say elsewhere, sensing her
writing 'hanging in space', before sending it; Nell, memorably, saying
'You never know what it is you are going to find out'.*

*I love all this indistinctness. It says so much. It is the misty morning: it
is where the sharpness of feeling seems to hang.*

*I sense in a strange kind of way how all this seems to be about me. It is
as if I am able to write this because of that. It is as if I wrote down my
notes when I listened to the others because it was me that was saying what
they were saying. I could only write down what seemed to be my words. I
can only say this now because it is only now that I am beginning to
recognise this. It is as if the words of those in the group actually wrote me.
I sense a becoming-Ken in the words that I heard and hurriedly wrote
down. As I write these words now it seems so clear that the collaborative
writing, listening, talking, listening, writing, talking, reading is energised
somehow by the words that I want to hear: it is as if, to use Mike's phrase,
I am drawing blood from others' creativity and in so doing transfusing,
giving some form of life to my always emerging and always incomplete
self. As I write, here, now, I am aware of my battle with my sense of self
and desperately search for words... the blood of others but somehow the
blood... it is as if I am hearing these words in a way that I want to hear
them, it is as if they are flowing in and out of me...*

Ken G

Flowing in and out and through the liminal spaces of minds, bodies,
pens, keyboards, physical place, carpet, smell, book titles, the air we
breathe, the shared particles of bodies left on paper and inhaled into
another's lungs uncritically and unconsciously: it is only when we stop and

ponder the layers and the sweetness of our desert that we begin to understand our process. We sense that we need other people to help us think (St. Pierre, 1997). Like puff-pastry preparation we fold and fold again, adding the rich butter that holds, separates and gives distinctive texture; we play with our material, allowing the folded layers to build as we prepare our chosen filling. With salivation we choose new fruits from our orchard, caramelise their sugars by taking them to the searing heat of another mind-body-spirit, a hotbed of critique and nurturing, before placing them with care into the waiting arms of our proud pastry. The apple and cranberry turnover is in the oven, ready to be savoured, contemplated and shared.

Collaborative Writing: it is what it is and it defines who we are, sometimes hiding who I am behind the barricades. Is there interdependence? Is there gratitude? Is there plagiaristic leeching? Or is it osmosis as through the shell of your egg?
When my written word is accepted as worthy of being part of your written word we are as children in the playground, platonic lovers slitting our wrists and mixing blood in a revolutionary bond. And yet I walk away, allowing the s/p/laces for considered connection. I am not devoured, I am enabled, lace bobbins twisted and manipulated to construct the celebration shawl that warms despite its transparency.
Scratching away—scratching a way down a longer road.
Mike G

Writers meet their writing as rupturing events cutting through the writing place that is itself created within space. It was Badiou (2007) who coined the term 'esplace', translated as 'splace', to describe this essential coming together of place in space (a structuration of reality?), and then went on to consider how events rupture this comfort. Our writing cuts through this splace with a freedom that is only contained by reflection from (on, to, with, beside?) our colleagues, troubling our own attempts to define and understand, setting us free to experience something more, that is both me and us, mine and ours.

SHE WANTS TO WRITE WITH ME
(on writing into conversations about collaborative writing)

Rats in the rafters, dropping ball bearings, eavesdropping
Eavesdropping....playing 'Chinese whispers'...

Catching fragments snippets, intensities

Drawing blood
Thrill, bounce, fantastic
Together

Couldn't do without
Each other, the
Chinese do it differently
Still about connection, friendship
Left field, exposure, excessive practice
Hoods up and down and the miracle of falling
Falling in love
Sue wants to write

   With me...

Blood filled thrills blood spills
Excessive exposing, inordinate fondness,
Falling, falling, falling for you, hoods up and hoods
down,
Doing it with you, doing it without you, doing it the Chinese way
She wants to do it with me,
I want to do it with her

   Jane wants to do it in twos and threes and lots of groups, Jane's a
floozie she's so up for this,
   Jane wants to do it with everybody, Jane wants to do it in Ammerdown,
Laugharne and Llanishen and Northumberland and Goosenest and
   Sifnos, Florence, Hawkswood, and even in Marina's garden in front of
the foxes, and tame radiologists

   Oops
   I wonder if I've gone too far, got carried away again,
   I'm supposed to be making theory, but I'm back in the unisex toilets
with Ali McBeal again and the Buddha and the dancing babies[4].
   I'm not making any sense
   I'm breathless, out of control Speedy,

---

[4] Ali McBeal was an innovative American TV comedy-drama series originally screened from 1997 to 2002 with Calista Flockhart playing the eponymous lawyer, occasionally indulging in spells of magical realism.

Un-professorial to say the least, possibly orgasmic,
Will I catch fire in the library under the gaze of Hildegard (of Bingen)
and her sisters…?

Oh Patti, Patti darling[5], we've gone too far again, you and I, we've
strayed into the realms
  the realms of voluptuousness, abundance and excessiveness

Too far, too soon, too quick, too hot, too rude… and much much too
overexcited…

But I do have to say to those boys… the ones with the comb-over
fetish…

Bugger bodies without organs,

I want my bodies stuffed with an abundance of ample, fully functional
organs…

I want my writing to rush out throbbing and whooping and screaming

I want

I want

I want

to write

together

with you

and then collapse into a heap of messy crumpled texts

and maybe light a fag…

Jane S

---

[5] Referring to Patti Lather, currently professor at Ohio State University.

Gestalt figure and ground illustrations of two persons meeting, their faces in silhouette leaving a space between, only become illustrative by their framing: it is only when contained within a clear boundary that the distinctive shape of a vase appears between them—the paradox of the container being dependent on containment. The paired writing between two people, as repeated call and response, appears simplistic when set against this zig-zag format that passes on words from one to another, and then again and again, through and to the full group. The two-dimensionality of the vase/faces illustration becomes multi-dimensional and the framing increasingly complex. And yet it is this framing, this containment that allows the reverberations to bounce off the complex surfaces of this 'splace', to recognise the paucity of causality and beautiful profundity of coming together (cf. Bachelard, 1964).

There's the writing in pairs and there's the writing in groups. The writing that takes you in unexpected directions, like bouncing off a trampoline. But it's more than the writing. It's about the relationships. And it's the way the writing keeps the relationships going.
  We talk.
  We write.
  We talk about writing.
  We write about talking.
  We talk about the talk that we wrote about.
  We write about the writing we talked about.
  We talk about the talk that we didn't write about.
  We write about the writing that we didn't talk about.
  We talk about not writing.
  We write about not talking.
  And then we write again.
  We write to each other.
  We write from each other.
  We write alongside each other.
  We write around each other.
  This way and that way.
  Writing, talking.
  Bouncing in unpredictable directions.
  Words trampolining.
  Not colliding.
  How is that?
  When we speak, the words inevitably collide, and divide.
  We stay in entrenched positions, more often than not.

When we write the talking gets better.
Nell B

Ann talks of this as political action, of being chosen by others, accepted, invited in so that we can hide behind each other's words ("hood up") while others talk of lovers meeting face to face and subsequently turning to their shared world side by side. I am reminded of the comparison between Levinas's and Lacan's views on encounter and co-construction of self, and the concomitant ethical positions posited: am I creating my self in the image of another so that I take on their emotion, their suffering, and indeed their responsibility (not to take on responsibility for them, but to be responsible for their responsibilities), or is it that I construct my self from the other in such a way as to become their competitor, as Lacan would have us believe (Fryer, 2004)? I want to align myself with Levinas, and yet I sense a closer fit with Lacan's position: so how can I accept this competitive element within collaboration? Only by noticing the paradox of its existence and letting it become an ingredient of this exquisite cuisine.

I think of the politics first of all as external to me and then without thinking I realise I am folded into the very living, pulsing bloodstream of power; it is impossible not to do this, there is something compulsive about this collaborative writing thing! Somehow I am finding my experience of this different to Ann's. Politics does not seem extra or excessive to me when I think about collaborative writing. I am forging them in to my practices, in this respect I am coming out. I am beginning to grow the confidence to say that this is what I do. I repeat it when the incredulous ask: 'Yes, collaborative writing as a method of inquiry'.

So this appeals to my transgressive (or is it subversive?) inclinations; I rather like the 'fuck off' that sometimes comes with the repetition, when I say again, 'collaborative writing as a method of inquiry'. The more I say this, the more I do this; the proposition becomes a prescription. And I begin to see unexpected others doing this too!
Ken G

Certainly this process troubles a narrative of repeating personal meanings that are inextricably linked with a conservative (and conservatising) understanding of identity. Instead of the developing symbolised story (words against background—figure and ground) being based on pre-existing personal archetypes, in this collaborative writing together we permit others' personal, sub-cultural and cultural archetypes to intrude, contain, rub up against and metamorphose our own meanings.

How are we gonna convince them that writing in a group excites us and inspires us? And then invite them into the collaborative writing world? Can they understand the pleasure and the excitement of writing together? To be honest, writing in a group is the only chance that I can hear the scratching sound.
    Ying-Lin H

I hope we have. I hope you can. As for now, the scratching sound is calling me again.

CHAPTER THREE

RIFFING OFF LAUREL RICHARDSON: TAKING THREE WORDS TO TWITTER

NELL BRIDGES, LAURINDA BROWN, JOYCE FERGUSON, KEN GALE, MIKE GALLANT, YING LIN HUNG, VIV MARTIN, SUE PORTER, JANE REECE, ARTEMI SAKELLARIADIS, JANE SPEEDY AND JONATHAN WYATT

One summer, soon after the 2009 International Congress of Qualitative Inquiry (ICQI) in Urbana-Champaign, Illinois, the twelve of us gathered at Ammerdown[1] to create an online collaborative writer's toolbox[2]. We decided to experiment by taking Laurel Richardson's ICQI 'Take Three Words' workshop online and onto Twitter. This gave us a haiku-like restriction of 140 characters including spaces.

Laurel's workshop exploring writing as a form of inquiry (Richardson, 1997, 2001) drew from C. Wright Mill's (1959) assertion that the sociological imagination comes most vividly into play at the juncture between the personal and the historical. Laurel's three assignments for us in this workshop were to write in three-word sentences about: firstly, a particular period of our personal life experience spanning about five years; secondly, what was going on around us in the world at that time; and, finally, both these phenomena combined (not limited only to three word sentences if we chose).

---

[1] See this volume, p.3
[2] http://writeinquiry.org/

The ICQI workshop had been fun to take part in, deceptively simple and incredibly powerful. After Ammerdown, we couldn't wait to get home and share these ideas with other colleagues and students. We thought we'd better let Laurel know that we were misbehaving in this way:
    jane.speedy@bristol.ac.uk emailed Laurel Richardson on 26th June 2009:

"Blimey, Laurel Richardson/UK's going bonkers/jane speedy starts/take three words/on twitter and/there's no stopping us/will send you/the outcomes if/we're not put/away forever - waaaaaaaaaaaaaaaah/
    Jxx"
On July 7th 2009, richardson.9@osu.edu replied:

"I'm a twitter/with your news/jane the speedy/queen of england/lady of means/for forging twitterings"

Laurel was clearly as badly behaved as we were, and so we began for nine days at the end of June 2009 (three days 'auto', three days 'ethno' and three days in combination) to take three words to twitter. In theory, we were limited to three-word sentences and 140 characters. In practice, we frequently came to double or treble our tweets in a row, as if 'a tweet a stanza made'.
One striking effect of this experiment was the cumulative sense of continuous cycle, not only of inner and outer worlds but of both the mundane and profound that makes up our everyday/extraordinary lives. This gradual accumulation of reflecting, thinking and feeling amidst the goings-on of our everyday lives produced an intense and compelling snapshot of day-to-day living and breathing in a way that much of the 'contrived' diary-taking/phone-in/blogging of everyday sociology experiments has failed to capture (see, for instance, Wood et al., 2002; Norton, 2009; Sternheimer, 2010). As Lefebvre (1991, p.15, quoting Hegel) often commented: "the familiar is not necessarily known".
In taking part in the three-word twitter, certainly we, the participants, have come to know ourselves differently, but more than that we have unexpectedly come to make known something more about (extra)ordinary, everyday life in 21st century Britain than was known before.
This experiment has shape-shifted considerably from Laurel's original ICQI workshop. By trying to 'Take Three Words' out of the conference workshop to negotiate our way online and offline into a Twitter group, we had become disrupted, disjointed and fragmented, but nonetheless intensely connected communicators. This way of writing, whilst retaining

the haiku-like distillation of Laurel's 'Take Three Words', had moved off further into the spaces between people and away from those spaces clearly occupied by any one person. This was becoming more of a collective biography, or perhaps collective auto-ethnography, not only troubling the imagined edges between 'auto' and 'ethno' but also disrupting the boundaries and causing landslides and slippages between subjectivities and collectivities. It led to an unexpected and surprising intimacy, an insight into each other's day to day lives that almost took on the flavour of 'reality TV'. We already knew each other well; we were all students, staff and graduates working within the same narrative research centre. Some of us had known each other for ten years or more. But suddenly we could see into each other's homes, we knew what each other watched on TV and had for dinner, and with whom; this was close-up intimacy on a different level at all sorts of times of day (and night—it was clear from the timing of our tweets that we had a number of insomniacs in our midst).

During the nine-day period of our twittering activities, the Wimbledon tennis championships were taking place in London where Andy Murray was the great British hope; the annual rock festival was taking place at Glastonbury and the British Queen asked for a pay rise. There were huge pro-democracy protests in Iran, during which the death of a young woman Neda Agha-Soltan at the hands of the Iranian authorities on the streets of Tehran was videoed and broadcast worldwide. In the USA, Michael Jackson died and throughout the western world, the financial/banking crisis continued.

In our personal lives, one of us got married and went on a honeymoon to Venice and another of us, a creative-writing teacher, witnessed an horrific, razor-slashing incident in the local prison. Meanwhile the birds twittered on and so did we...

janewriting
Early morning heat/disturbs me. i/listen to ticking/clock, calling wood-pigeons/chirping house martins/in the eaves/ideas racing through/ my brain calling/me to twitter

artemi89
It's gone mid-day/I sit embittered/ have not written/but only twittered./Just finished printing/preparing for meeting/MUST slow down/create writing time/

Nellbridges
Virginia was wrong/never mind room/TIME of one's own.

Laurinda
End of term/one week left/in my office/
Surrounded by paper/most is important/certainly to students/their writing beckons/time to mark/

janewriting
Furious rain soaks/the earth and/tomatoes grow fat/will need more/sun and i/would love a/cracking thunder storm

suecrowandmoon
Hearing you all/move about planet/warms my heart/I'm with Nell/
Love my room/give me space/good old Virginia/she could swing/when not sinking
Sorry about that/was joke unforgiveable?/
Still dry here/last night's hay/baled and gone/ravens patrol field/ stabbing beaks ready/all beware!

Nellbridges
Sinking's a choice/I'm with Virginia/stones in pockets/the quiet Ouse/I've been there/kind of pilgrimage/stood on bank
Sent too soon/pushed the button/send by accident/sold her short/sister across years

suecrowandmoon
Low flying p(l)ain/over hay field/shatters peace here.
Reminds me Fairford/Gulf war demo/Tony Benn speaking/bombers takeoff
Suddenly find I/can't breathe in/can't breathe out/choking sobs tearing/their way out/
Was I angry?/Was I weeping?/'course it's both/Remember Iran/still my heart

artemi89
Dinner was lovely/stuffed tomatoes & peppers/whole lot gone./Touch base quickly/
(room is great/if you have/time for it)./But not now
Thing with time/is you choose./So, right now/I won't twitter./
Instead will watch/Wimbledon highlights./First time this year.

suecrowandmoon
We have wasps/bigger than humbugs/cruising past window/dive bombing balcony/said to be/relaxed not grumpy/
Not that I/want to find/if true!

Laurinda
It asks me/what are you/
Doing when now?/In the moment/I am typing/Twitter answers itself/its own question
Like a mirror/Twitter gazes into/its own face/staring back at/its own face/what are you/doing it asks.

vivmartin
Michael Jackson dead?/He was 50/I recognised him/Someone younger/Child at first/The Jackson Five/Black to White

Laurinda
Glastonbury plays Jackson/In the rain/Snippets of songs/through my mind/Moonwalking to work/To Billy Jean

mikesonthecase
Storm brewing for/michaeljackson alone - complicated/black peter pan/elizabeth taylor wept/her friend dead/a little boy/he's real 2 her

nellbridges
Not Peter Pan/just a dream/a stolen childhood/
Like so many/yet so unique/an attempted reclamation/like so many/yet so unique

borisovski
Michael Jackson fifty/another person outlived/sadly not out-famed

janewriting
Snatching time twittering/party preparations continue/sister says spoiled/by rain and/brother in law/getting flu 'deliberately'/I watch rain/and hope for/a weekend without/a family storm

artemi89
Day keeps improving/Forgot a fork/Eating lunch with teaspoon

speedovski
TING TING TING!!!/just a reminder/auto one more/day - then it's/ ethno, altho/we crossed line/with Michael Jack/
Maybe music seeps/beneath these auto-ethno walls/anyone for madrigals?
Show support for democracy in Iran add green overlay to your Twitter avatar with 1-click - http://helpiranelection.com/1:59 AM Jun 25th from Support #IranElection

tweetylin
On telly michael/jack discussed, picked/over by paparazzi/shutup white man/we say, but/honkey doesn't stop/probably went 2/Eton (damn nearly)

suecrowandmoon
Where's Iran gone?/Does anyone know?
Does anyone care?/eclipsed by celebrity?/No longer 'sexy'/we're fickle friends/low boredom threshold!
Exhausted again today/from blowing on/embers of love/sitting with father/whose forgotten me/Altz cruel disease/all infected does/he miss me?
Iran displaced by/celebrity death toll/ Even Farrah lost/out to Michael/ Even exams lose/out to Glasto/Even fathers eclipsed/by our lovers

speedovski
love lies bleeding/forget me not/ox eye daisies/red hot pokers/deadly night shade/purple fox gloves/lavender and rosemary/in remembrance

janewriting
Stagger back home/overburdened by food/having grossly overestimated/friends' consumption capacity/graffiti on pavement says/less is more
Temperature is soaring/too hot to cook/will tell friends/less is more

vivmartin
Just tried moonwalking/instructions in Guardian/forgot to look/behind. Cuppa tea/spilt on carpet/off to Supermarket/will walk 4wards

borisovski
Thirty minutes spent/shelling stupid peas/next time shelling/with explosive device/
Recommend frozen ones/available at supermarket/Peas that is
Twitter has revealed/boring state of life/am now planning/round world trip/emailed bank manager/Please send/massive cash injection

nellbridges
World outside twittering/this time birds/have been at/it since 4.30/no delay there/hear & respond/show and tell/in same space

suecrowandmoon
Twitter has helped/me2 hold/you in mind/Would other form/have worked as well?
The light touch/of 140 characters/means I've written/not put it off

speedovski
Ting Ting!!
Sunday ethno day!!/Observer all wacko/jacko n obama/black male icons/both really pretty/both really clever/at what they/do - America dominates!

tweetylin
Michael Jackson died/the shocking news/fans sad& mad/he is crazy/he is mad/may be sick/but so what?/he is Michael Jackson/gotta be him

suecrowandmoon
On the radio/On T V/Mentioned @ Glasto/Talk in supermarket/overheard in gallery/Unpicked over wine/drunk with friends/Poor dead Michael

vivmartin
In Iran people/die in protests/in Birmingham lightning/strike kills boy/elderly man dies/amidst ordinary mundane/life extraordinary things happen

jonathanwyatt
Murray winning/Brits be proud/could he win?/Nadal's injured—shame/Federer's king will/he topple?/centre court now/roofed so - no/rain this year?

suecrowandmoon
On Desert Island/today luxury chosen/was eyebrow Tweezers!/2 mins
later news/from Iran tells/arrest embassy staff/whose reality counts?

speedovski
Obama gets climate/change bill thru/now health to/go wot do/our boys
do?/NADA
Who shall/i vote 4?/but people r/dying for the/rite 2 vote

nellbridges
I get older/I get bigger/men get keener/what's going on?/What's their
idea?/Large portions expected?!

artemi89
One daughter's birthday/Another to Russia/Trouble at school/Friends
to dinner/House a mess/Work deadlines accumulate

speedovski
Jacko family prowl/nastydad has nose/Sista Janet (who/accused Jacko
publicly)/has neverland nose/tabloids last pic/sees Jacko noseless/oh!

janewriting
back from inner/space and family/to outerspace/and prison and/reading
between the/lines the royal/family cost £41.5m/per year and/last year
liz/dipped into a reserve/the £7.9 million/deal not enough/she intends
to/ask/for a rise/what a rise!/as the men/inside say

jonathanwyatt
Who's for 4s?/I'm for 3s/bees knees threes/singles on telly/murray on
top/one night stand/covered up court/courting with us/our tennis love

vivmartin
Sweeping cobwebs from/the edges of/my my my/mind 3s not 4s/all on
board/all on board...

speedovski
TING! TING!/one more ethno/day 2moro then/parting with
simplicity/wot sweet sorrow/we shall choose/2 integrate all/3's or 4s/or
even mores/liberty hall!

Laurinda
When is tomorrow?/A child dies/Infected with swine flu/the numbers
mutate/alongside the bug/last heard 3000/now it's 6000/can't take it in

Neverland replaces graceland?/Why not and?/News offers dichotomies/
when did news/become assertions?/Ask meaningless questions?

roughtor
When Twitter rules?/ Who needs media/to spread word?/Facts already
talk-ins/people sharing feelings

jonathanwyatt
Didn't sleep well/Murray's struggles lingered/More than Gordon's/And
his gang's/More than Iran's/More than Jackson's/His are over
Andy's superstitions triumph/Not eye candy/Sniffs the Guardian

borisovski
Michael's debt? wealth?/children? house? probate?/for god's_sake/leave
them alone/world is nosy/celebrity can never/rest in peace/it's a job
Swine flu parties/all the rage in/middle England beating/tupperware
and ann/summers. heat wave reduces/Banksy museum queue/GDP down
2.4%

janewriting
Cannot twitter chirpily/tonight still removing/self from auto/during
afternoon break/a learner was/slashed with razor/by two others/
Staggered out of/toilets blood everywhere/classroom cordoned
off/police investigate assault/
We all make statements/more tomorrow while/search for blades/and
other evidence/
Victim did not/see attackers (he/cannot say for/fear of repeat/or worse)
and/I am tired/of life imitating/art so I/say good night

nellbridges
Oh my dear/oh my heart/is with you/and with him/poor hurt
frightened/soul, and strangely/with them too/what brings them/to this
place?

speedovski
Forget Twitter for a moment. News can get too close to life. Hope today is better than yesterday.
Thinking of you.

suecrowandmoon
Today I nearly/died: White van/pulled across in/front of car/me in passenger/seat inches from/impact @40/mph. That was/12 hours ago/
I'm still tingling/as if/fear has made/me inhabit my/body differently, at/ least for a while/
Maybe no bad/thing 4 a/woman losing touch/with her body?/maybe that's what/Carol K would/say: 'you (nearly)/hit me and/it felt like/a kiss'.
Speaking/the fear out/loud helps me/uninhibit part of me./
In the meantime/huge moth sits/quietly by window/Possibly condemned 2/die in house/by virtue of/its size. I/think how I/might lend a/hand

vivmartin
Combine the ethno/and the auto/make me homesick/why? human brain/a mysterious area/I wanna cut/it open to/see what's inside/must be xxxxxxxx

speedovski
Taking three words to twitter/some loved it/some petered out/some didn't really start/
And as for/Speedy, Crow, Nell/Tweetlin, Laurinda, Jane/and Art... What/ a bunch of/old internet tarts...

Keeping 'auto' and 'ethno' separate for days and days did not really happen as the inner and outer, the mine and theirs, the co-implications as Bronwyn Davies (2010) would say, slipped and leaked and slithered out and about in our daily lives; but as a snapshot of what we had for dinner, who nearly died, and the impact of us in the world in us, this was a slice of everyday lives and philosophies like no other. Towards the end our structure faded into an elegant, quirky, typically British kind of chaos, as we were just left with a few faithful tweeters continuing well beyond our nine-day experiment to enjoy the writing and the connectedness:

mikesonthecase
And even I/sat and watched/ Murray lose 2/American who can/ manage 2 give/him the run/around. Wondering could/we cope with/success? We'll never know

borisovski
Public sector workers/asked to freeze/their pay. But/ bank bigwigs still/getting fat packages/from public purse./So much 4/fair play

nellbridges
Standing stones commemorate/the fallen of /7/7. New stones/evoke old stones/ring of brodgar/callanish and carnac/spirit of place/and of time

speedovski
Insomniac Venice moment/ finds compelling talk/of standing near/ death sweetpea stones/
Biennale meanwhile provokes/and Venice stones/rise majestic and/quirky avoiding masses/
We meander along/back alleys and/quiet canals not/hand in hand/no pink flags/here squid in/ink for lunch/
Death in Venice/life goes on/tomorro more art/then the Lido/then home Easyjet/using up the World

suecrowandmoon
I write 4/me, and 4/anyone who reads/me. Can't resist/ answering Jane's who/are still writing./
Love this contact/and the rules/and also breaking them!

Laurinda
On violence and/mourning while rain/soaks the earth

jonathanwyatt
Make sense of/teacher attempting murder/more killed in/Afghanistan against the/warning that there/will be more/reading judith butler

artemi89
Twitter in tatters?/virtual community virtually/absent? Ground rules/ misunderstood? Ignored? Revised?/Who writes to/whom? And for/what?

CHAPTER FOUR

CALL AND RESPONSE ON EMAIL
BETWEEN AND BEYOND THE TWO

KEN GALE

This chapter describes and critiques processes of writing that might be labelled 'call and response'. Participants in this form of collaborative writing exchange texts, typically via email, to which others in turn respond. There might be one other writing participant (e.g. Gale & Wyatt, 2009) or more than one (e.g. Gale, Speedy & Wyatt, 2008; Wyatt et al., 2011). A fellow participant in such an exchange might respond directly to what others have written, working with the ideas, stories, figures or form of the piece(s); or they might work with the writing's 'echoes', the images or memories it prompts, allowing others' writing(s) to lead us elsewhere, somewhere, anywhere. Such writing might also be described as a form of collaborative writing as inquiry (after Richardson, 1997; Richardson & St. Pierre, 2005 and others), where participants do not know where the writing will take them. They write, together, in order to find out where they are going and what will be created, always, though, with an awareness of the other(s) as audience, witnesses and collaborators. The writing might also be conceptualized as taking place in—and creating—the spaces in between. This chapter explores the forms that such writing might take and its potential as a way into collaborative writing; and it examines its possible risks and limitations.

***

Feeling my way into writing this chapter I am finding myself pondering the phrase that attempts to catch what I am trying to do here and how the idea of 'call and response' can be used to describe a particular kind of collaborative writing. I am drawn, first of all, to the apparent simplicity of the call and response conjunction, which suggests a pervasive pattern of democratic participation. Here we are communicating: I call you, you respond, that's it. I love the way we complicate it in this book and I search for its complications. We feel our way into call and response and begin to wonder, is that it? And, of course, in answer to my call here the response is, of course not.

I am opening a door. I know it will never close. Shall I fling it open? Shall I ease it open and slide in around the jamb? Shall I breeze in as if there is nothing going on? Nothing to think about? Nothing to theorise? Nothing important to respond to?

Already I know that my door metaphor is a kind of call. Already I am thinking of Althusser and his analysis of a simple 'Hello'. Althusser's theory of interpellation (1990) starkly and clearly claims that when another person responds to our 'hail' that person ceases to be an individual and is turned into a subject. This approach, that highlights processes of subjectification, takes all the innocence out of communications, it puts love, sincerity and authenticity all on trial, the 'democratic participation' suggested above becomes a cliché that can only vainly attempt to resist the diffractive possibilities of a way of thinking and an aesthetics of becoming that challenges custom, habit and the conformative restraints of the normative. How can this self break free of the self that is always being hailed by a world of others in relational spaces that always 'see' the self and represent it in particular ways?

So now, as I continue to open this door, I sense hesitation, I cast my mind back to previous collaborations and I begin to wonder about them: how did I hail and how did others hail me? In what sense was there a self there that was performing its self? And performing its self in particular ways? And as I drift in the liminality of this shifting door space, the sense of hesitation palpable in my becoming, I also feel good. I feel the self that is writing its self here and now beginning to re/member, beginning to re/collect and to re/construct. I share with Foucault a sense of the politics of these moments. I have a knowing that processes of subjectification are rarely benign and I write into this emerging space with gleeful nakedness; I am aware that this writing in its becoming will place me again within those always transmutating assemblages, I will be hailed and I will hail, and although there will be a politics there I feel that I will again be washed on a wave that carries the politics of friendship. Tillman-Healy (2003) has provided us with the rhetoric of 'friendship as methodology'; I am happy to work with this phrase as a simple motif and as I begin to write into the space that asks me "What is call and response writing?", and with Ron Pelias (2007) I ask the question "What work does this (call and response writing) do?", words like 'friendship', 'care' and 'love' populate these nascent becomings.

I have already revealed that I want to talk of call and response writing both as working within and as creating 'assemblage' (Deleuze & Guattari, 1988). So, when talking about the insidious nature of processes of interpellation,

> "Althusser argues that the pervasiveness of (this) language goes largely unnoticed by our sentient and perceptual minds; the objects of the external world somehow enter our consciousness, they become internalised, and then we are... "hailed" by them when they reappear." (Gale, 2009, p.161)

Hailing, calling and responding, occurs within the complex 'intra-actions' and 'entanglements' (Barad, 2007) of discourse and materiality. We have a language that grows and in its growing it nurtures embodiment and brings these 'objects of the external world' within our grasp. In our 'response' to these 'calls', we are becoming in our awareness of shifts in our corporeality. We sense in our writings how we are entangled with other bodies, that forces are at play and that when the call and response of writing takes place it is the body in space that cries, that laughs and that shivers with the vectoral vibrations of the renewed energies of affect, of creativity and intuition.

In a chapter entitled 'Body to Body', Tami Spry writes in response to a 'call' from Ron Pelias:

> "Ron, I, too, cherish the physical presence, to "be alive to what bodies can tell." But we're not together physically as a group; for me, that is the point of this kind of writing process. I find it working as a performative process of writing into being, exploring the advantages and limitations of doing reality/communication through language, the heartbreaking processes of a methodology of the heart." (Gale et al., 2012, p.66)

I find the physicality of Tami Spry's language so powerful and evocative; it does not simply talk to or write itself on my body, it is the becoming of my body. As I read and then write these words, once again my body has changed, it is different and it is alive in a new way. In that 'Body to Body' chapter, indeed in large parts of that book, the immersion in the rainstorms and deluges of our performative collaborative processes of call and response produced many life changing moments; my body was always moving, shifting and dancing with the words that plaintively sang to me, to the rhythms that pumped out of troubled hearts and to the riffs that in their insistence pushed me into seas of exotic vibration on waves of flowing viscosity. Tami Spry also picks up on the complex nature of this immersion as she reveals "when under stress and duress, I feel the written body of this group waiting to embrace" (ibid., p. 67). I also sense the intensity of this 'embrace': as Tami Spry says "we're not together physically as a group" and yet we engage in the entangled complexities of these calls and responses, we both create and come alive in this 'written body'. I love the way in which the intense tactility and physicality of the word 'feel' in Tami's writing, brings alive the affect and sensuality of this 'embrace'. It is in the heat and light of the phosphorescent cauldron of this brief remembered moment that the naked power of call and response writing comes alive. The word 'feel' is not there simply to evoke, it is generatively there in the performative vulnerability that is exposed, lived and multiplied as the line between language and materiality, for a brief candlelit moment, is beautifully erased.

So it is in this intensely complex place that we are calling and responding and, at the same time, re-writing, re-creating and re-conceptualising call and response as a genre of collaborative writing. Bland or simplistic explanations cannot be offered about processes that are potentially so complex and entangled and in this respect call and response cannot be characterised simply as succession or as the interaction of distinct phrases as in, for example, the exchange between verse and chorus often found in certain musical forms, where the interactions between phrases takes the form of commentary and repeated response. We learn from Deleuze (2004) that with repetition there is always difference, each new response, if you will, might well be a repetition of an earlier 'call' but equally each repetition exists in multiplicity as a new encounter and hence is exemplified through and as difference. In a well-known passage, Deleuze describes working with Guattari and offers a telling and illuminating picture of the flows and indeterminacies of call and response as intra-action.

> "We were never in the same rhythm, we were always out of step: I understood and could make use of what Felix said to me six months later; he understood what I said to him immediately, too quickly for my liking— he was already elsewhere. From time to time we have written about the same idea, and have noticed later that we have not grasped it at all in the same way." (Deleuze and Parnet, 2002, p.17)

We have engaged with *How Writing Touches* (Gale et al., 2012) and it seems that how it touches is never the same: each new intra-action floods new words, evokes new feelings, creates different impacts; difference is always in repetition. Each time our writing touches it does so in a different way, as Deleuze notes of Guattari, "we were never in the same rhythm" (Deleuze & Guattari, 1988, p.158). With the space between each new exchange something has elapsed, the space 'between-the-two' (Gale &

Wyatt, 2009) is a space of intensive multiplicity, it is a space of becoming in which each assemblage of bodies, forces, encounters and language moves on, transmutates and is always in flow.

In creating a "conversational distillation of a year of writing" (p.317), Gale and Pineau also show that the intra-actions of assemblage can be nurtured and made more complex through "the overlapping rhythm of (our) letters" (p.318). In this writing, the call and response works within the play of concept, percept and affect and nurtures a complex exchange between different philosophical positions, which in turn is generative in the becoming of a new and emergent praxis of inquiry.

> "Working with a Deleuzian practice of conceptualisation, and from the epistemological stance of performative writing, we attempt to give a flavour of the intensive frisson that emerged in the spaces that opened up and the becomings that unfolded, when our collaborative writing practices were set in motion. Our growing methodological awareness arose from the coming together of the Deleuzian and the performative as we recognized a productive intersection of our disciplinary and writerly perspectives."
> (Gale & Pineau, 2011, p.317)

The synthesis of ideas and practices that emerges from the intensity of these 'overlapping' calls and responses also fuses affective and evaluative dimensions and forms within claims for a new and constantly differentiating praxis of collaborative writing as method of inquiry. Through these mediations, the call and response creates the opportunity for new forms of theorising that move beyond the abstract in their gradual emergence within the writing.

It is the living with opportunities and transversalities of this kind that is the energising force of a becoming group of writers qua assemblage. Susanne Gannon provides an example of the day-to-day living force of such an assemblage when she describes her thoughts and feelings, working with "a daisy chain of quotations", as she prepared herself to write with us and Deleuze about collaborative writing. She says of the quotations,

> "I thought I would delete them. How could they still be relevant when such a chunk of time has passed? How many people—a hundred, more—have I had to interact with in a single week at work? Does each interaction overwrite the lingering ones that are not yet complete (or in this case, not yet begun). But instead I'll keep them here. I'll work my way up to them, write my way in, and muse around them." (Wyatt et al., 2011, p.45)

The gentle, inquiring rhetoric of Susanne's writing alerts us to the fragile and always mutating transversality of the calls and responses of this kind of collaborative writing. As a four (or was it a five?!), we had hardly met and yet, as we wrote, the intensity of our exchanges energised a huge spring tide of writing that flooded the increasingly intra-active spaces of our nascent inquirings into the assemblage of our emergent collective selves, Deleuze, collaborative writing and more (Wyatt et al., 2010, 2011). In this sense, we became aware of the power of collaborative writing as a method of inquiry. In our early writings (Gale & Wyatt, 2007, 2008), Jonathan and I began to realise that what we were doing together in our emergent between-the-two was somehow creating and building a form of collaborative writing as a method of inquiry, taking Richardson's (1997) important methodology beyond the relatively singular consciousness and practice of her study. In becoming heavily reliant upon and increasingly in love with Deleuze's "logic of sense" (1990), we found our collaborative selves writing more and more into the not yet known, in part fuelled by the awareness and growing confidence of writing to and with one another. For the writer, the one who makes the call, the performative nature of this experience is strongly implicated and tangibly informed by the sense of the other in the growing complexity of the collaborative milieu. After writing in this way now for seven or eight years, the sense of writing to/with Jonathan remains powerful, complex and highly indeterminate: this sense is both material and discursive, it is of my body and of the discourses that emerge from our work and that help to construct us in the always becoming of our collaborative process. As I write this response to the call to write this chapter, I continue to ponder and wonder what it is that is calling me as I write. It is as if writing to/with Jonathan is for me a means of writing to and with the world: no other writing is ever easier or more fulfilling.

PART II

THE SPIRIT(S) OF COLLABORATIVE WRITING

CHAPTER FIVE

PROLOGUE TO PART II

DAVINA KIRKPATRICK
AND JONATHAN WYATT

"(l)andscape is where the past and future are co-present with the present through processes of memory and imagination" (Jones & Cloke, 2002, p. 82)

Jonathan writes:

The landscape of collaborative enquiry is full of multiple worlds, and voices and ways of being, reminding me of Jones's words.

Outside the TV room, in the most comfortable chair I can find, the breeze is brisk and the sky dull. Others are scattered around the house and grounds, taking a break from writing prologues. I'm feeling the pressure to make progress, having taken too long to get started and knowing that I'll miss tomorrow morning's writing time.

Sue and Jane have taken on the challenge of heading along the dimpled, puddled path towards the monument at the top of the hill. By the back door here there's a warning notice that in the fields en route to the monument there are steers, which have been known, it reads, "to chase people". We hope to see Sue and Jane for tea. Early this morning, Tess and I took a turn around the grounds, passing the cows in the nearby field. There was a fence between them and ourselves but, in any case, they paid us no attention. They stood sturdy and uninterested. They remained our unseen companions even as we turned the corner.

Davina writes:

This section of the book carries a sense of both felt companionship and risk.

Jane Speedy (Chapter 6) argues that all writing is collaborative, that we are always already in relationship with others as we write; we're never alone.

There are the choices we make as collaborative writers about visibility, the extent to which we make ourselves 'known', that Porter and Rippin write about (Chapter 7). Hoods up or down? What shall we reveal? What shall we keep hidden? And what conditions are in place to enable us to make such decisions?

Where does writing into and from our ghosts take us in our inquiries? The playful presentation of being alive, dead and ghostly seems to create a slippage between worlds—life, afterlife, trace in the 'Obituary' chapter (Chapter 8). What happens when we play dead to our writing companions? Through the genre of the obituary, and what it leaves behind, Gale, Speedy and Wyatt explore the companionship and abandonment of writing themselves out of and then into, differently, their relationships. This chapter is both playful and painful.

In 'Mapping Spectral Traces', Karen Till talks of how "past presences occupy the realities of our lived worlds" (Till, 2010, p.2). What draws my attention is how past presences both reside in place and within us and how these presences are recalled, maybe an articulation of 'splace', after Badiou (2007). How mnestic traces are inscribed, impressed, overlaid (with reference to the metaphorical, artistic possibilities of Aristotle's wax tablet and St. Augustine's storehouse). The affect of meme and anamnesis, recall and recollection (Ricoeur, 2004), eidetic memory, affective/sense memory, "the otherness of memory" (Sheringham, 1993), on the interaction between people, objects, place and story.

Jonathan writes:

The steers are always in the fields; they may or may not turn on us.

It's tea. It's time to re-gather, though my companions have been with me throughout this writing. I need to check that Jane and Sue have returned safely.

CHAPTER SIX

COLLABORATIVE WRITING AND ETHICAL KNOW-HOW: MOVEMENTS WITHIN THE SPACE AROUND SCHOLARSHIP, THE ACADEMY AND THE SOCIAL RESEARCH IMAGINARY[1]

JANE SPEEDY

It may seem incongruous to come across a 'sole-authored' text amidst a book about collaborative writing. For my part, the contradiction 'plays' eloquently with what it might mean to be/come a singular-yet-silted-up-accumulation of a human being. This chapter represents not so much an assemblage (although that too) as a collectively auto/biographical constellation, accumulation and distillation of the traces that have remained lying around and about after many decades spent engaged with collective, collaborative and participatory writing.

By themselves, these sediments and dregs do not amount to much and certainly do not fit together, but as they have accumulated over time they have come to represent something of a body of work. Hence the conditions of possibility surface for me to give an account of the very particular kinds of ethical know-how[2] that I have witnessed emerging from many groups of people writing together collaboratively within (and to some extent against) the Academy.

This chapter draws on feminist sensibilities, narrative and poststructuralist

---

[1] This chapter was originally published in the journal 'International Review of Qualitative Research', 2012, 4, pp.349-356

[2] The term used by Varela (1999) to describe an ongoing, everyday and responsive ethical practice of continual, contextual, ethical becoming, as opposed to an ethical morality or set of principles, for instance.

ideas, therapeutic practices, utopian methodologies and multiple-writing accumulations over time to suggest that the continued and explicit practice of collaborative writing amongst social researchers alters the academic spaces they inhabit and the ethical know-how that they come by. In time, the (albeit fragile) emergence of this different sense of scholarship and scholarly work and even, perhaps, of what it means to be a human being amidst human beings and other elements can begin to rework and expand the social imagination.

I wrote the abstract for this chapter in August, 2011. I had taken myself and my dog Rubi on a writing holiday to a cottage by the sea on Pen Caer, the westernmost tip and bleakest part of wild, west Wales. I wrote the abstract sitting next to the woodburner in the cottage living room with my feet up on Rubi's back—strange then, that the abstract should start with mention of a 'sole-authored' text, since I wrote it in such a shared ruminative space—co-authored emotionally with and by Rubi and geographically with and by the gnarled treeless landscapes of northern Pembrokeshire. This is a landscape I do not live my daily life in, but one that I frequently escape to and that I know like no other—I spent all my childhood holidays there, since which time it has become a national park and thence a landscape that has changed very little over my lifetime. It is a landscape untouched by twenty-first century technologies, with a skyline free of pylons, an absence of high-rise buildings and a road system folded gently into its hillsides, unscarred by three-lane motorways.

I am writing this introduction to the chapter, accompanied once again, with Rubi at my feet and by a pair of chattering magpies in the pear tree, as I sit on the deck of my north Bristol back garden in May, 2012. The background soundscape of the city: a heady urban blend of sirens, motorway traffic-buzz and children's voices from the paddling pool across the road in the park. When I write here at home, I write out on the deck, or at the kitchen table in the sunny south-facing back of this rambling Victorian house. This is my day-to-day landscape, yet its streets are not inscribed on my heart and mind in the ways that Pembrokeshire is. I do not dream about Bristol. I live here. I believe it is a great city, not least because of its proximity to Wales, but I am in love with Pembrokeshire. Pembrokeshire connects me with my family of origin, all of whom are now dead. Bristol is where I currently work and live my daily life within my family of choice. Thus, both these pieces of writing, the abstract and the introduction, are written by the same woman, accompanied by the same dog, but are clearly very differently geographically situated and hold different connections to my personal history. The feminist poet Michelle Roberts writes compellingly of "all the selves I was" (1995) but whilst I brought all the selves I was at the time to each of these pieces of writing, the two geographical, historical, and emotional collections that made up these two singular spaces in my life, the abstract-writing space and the introduction-writing space, were not necessarily the same collections of selves. Indeed, both pieces were written for and in the imagined company of different audiences. The abstract was written in response to a request from two friends and colleagues, Jonathan Wyatt and Ken Gale, as a contribution to a special issue of the journal 'Qualitative Inquiry'. I had those two colleagues and the journal editor, Norman Denzin, very much in my sights as I wrote the abstract. This introduction was written 9 months later, the weekend before the 2012 International Congress of Qualitative Inquiry (ICQI) was due to take place in Urbana-Champaign, Illinois. This was a congress where I felt at home, and was a scholarly gathering I had every intention of joining when I wrote the abstract. At the time of writing, I had the audience of my fellow collaborative writers from Europe and North America in a proposed Congress panel and journal special issue in my mind's eye as well as a room somewhere in the Illini Union building and an audience comprising some of my fellow 'season-ticket holders' for collaborative-writing contributions to the ICQI congresses. I could imagine it all clearly. I could see the faces of the panel and some of the faces in the audience and some, although not all, the selves they brought. I could hear the 'noises off' from other rooms down the corridor in the Illini Union building, the muffled sounds of clapping and of laughter from other presentations. I could imagine the view from the windows across the campus. This was another space that I knew well—a scholarly home from home.

If spaces comprise multiplicities, or as Massey (2005, p.9) says, a simultaneity of "stories thus far" then each of these spaces I had imagined myself into whilst constructing the abstract and introduction was awash with simultaneities of selves and stories. Each writing space, so-called "sole-authored" by all the selves and stories Jane Speedy brought to it, was in fact co-peopled to the gunnels.

"What is an author?", Foucault asked (1977). A simultaneity of all the selves she had ever been and stories that had ever been told alongside /about/with Norman Denzin, Jonathan Wyatt and Ken Gale in the case of the abstract to this paper, plus all the selves and stories connected to the ICQI collaborative writing panels and audiences for these introductory paragraphs. Despite being written thousands of miles away from my collaborating co-presenters and audiences, this abstract and introduction were clearly conjointly written.

The act of naming the spaces we are writing into as collaborative writing spaces, then, is an act of making these communities of selves, simultaneities of stories thus far and communities of co-writers and audiences explicitly available to scholars and their readers. It is an act of acknowledging the inhabitants of some of our academic silences (Mazzei, 2007).

Talking of academic silences, the writing that appears in academic journals often appears as a seamless uninterrupted stream of academic thought. Academic writers of introductory paragraphs such as these rarely mention the environment they are actually writing from and almost never lose their focus and meander out of the window into the gardens beyond or get interrupted by events in their domestic lives—and yet, just as I am returning to these introductory paragraphs a week or so after starting to write them, the front doorbell rings and the postman arrives with a timely parcel sent by Jonathan Wyatt containing a copy of 'How Writing Touches: An Intimate Scholarly Collaboration', signed by each of its five authors: Ken Gale, Ron Pelias, Larry Russell, Tami Spry and Jonathan himself. This is a book I feel familiar with, having heard much of its contents presented by the co-authors at preceding ICQIs. Nonetheless, I stop what I am doing to leaf through the book and step a little into the imagined lives of the authors and read the comments from the 'great and the good' on the back cover. Norman Denzin says: "collaborative writing is a relatively new writing form in which writers write themselves into each other's lives".

And I find myself sitting on my deck in Bristol, in conversation with Norman Denzin in Illinois.

"It's not new in Bristol, Norm," I find myself muttering out loud. "And there is space in this writing. There is an open invitation to join in with these lives—to imagine ourselves into the gaps and cracks between these voices. This intimate 'writing that touches' both touches and includes us all. It is the open imaginative spaces for the inscription of readers' and listeners' lives into this collaborative writing—the fact that nothing is closed or fixed—that makes its touch so compelling."

Our Narrative Inquiry Centre (NIC) at the University of Bristol actively encourages an abundance of collaborative writing courses, groups and pairings (Reed & Speedy, 2011) and hosts a collaborative writing website for the British Higher Education Academy (http://writeinquiry .org). Indeed, many of the contributors to this special issue—the Bristol Collaborative Writing Group, Jonathan Wyatt and Ken Gale and myself— have helped to constitute and been, in part, constituted by this centre of collaborative scholarship. I have noticed over time that our culture of collaborative writing has fostered a different and radical sense of ethical know-how or wisdom (Varela, 1999) in the form of unfixed and open writing spaces and an acute awareness of the ways the academy privileges, in its practices, conventions and career trajectories, a sense of competition between fixed and distinctive 'voices' (Jackson & Mazzei, 2009) and a lack of collaborative practices (Speedy, et al., 2010; Sakellaridis et al., 2008)—even the conference software for the 'International Congress of Qualitative Inquiry' (ICQI) fails to recognise 'Bristol Collaborative Writing Group' as a single-yet-collective author.

The collaborative writing environments established in Bristol hold biographical and historical traces of earlier European socialist feminist (Haug, 1999) and contemporary Australian post-structuralist feminist forays into collective memory and collective biography work (Davies & Gannon, 2006). As director of the centre, I bring a background of second-wave, feminist allegiances to 'the personal as political' as well as firmly held beliefs in cooperative political and community movements and a commitment towards "utopia as method" (Levitas, 2007) in social research. This juxtaposition of values and methods privileges the collective and the connected over the singular and the distinct, somewhat against the grain of the academy. This form of collaborative writing with 'hoods up' (Rippin & Porter, 2010) allows a collective identity and anonymity of ownership and authorship not available to the 'call and response' writers of the 'how writing touches' book, which is written in five distinctly authored voices (albeit each voice includes shards of the others).

There are then, two different styles of collaboration represented here—the first 'call and response'[3] and the second 'collectively inscribed', each arising from different technological, geographical and methodological circumstances, and also perhaps different understandings of what comes under the heading 'writing'. The 'collective' writing includes and even privileges, all the crafting—the literary rendering and interweaving of the accumulated pieces of simultaneously written text, all the "writing stories" as Laurel Richardson (2001) would call them, as part of its collaborative ethos. The 'call and response' writing emerges as a dialogue between different voices and the interweaving, editing and selecting of them is undertaken backstage, hidden from the audience's view. The 'call and response' writing is the result of individually named and owned email exchanges; the collectively inscribed writing emerges from the collating and interweaving of individually written texts in response to the same

---

[3] See Chapter 4

context, theme or issue, rather than in response to each other.

And yet, despite these differences in construction, both forms of collaborative writing offer similarly evocative invitations to readers and listeners to scramble into the imaginary spaces between the accumulation of lives they are presented with, gathering up stories and selves as they go.

It is perhaps this imaginary space that opens up the different ethical practices and processes for collaborative writers and scholars that I have been most heartened by as a teacher/scholar in higher education. It is this compulsion to imagine and inscribe and connect our selves and our stories into and around the writing and lives of others that generates a radical, subversive space within the academy. Collaborative writing asks difficult questions about the structures and hierarchies of modern universities and societies and about what it means to publish scholarly work. The innovative contribution that collaborative writing (as opposed to other forms of writing as inquiry) makes to qualitative research methodologies is its explicit attention to multiplicities and connections. In focussing on the multiplicity and simultaneity of stories and selves that are brought to the chosen theme and/or space between writers, collaborative writing opens up these multiplicities for the scrutiny of all writers and readers whose work is engaged with the opening of imaginative and other spaces between lives. The work of collaborative writing groups draws explicit attention to the myriad 'inhabitants' of academic silences; to a contemporary widening of the social imaginary and to an acknowledgement that all the 'new' ethnographies—particularly the auto-ethnographies—are collaborative, performative and emancipatory methodologies. In shucking off the mantle of the esoteric and distant narrator and eschewing the development of their own distinct 'voice' or 'brand', collaborative writing methods offer an invitation to research users to engage with the academy as a facilitation service in the development of their own forms of scholarship and ways of knowing (c.f. Speedy and the Unassuming Geeks, 2005). If scholarship is becoming more intimate, more personal and more interconnected and if academic writing includes myriad opportunities to imagine ourselves into and between each other's lives, the relationships between researched and researcher that have taxed us all since Denzin and Lincoln's (2000) "crisis of representation" become more spacious, more connected and more potent sites for discovery.

It is this potency that I have noticed in the culture of collaborative writing that pervades our research centre: auto-ethnography and poetic, performative and other forms of writing as inquiry are also taught within our doctoral programmes, but it is exposure to collaborative writing communities that generates the most radical and emancipatory shift in people's work and in their sense of scholarship. Students and staff engaged in these communities become differently connected with each other, presenting radical challenges that often crash into or through the university's established career structures and ways of working (Gale, Speedy & Wyatt, Chapter 10).

As I read through what I have written here in the abstract and the body of the text, I am struck by all that has been left out. I have played across different writing and reading times and spaces, including making reference to the process of writing this piece, but I have left out the most massive changes to all the selves I might bring into my writing that took place between the writing of the abstract and the writing of the ensuing paper. These two pieces of writing were written by the same woman but were very differently inhabited and embodied. The woman who wrote the abstract was curled up in front of the woodburner with her feet stretched out on the dog at her feet, anticipating her attendance later in the academic year at ICQI. The woman who wrote the rest of this paper on her deck had clearly not flown over to the USA to attend the ICQI. She had no intention of moving out of her own backyard, or of curling up anywhere. She was sitting bolt upright on her deck in a wheelchair, typing with one hand. The massive stroke that had befallen her between the writing of the abstract and the compilation of the rest of the chapter—an overwhelming and defining experience—had been quietly left out of the text. She wrote as if from the same body (the default position of bodies—the body readers have imagined her inhabiting throughout this text thus far—being 'able-bodied').

This disembodied writing about writing rang false, by omission, as I re-read it. The six months with my colleagues and students waiting to find out if I was going to make it to the ICQI in May 2012, an important date in our research centre's calendar, had somehow been washed out of this text, but these bodily changes were inscribed between the lines as I read them, perhaps written in larger writing as a result of their absence. The body written into and out of the main text, being a broken, spoiled or (dis)abled body, hidden quietly away in the backyard, not ready yet for public display.

This volume is about collaborative writing, and yet all writing is collaborative, insofar as all writing is an embodied and imagined accumulation of selves and stories. All writing, to quote Gale &Wyatt (2009) is about love. All explicitly collaborative writing is about bringing what Weems (2005) describes as the "imagination-intellect" into play and extending the social imaginary of the academy; collaborative writing is about engaging with the highly subversive activity, much neglected amongst scholars, of building loving communities within and across groups of writers, across disciplines and themes and across continents. To write collaboratively is to engage with reconsiderations of scholarship and of what it means to be a human being living amongst other human beings and other species and elements on this planet.

CHAPTER SEVEN

HOOD UP AND HOOD DOWN WRITING: ANONYMITY, COMMUNITY AND IDENTITY

SUE PORTER AND ANN RIPPIN

Introduction

In this chapter, we explore the questions of disclosure and exposure in the context of collective writing, drawing on our experience of writing in collective biography (Davis & Gannon, 2006) and other collaborative writing groups, including a group of women writers who convened to produce a collaborative biographical account of love. We question the interplay between the collective and the individual, what is disclosed and what remains unspoken (and possibly unspeakable) in these writing groups, the anonymity of the dispersed self when the individual can get lost in the crowd of the edited text, and the ways that we can track how individuals and individuality are always under negotiation, constantly under erasure.

Before discussing our thoughts on this form of writing we offer a definition of collective biography itself.

Collective biography

Collective biography as a method draws upon the earlier memory work of Haug (1987), in its form of bringing together a group of 'biographers' to share memories of a common experience, and through talking and writing develop a collective 'biography' which "produces a web of experiences that are at once individual, connected, collective" (Davies & Gannon, 2006, p.18). The method utilizes cycles of talking, writing, reading and responding, seeking to find collective experience in the accounts of lived experiences. Richardson uses the crystal as a metaphor for new and different forms of qualitative writing practices: collective biography is one such form of writing, a crystal face through which the individual writers reflect, refract, grow and change both collectively and individually (Richardson, 1997, p.91). The many angles and variations in the shapes and forms of crystals give us a sense of the diverse, multiple voices of a collective group of writers. However, crystals can also bend light and it's the bending and blending possibilities of collective writing/biography groups that offer opportunities for individual writers to speak out in ways they may not be able to do elsewhere.

Hoods up, or hoods down?

One of the aspects of collective biography that has caught our attention is that of the dispersed self; the loss of the identifiable individual within the edited text, an anonymity, whether sought or not, the specific absorbed into a textured whole. The authors have come to call this 'hood up' or 'unhooded' writing. Writing with the hood up allows the author to hide herself within the jointly owned and authored text, unhooded writing comes when the safety, and maybe the acceptance of the group, enables an author to gain confidence to speak out from collective anonymity.

There is an advert for a private pension company in the UK that features a cloaked woman (a Scottish widow). In her full-length, black cloak and voluminous hood she looks mysterious and otherworldly—she could be death or the maiden. Towards the end of the advert she turns to face the camera and lifts the hood from her head, exposing her face and a mane of dark hair, her eyes meet the eyes of the viewer. Her face fills the screen.

A core issue for collaborative writing groups in our experience is how much to trust other members and make oneself vulnerable and how much to hold back and protect the self, and, when the group shares its writing, how much an author chooses to hide within the group, and what this enables her to write, which might otherwise be unspeakable.

Subsequent to writing in a larger collective biography group, we two wrote the following piece exploring this hooded and unhooded tension, before reflecting on the experience of writing in these two modes together.

Writing with my hood up

There are, as Wordsworth (2006) said, "thoughts that do often lie too deep for tears", thoughts that can take the skin off your knees, thoughts that will take a razor to your ear, leave a perfect blue imprint of four knuckles smashed across your cheekbone. There are experiences for which, for all we cope and manage and deal with them, can still, if they catch us unaware, in an unguarded and unprotected moment, reduce us to tears or cause us to stammer and stutter and blush. We understand that in polite society we should keep these words and experiences to ourselves. We know that alluding to them would risk opprobrium from our colleagues, perhaps even sniggering, certainly deep embarrassment, which we do not want to cause. But, nevertheless, these thoughts and experiences exist. And if they are there for us, then it stands to reason that they are there for others. Ann writes:

I cannot be the only one in my organisation nursing and nurturing elaborate revenge fantasies against the powerful and power-wielding, for example. I put my hood up and write:

Let us imagine a golden boy strolls into my classroom on a sunny October morning. Let us imagine all the lyricism of the poet of the Song of Solomon could not do justice to his golden skin, his doe-like eyes, his honeyed-breath, his subtle form. Because of my particular institution, let us imagine twisting and trailing and winding about him like musk is his wealth and position and provenance. Let us imagine his smile. Let us imagine, next, that we find ourselves in a smaller and more intimate tutorial room with him. Let us imagine that he then comes to our unshared room for a little help with his assignment.

And let us snap shut our imaginations right there.

Another example. Let us take the case of the polycystic ovary. Try to imagine quite what a useless specimen that is. Consider the monthly torment to the infertile woman of the fruit of that malfunctioning organ being precisely nothing. Let us imagine the darkness and the pain and the hollowness and the lack and feeling of incompleteness that goes with that particular repeated monthly failure. The pain of other people's baby photos and moans about the paucity of good schools. The pain of separation from someone you never had.

As someone trying to explore the world around me, as a (quasi) social scientist, these phenomena might well concern me: transgressive love and infertility; hidden but powerful motivations; social phenomena. As a social scientist, I might want to say something meaningful about either. I might as a researcher want to climb inside a painful experience, see it and feel it from the inside out, and not just through the telescopic lens of survey data. I might even want to speak from out of my experience. And so as a career academic as well as a searcher after knowledge, I must share my knowing with the wider world. Knowing isn't enough. I need to disseminate my findings, publish them in a wide, almost boundary-less community. But there are some things about me that I might not want that community to know about me, even if I want them to know about it.

Collective biography allows me to explore and to re-present those explorations in an inhabited way, which will provide testimony, thick description, compelling data for those who truly want to know rather than merely count, and simultaneously to keep myself safe, protected, whole.

By keeping my hood up, I can safely reveal myself.

Unhooded

One of the writers in one group we are a part of, the 'Love' collective biography group, noted in her own process of 'will I? won't I?' at the end of the first day, deciding how 'unhooded' she wanted or dared to be with her writing companions:

So where am I in all this questioning?

Is 'love' yet another arena for self-doubt and uncertainty?

Waiting to make sure the invitation is aimed at me.

Glancing to check I'm doing ok…

How much should I reveal?

What will happen if I expose how I really feel?

Should I just play the 'being-cool' game?

What happens when Sue takes off all her clothes and stands on the canal bank naked?

She then wrote about 'standing on the canal bank naked':

What happens when Sue takes off all her clothes and stands on the canal bank naked? I'll tell you what happened:

We went for a walk. We were still playing at being friends, being neighbourly. I don't remember who suggested it, the walk in the dark along the towpath, over the lock and onto the canal bank. Lying together in the still-warm grass I watched the rain falling on one side of the (ship) wide canal. I swear it never rained on us as we lay there. Not that I would have minded the rain. It was 1976, a long dry summer, and rain became just a memory to us.

There was a magical feeling about the night; everyone else in bed in the farmhouse we shared, the lights out in the houseboats moored by the lock. Seeing the edge of the rain shower—being protected from it—seemed to perfectly fit the mood. After all, if I could have you like this, then I could have anything, everything.

When we finally rose to return home I couldn't bear to put my dress back on, but strolled wrapped only in a shawl, the long silk fringes sliding on the backs of my naked calves as I walked, bare footed and bare arsed.

I remember too our perfect parting—you standing in the doorway of my half of the house, silhouetted against the moonlight. The white horse in the paddock moving to meet you as you walked past to your own door.

I lay in my wide bed later, awake and thinking of tomorrow, and tomorrow. A long moment of trust-without-fear, rare and seldom repeated.

It was this piece of writing that gave the writing group a descriptor, 'bare-arsed', for writing that was intimate and unhooded. For there are layers of choices to be considered here, regarding both content and process: the exposing or risky nature of the content of the writing; and am I to be identified as the writer.

Sue writes:

Whereas in some other aspects of my life I am happy to sink into being unseen as an individual, indistinguishable from the group, when it comes to my writing then I notice I cannot easily let go of one aspect of authorship—that of the performance. Seeing my words on the page, nestled into the words of others is ok, in fact it's just fine. I can follow my words across the page and have come to enjoy the point at which I lose a sense of whether I wrote what comes next, or whether it's another's words that chime in so harmoniously that neither of us can tell the difference. Hand in hand we can travel as a group through the watery medium of the text, just occasionally one person may come up for air, but then sinks back into the shoal of authors, the collective.

No, it's not the seeing, it's the speaking that I can't want to let go. I want to speak my words, to perform myself. Even when I'm speaking the unspeakable, the shocking, the vulnerable me, I want to be the one that performs me. The socially transgressive act of performing that which has been silenced (Park-Fuller, 2000, p.26) turns the telling into an act of self-liberation. I am attached to my performance; to the space it creates for me, around me, to the line, the direct look it throws to you, the audience. The invitation is to see an aspect of my identity, which I perform for you, with you, in the moment of the speaking/listening.

I lift the hood, let it fall back onto my shoulders, exposing my face.

Pause for reflection

So, did the ground move for us as we reflected, wrote and rewrote about our experiences of love? There may have been some seismic disturbances but we can perhaps agree with Haug that:

"Writing stories is fun... it expands our knowledge enormously, sharpens our social perception, improves our use of language, changes our attitude to others and to ourselves." (Haug, 1987, p.71)

But this form of inquiry is not unproblematic, and one of the problems it raises is what we have described as 'hood-up' or 'unhooded' modalities of writing. Insisting on retaining an individual voice is important for certain political groups that need to tell specific, differentiated, embodied stories from particular perspectives. So, while we might find an unbounded, collective, encountering identity very attractive, it needs to be worked by and with this subjectivity and be prepared to contribute to action for social justice.

The email exchange

One of the joys of collaborative writing can be the possibility of making great friendships, which are enhanced through an appreciation of another person's outlook on life, but also of the quality of their writing. We met together and wrote and talked about writing on a number of occasions. We were expecting, therefore, that it would be a fairly simple matter to write something reflective and analytical about the hooded/unhooded writing quoted above. But, despite a number of meetings and sincere promises to produce a draft, we found it almost impossible to write the meta-account of our work together. In the end, we both undertook to converse about the task via email. This is the exchange that followed:

On Tues, January 8, 2013 19:49, Sue Porter [UoB] wrote:
Well, it feels as if our title should be shrouded, rather than hooded...
I write this struggling to keep a spirit of inquiry, rather than get lost in self-blaming and frantic scurrying around. I am finding this the most mercurial chapter to pull into being; just as soon as I feel clear about it, it shape shifts and dissolves away. I think I know what we have agreed, what I am to do, and then I can find no trace of my notes, no reminder of even the first steps. I am left wondering, is it my imagination that caused it all to feel so clear? My chaotic state that has allowed the clarity to slip and fade away? We had a great plan, the latest of several, and yet now I cannot find even a coherent sketch.

What of this project wishes to remain obscure? What was it that was exposed to view, for a short while and while we were together, yet slips back into shadow once we are apart? It is as if we need proximity to each other to conjure it out of hiding. A metaphor for collective writing maybe—that some things can only be sustained in relationship.

What I do remember is that we said that we would email each other daily for the next week, and see what new material surfaces, and so, a little late, here is my first contribution to the exchange. Tiny, confused, rather ashamed of itself, but a first step.

And I notice that, in admitting my not knowing, in confessing losing my notes of our conversation, I change in-turned shame into excitement.

Making myself vulnerable is an important aspect of our writing relationship, feeling exposed feeds me, keeps me sharp. Hood off.

x Sue

On 10 Jan 2013, at 09:01, AJ Rippin, Department of Management wrote:

Well, as ever you have put your finger on it. I think mercurial is the perfect epithet. I clearly remember having a conversation with the women writers on another project and thinking, "Sue and I must write this paper; it has a real contribution to make about the need for self-protection in a bruising academic world, and the need to find the strength and courage to shout loudly from centre stage, and the difficulty of doing both." But I can't remember the details. I can't remember what made me think that, or what exactly our contribution should be.

And, I notice I had completely forgotten we were going to do this—our one action point on this chapter. I got back to my desk and then everything vanished.

And this is odd, because I love the chapter and I do think it has great things to say. I love the quality of the writing. I love the subversion of writing in the face of the academy rather than for it. So, why can't we finish this chapter?

Do you know what it makes me think of suddenly? Penelope weaving that tapestry or stitching that embroidery every day and then undoing it every night to put off her suitors and to protect her relationship with her husband. Is that what we are doing? What are we protecting? Who are we protecting it against? And another Classical myth.

This feels ridiculous. There is a paper here about not being able to finish. Another about the need to be in-relationship. Another about Classical myth and archetypes. Again, you are right. I wanted to dash off and think about Mercury and Penelope.

I have a great friend who says that it is the curse of academics that they are always writing about something that they are no longer interested in. This isn't the case here. We get great energy from this. But, and here's a thought, maybe from the performance of it, and not the writing about it. Perhaps that is where it really exists. And another hare is set running.

But will we ever finish the original one?
And it is not as if the clock is not ticking...
A x

On Sat, January 12, 2013 5:17 pm, Sue Porter [UoB] wrote:
Collective writing as performance...
Reminds me of clowning, with a small group or a partner. The whole business of letting go of 'trying to get it right' is itself an effort. The focus on allowing what arises to flow through the clowning, while keeping a relationship with the audience and your partner(s). These are difficult balancing acts—the acrobatics of staying in-relationship. You could say the circus of collective writing is transgressive in the 'serious' setting of academic writing, and clowns frighten the adults more than the children.
So, if I draw on my clowning experience, then I'd say we could seek to just go with it... playing into who we are, rather than who we think we ought to be.
x Sue

On 24 Jan 2013, at 11:37, AJ Rippin, Department of Management wrote:
I think this is vital—the notion of being in relationship in this kind of writing. If we really want to remain open and in the moment it runs directly against the requirements of academic writing which has to be finished, hermetically sealed and not open to debate—hence my reviewers' comments on being tentative that I have received recently. Our writing is about opening ourselves up as a resource for people to work with—about sensitive and emotional areas—living with disability; childlessness, erotic charges in the classroom, having bare arses. The writing is done in relationship to each other—including our lovely outings, which we no longer seem to have—and our growing and changing friendship, and relationship to the reader—what we seem to be modelling and evoking is vulnerability—like clowning. Like performing a text. Like performing anything, I suspect.
Hope this makes sense.
A x

Writing this email exchange allowed us to discuss our work and acknowledge the fact that we would much rather write than write about writing. We both found relief in this acknowledgement which is difficult for practising academics to make, that we were reluctant to theorise about something we loved to do, like smashing a Ming vase to see how it was made or pulling a plant up by the roots to see how it was growing. But it allowed us to highlight two themes underpinning what we found compelling about collective writing: risk and vulnerability that requires us to keep our hoods up, and the need for witnessing through producing performative texts that requires us to keep our hoods down. We develop this further in the following section.

Risk—Hoods Up

There is for some a particularly generative aspect to collective writing, an excitement that comes at least in part from sustaining the exchange, staying in-relationship with other writers, as well as the subject, which contrasts strongly with the pressures of academic life. As we have touched upon in our email exchange, the mores of the academy, and specifically the Research Excellence Framework (REF) audit currently operating in the UK, drives us to competitive behaviours such as the political scramble to be submitted to the audit which is dependent on the 'quality' of research 'outputs' and to be recorded 'first' author, who can claim the writing as part of their REF return, and so on. This can 'flatten' and reduce the experience of writing from a creative/responsive act into a simply instrumental process that churns out the journal articles, reports and conference papers. In the world of REF writing there is little space for multiple authorship and explorations through writing without targets. While Principal Investigators and their successful work teams are lauded, there is little scope to insist on the truly collaborative where individual contributions merge together and no-one can claim 'thought leadership'. In the face of this normalising process of academic evaluation why would anyone want to submit their experimental, gorgeous writing to be taken apart by reviewers, to have the heat and excitement taken out of sharing it by the delays in publication? To write in this way becomes a subversive act rather than a valid methodological choice.

However many collaborating writers, in academic and other fields, are engaged in exploring a form which challenges our individual selves (even as we, along with Deleuze, treat this individuality as a process of becoming rather than a settled state), and offer a we-ness which is a recognition that:

"The *I*, as a psychic individual, can only be thought in relationship to a we, which is a collective individual: the *I* is constituted in adopting a collective tradition, which it inherits, and in which a plurality of *I*s acknowledge each other's existence." (Stiegler, 2004[1]).

In collaborative writing, recognising, working with and unravelling our separate subjectivities is part of the ongoing work of staying in-relationship, which is catalysed by the writing, listening and responding process. In this way, collaborative writing can be said to be *writing as a way of being in the world* (Wyatt et al., 2011, p.106)), as an ethical practice of co-operation, an expression of reciprocity, and as such it is risk taking, and challenging, sometimes taking us beyond our comfort zones.

Risk is central to our understanding of both the practice and the value of collaborative writing. As we have seen, this can be a way to say the unsayable, itself a risky undertaking, and it can be an intrinsic part of relationship building with co-inquirers. The idea of facing a risk down and overcoming it can suggest that this form of writing is therapeutic, a term which opens the writer up to the charge of being unacademic, and which is to be avoided (Rippin, 2006). The notion that therapy is ever absent from our attempts to make sense of the world through scholarship, research and inquiry is questionable, as is the idea that this would be a bad thing. As hooks says of writing in general:

"One can have a complete imaginative engagement with writing as craft and still experience it in a manner that is therapeutic; one urge does not diminish the other." (hooks, 1999, p.14).

In considering whether to disclose or withhold, one of the ways in which we can think about decisions the collaborative writer makes relates to 'risk': risk to the writer, and risk to those with whom she shares her writing.

Berman (2001) writes about sharing what he terms 'risky writing' in the context of the classroom. He makes the argument that self-disclosure can be therapeutic, can lead to "self-transformation", and be generally beneficial to the writer and her audience. However, as the term 'risky writing' suggests, Berman also emphasises the risks involved in this sort of self-disclosure in a group setting. Like Ann's example of academics writing about their feelings towards their students, we may write in order to understand ourselves and also to be understood, but we cannot always predict or control the impact of our words on others. Benjamin, for one,

---

[1] This was a lecture, hence no page reference.

talks about the *Nachleben* or afterlife of a work of art going out into the world beyond its creator's control, open to interpretation in ways that he or she never contemplated (Pryke, Rose & Whatmore, 2003).

Berman suggests that "Risky writing threatens nothing less than the writer's identity and self-respect" (2001, p.9), and that shame can be a key emotion in risky writing. Even when the writer has done nothing wrong, if the disclosure relates to a shaming experience such as sexual assault, our fear of being shamed may cause us to remain silent, freezing the shame inside us. The alternative is to risk the buffeting and vulnerability caused by releasing negative feelings of fear and anger, and the possibility of being re-traumatised. Writing about infertility and the polycystic ovary, for example, calls into question identity and validity as a human female, albeit in an essentialist and reductive way, but one that is nevertheless painful. Additionally, particularly in the early stages of a writing group/relationship, we may fear that self-disclosed experiences will lead others to judge us, and that our listeners will be critical, or fail to keep our confidences.

Marian MacCurdy writes about the reasons to facilitate opportunities for self-disclosure in writing, starting with a desire to give school students "the opportunity to tell their truths" as a way of discovering that they can have some control over their own lives; offering the opportunity for reflection and insight and planting the seeds of agency and change, a chance to remake the self (MacCurdy, 2002, p.197). As Berman writes of his student Diana:

> "It appears, though, that writing about molestation has allowed her to express the heretofore unexpressed and thus to construct a meaning that will provide aesthetic satisfaction and psychological relief." (Berman, 2001, p.12)

Baumlin, Jensen & Massey, in an article on the ethics of growth, write that:

> "a more sophisticated approach to autobiography would reveal the simultaneous presence of two rhetorics. One, a rhetoric of identity, seeks out the stable, knowable characteristics of the self; the second, a rhetoric of transformation, discovers those moments in time, typically crises and 'conversion experiences', when the self is changed and identity thus remade. Identity ranges across a continuum of transformations." (Baumlin et al., 1999, p.206).

This tug between the known and the changing is at the heart of choosing whether, how and when to disclose when we write, at least partially in order to discover what we know and who we are.

Risk, then, emerges as a central concern of our writing. Through the metaphor of writing with our hoods up or down, we can explore issues of risk, safety and vulnerability. These are not, we would insist, by-products or perils of this form of writing that need to be avoided or require elaborate self-defensive routines. They are intrinsic to the collective work that we want to do to make our experience of being in the world and embodying certain social phenomena such as disability, infertility, and the moral hazard of eroticism in the classroom available to others as rich, contextualised data experienced through very particular bodies.

The challenge could be made that all writing carries the potential for this sort of riskiness, but it is our contention that writing in the collective makes for a safer space to explore this. It provides a protected space for the unsayable to be said in powerful ways, including in performance, which we now come on to consider.

Performative writing—Hoods Down

One of the forms of writing that appeals to us as contextualised, embodied women writing in the form of collaborative writing, which might be termed 'The Bristol School', is performative writing. We take our starting position from Spry's work, in which she insists on the centrality of three elements: writing from a particular bodily experience; writing as craft and the importance of performance, what she calls body-page-stage. Evocative writing, which is intended to move the reader, is also written to move the listener. Witnessing, which is part of the Bristol model (see Chapter 19), requires those who witness to be those who will listen and take the narrative seriously. As we have seen, this became an element we explored in our email exchange. Sue is clear about this and the links to another of her inquiry practices, clowning:

"[It r]eminds me of clowning, with a small group or a partner. The whole business of letting go of 'trying to get it right' is itself an effort. The focus on allowing what arises to flow through the clowning, while keeping a relationship with the audience and your partner(s). These are difficult balancing acts—the acrobatics of staying in-relationship. You could say the circus of collective writing is transgressive in the 'serious' setting of academic writing, and clowns frighten the adults more than the children.

So, if I draw on my clowning experience, then I'd say we could seek to just go with it... playing into who we are, rather than who we think we ought to be. "

And Ann expands:

"Our writing is about opening ourselves up as a resource for people to work with—about sensitive and emotional areas—living with disability; childlessness, erotic charges in the classroom, having bare arses. The writing is done in relationship to each other—including our lovely outings, which we no longer seem to have—and our growing and changing friendship, and relationship to the reader—what we seem to be modelling and evoking is vulnerability—like clowning. Like performing a text. Like performing anything, I suspect."

The recipe starts to emerge: letting go of injunctions to 'get it right'; reclaiming the idea of performance from a top-down injunction to 'perform', to an invitation to a conscious practice of embodied writing; and staying in-relationship, as Davies writes:

> "Collaborative writing is
> to be co-implicated with the other
> to be present
> to be assailed by thoughts by being
> to be singular   to exist in the space of writing with"
> (Wyatt et al., 2011, p.131)

We understand this as an ethical practice of co-operation; the practice of staying open to oneself and the other(s) in the writing relationship, as Davies and Wyatt write:

> "Such a conception of ethical practice takes me, again, to listening, listening both to oneself and to the other, listening not just for meaning, but for affect, for modes of existence that include and go beyond rationally acquired knowledge (Nancy, 2007). Such a listening is not categorical and self-referencing, but involves listening to thought with an openness of mind, with openness to differentiation". (Wyatt et al., 2011, p.112)

Performance, then, becomes not just an exhibitionist 'look at me' practice, but an ethical choice and a scholarly practice. We meet others and share in their experience without judgement, and we learn to listen in a way that is more sensitive than carrying out the most rigorously constructed interviews or focus groups could ever be. Spry says that once you know that writing comes from a particular body, things change (Spry, 2001). It is much more powerful, then, to have that body performing a text, to write and perform a piece with one's hood down, than to have some of the affect bleached away by an 'other' giving the performance. Being seen and heard is of crucial importance in the collaborative, performative writing that we want to do. It is not that either mode of writing is better. The point of our contribution is to insist on the importance of holding open the possibility of both forms of writing for researchers to decide which is the most appropriate for them, and why, depending on what they want to investigate and how they want to engage their readers. It is a challenge to the increasing tendency of the social sciences to mimic the natural sciences in restricting our choice of methodologies and modes of writing.

CHAPTER EIGHT

NEGOTIATING THE STORMS OF NOMADIC COLLABORATIVE WRITING: THE OBITUARY AS METHOD OF INQUIRY

KEN GALE, JANE SPEEDY AND JONATHAN WYATT

We'd been writing together, publishing a paper called 'Gatecrashing the Oasis' (Gale, Speedy & Wyatt, 2010), with Ken and Jonathan cast as nomads and Jane as their ally helping them as their supervisor to infiltrate the oasis as academia. Then Ken and Jane fell out and we all fell silent. So Jane decided to take matters into her own hands:

Jane

Jane Speedy, the innovative British text maker, died this morning in bed accompanied by her dog, Rubi and her silver laptop. She had spent much of her life engaged with the construction of textual spaces to step into and perform from. As we write, the cause of death is unclear, although it is thought that she had woven herself into a textual mesh too thin to carry her weight and had simply fallen through her own words into the silence. Known for her collaborative projects with a range of people, both living, dead and totally made up in the moment, she had been working, at the time of her death, on a collaborative piece that was thought to have fallen into intertextual difficulties, concerned with a nomadic plot to disrupt the day-to-day boredom and assumptions of academic life.

Jane's writing life had started with letter formation at the age of four with a big, thick, china-blue crayon and a roll of lining paper and had moved on through an unhappily ink-stained Marion Richardson sentence construction phase, emerging in adolescence into glorious over-the-top, turquoise, italic poetics. As an adult she had moved inconsistently between green inks on yellow paper, gaudy pink and purple gel pens and a series of much-loved silver laptops. She had always gone too far. Jane's bedroom is not being treated as a crime scene and foul play is not suspected. The text police are currently investigating any signs of nomadic activity in the area, as they believe that the intertextual difficulties she was experiencing may have involved a group of travelling nomads. It is thought that some outbreaks of writing against the grain earlier in the year, in and around one of the closely guarded inner oases, may have been linked to the cause of her death.

Although, as we write, we are still waiting for a coroner's report, we are able to reveal that textmakers, rather like Tamagotchi toys, are known to simply fade away eventually if starved of response for too long a period of time. Indeed, the international commission on human writes recently recognised and condemned prolonged silence as a form of torture that was being used against renegade textmakers in a number of textually constrained and constraining parts of the globe. Jane Speedy may simply have given up the ghost through lack of response. She is survived by her partner Sarah and daughter Esther, her dear old dad and her dog Rubi, a large number of unfinished projects and a beautiful silver laptop.

Jane is dead, long live Jane! (Ken)

In that early writing that Jonathan and I did together for the EdD programme and what became our first publications together, we all (Ken, Jonathan and Jane) played with the idea of Jane's presence or absence in Ken and Jonathan's early nomadic wanderings. I remember claiming with great conviction that I wrote without any sense of Jane being there. I still believe in that unawareness as I reflect on it now.

Jane, it was as if you brought yourself alive! Your living self entered the work that we were doing, offering a presence, that, at first, I think we were unprepared for.

I see you differently now. You no longer simply represent—although of course in part you do, as woman, as supervisor, as 'head honcho', etc. —you are lived experience now, it is your friendship that fires this methodology. Is it that simple? Is it just that we have come to know each other, that we have become, or are becoming friends? This term embodiment keeps coming to me: it is not knowing you Jane it is *a* knowing and therefore for me it is about sense.

It is about our work together, it is about not knowing and therefore it is about living more and more in haecceities (Deleuze & Guattari, 1988), in the wonderful world of sense and value that always refuses to be tied down in categories of self or taxonomies of action, it is that lovely growing feeling of being able to perform self through the writing and to write to break down the division of self and writing that is a space of illusion.

Jane.
Dead?
How could that be?
Never.

Jonathan

Jonathan Gunning Wyatt, nomad, had his quest for life interrupted, after weeks of passivity, on Sunday 16 November in his guinea pigskin home on the Abingdon steppes.

His passing was brought on, finally, by abnegation of responsibility and lack of agency, both of which have been variously ascribed to a surfeit of post-structural doubt, an acute loss of faith and too intense a taste for mourning (Derrida, 2003). This most recent extended period of tameness was not the first such episode in his life. On this occasion, however, his inactivity proved too much. Having remained silent while his erstwhile playmates and collaborative writing partners, Drs Ken Gale and Jane Speedy, slugged it out in an altercation that led, tragically though indirectly, to the late Dr Speedy's own untimely end, he realised that his complicity in her death was undeniable and he turned his absence of presence upon himself.

For a number of years, Wyatt had not been sure of who or what he was. The nomadic life, despite its profound joys and discoveries, had left him disorientated and lost. In one moment, he would be clear that he was an individual of the humanistic kind or, perhaps, at least, a unique existent (Cavarero, 2000), while in another he would be struck with sudden, vital and liberating clarity that he was neither of these but was instead a small, rusty but significant cog in a machinic assemblage; a flow, an intensity, mulitiplicities (see, for instance, Deleuze & Guattari, 1988). And then, maybe, as he reached to pat his camel kindly on the neck, he would be struck immobile by his binary thinking and unable to hold these two alternatives as anything other than mutually exclusive. This initial, merely chronic, doubt gave him both ethical and agentic difficulties, which he was ultimately never able to resolve.

Gale, his great ally, relentlessly took him to new regions of Deleuze and, when they reached the Great Oasis with Speedy's steadfast support and could officially begin playing with Speedy, it seemed as if there would be no end to this adventure.

Tragedy swiftly arrived, however. Speedy, in that much raked-over incident, told a story of Gale that Gale took to mean both that she saw him as a separate, individuated being, a "Ken-as-only-Ken", and that she was suggesting his claim to haecceity was untrustworthy.

Gale recovered well from this terrible time and in his later response to Speedy's loss, he wrote as if Speedy was not gone at all. However, for Wyatt, the loss of Speedy was too much. The phrase from their Speedy obituary, that, as a textmaker, she maybe had "fade(d) away eventually... starved of response for too long a period of time" stayed with and haunted him to the end.

Wyatt is survived by the ever-tolerant Tessa, budding writer Joe and established teenage socialite Holly. His dear friend Ken, of course, remains to tell their continuing tales.

Ken

Coming to? Awakening? What is this? Where am I? This is strange, very strange. All these people, a crowd packed together in seated rows. I know them! God, I know them all! What is this? Where am I?

And that amazing view, those swallows darting and skimming past the huge window in and out of vision; they are appearing from all sides and in the distance, they seem so free in their aerial dance… and down across the fields, that beautiful wooded valley. It is so rich, so green, so incredibly alive, glowing in counterpoint to that iridescent blue sky. This is so lovely, why aren't these people watching this beautiful peaceful scene, they seem unhappy, sad, distracted, distracted by what? That box? That long wooden box, is that what they are looking at? My God, a coffin, flowers, shiny handles, yes, that's it! What is this? Where am I?

It's a funeral obviously. I seem to be above all this. In the sky? On the ceiling? I don't seem to be alone in all this looking down. I remember thinking about this when my mother died, I imagined her there, above, detached, withdrawn but yet able to see. Died? Dead? Am I dead? Is that what is happening here? Where have I been? What have I been doing? When was I last alive?! That sounds ridiculous, I feel alive now! I am going to have to work on this; is this to do with memory? Is this to do with living in another world? Am I going to be able to make any connections here? This is *my* funeral. My funeral and I am still alive?!

I am beginning to think myself into this situation. In my emerging presence I am beginning to sense myself in a shifting world of ethereality and corporeality. Thinking again! Just leave those thoughts for the moment, just be in this situation; look, what's unfolding now? Someone is talking down there. But I can't... is it that I don't want to hear? I can feel myself with others, here, with people who have died. Is that Jane? Jonathan? Of course they died didn't they, my nomadic mates who couldn't stand the pace and just popped off. I remember their obituaries, written by someone else. Their real obituaries, for me, was all the lovely writing that they left behind, writing that we shared, that coaxed and teased us into other worlds of inquiry.

I don't remember (actually) dying. I am living somewhere in between extensive and intensive bodies.

Obituaries. I remember those elegies to Jane and then Jonathan, my erstwhile pals and conspirators; they were so full of re-membering. It was as if, after the initial disbelief that they had both died, that the writing kept them alive. That's it, the way that the writing helps to re-member, to re-configure bodies, to change the emphasis of presence but essentially to maintain the feeling that they are still there. I wrote with Jonathan about this some time ago, focusing upon the way in which his writing served to keep his dad alive and how through our shared writings, it helped me, in turn, to bring my dad back to life. Jane, Jonathan and now me, floating in this strange ethereal place, unsure of the in-between-ness of it all but sensing an acceptance and an enjoyment of these new (are they?) virtual moments.

In all this living and dying, I sense the tide changing, no longer slack. I am in repose on this beach; I no longer wistfully look out at distant rocks and islands and long to bring their sunny vistas alive on my body. I can enter this water. It is as if this swimming, this flying in warm, intoxicating water will simply take me there; I will adventure with other travellers, I will become the nomad that I simply wrote about. Perhaps this will really be my death, no longer absorbed in imagery, no longer drawn to the lonely writer's desk, no longer strung up by those words. Perhaps then there will be another obituary for me to read. I will stop writing and... and... ah there it is, the 'flying' poem:

> Standing at the edge
> of a very tall building,
> feeling the ability
> just to step off,
> the gull wings stretched,
> immediately lifted

by the breeze
sweeping across the parapet.
My vertigo holds me back
The backs of my legs
shiver.
The great fear of falling
The great envy of flying
To fly
To fly
To fly

Jane (as narrator)

And meanwhile over on another cloud... a little to the left, slightly overlooking the cloud Ken is flying around... two translucent wraith-like forms (one short and stubby, the other long and wispy) are engaged in casual, but intense, conversation...

Jane: How's the ghost writing coming along?

Jonathan: I'm beginning to get the hang of it thanks. It's been a bit odd being out of a body, though. I keep trying to use hands I haven't got to pick up pens I cannot grasp...

Jane: I know what you mean... I still can't really write completely telepathically and sustain any sense of form or content. I still have to imagine paper or parchment and then think onto it in green ink. I've always, secretly, thought in green ink but now I'm really coming out of the closet about that—Veridian—out and proud. The unicorns can do it standing on their horns of course (writing telepathically, I mean) but then they've had centuries of magical realist practice and since they never 'really' existed they don't even regard magical realism as a subversive form of social inquiry (see Bowers, 2004), for them all this is just obvious, everyday stuff.

What did you think of Ken's contribution?

Jonathan: Great quote. Great writing. Pity he didn't like the obituaries though. I thought mine was a masterpiece. Is he dead yet, do you think, or somewhere in-between?

Jane: Well, he might be dead, he is flying about the place. He seems too convinced still of the fixed differences between death and life to be truly dead in my book.

Jonathan: Truly dead in your book, eh, there's a thought. Give him a break, though, he's only just arrived... and may even be just visiting. It is hard for people to grasp that we are all born dying... not the gargoyles of course, who were probably always dead, but people, human people have a tough time adjusting to this existence here...

Jane: Mmmm, it's not just that that worries me though, it's all this privileging of life over death. As the first to die, as the most dead of the three of us... (even if I did die just to get your attention... did I ever confess to that? I was jealous you know, you two seemed to have really taken off without me, seemed to be off with all your cool, North American friends and I couldn't think how to get you to notice me any more... and then I thought, I know, I'll die, that'll cause a bit of a stir... and it did— trouble is I ended up dead and that takes some getting used to. I've just been through the longest silence ever).

Anyway, next thing I knew you died too, which was a complete shock, but I've had the longest time to get a bit of altitude on all this—to really appreciate all the dead and forgotten creatures—not just humans, but albatrosses (why are there so many here, by the way?), centaurs and gorgons (to name but a few). I don't write to stay alive, or to keep people alive, I write to remember, to not be forgotten. I write to haunt... I write to see over into the edges of what I couldn't see if I remained alive, bound to conventions of time and place (or "splaces" as Badiou (2007) would describe it). I write now as somebody not just in a body without organs but out of body, not so much embodied as deadbodied... but am I going too far? Anyway, I'm well and truly dead. Being dead, becoming dead, is a line of flight that takes me right out of my 'self'... and yet the funny thing is, going back to Ken's writing, listening again to some of what he was saying... I still have edges... and the same sense of humour. Unexpected that, telling bad albatross jokes even when I'm dead...

Should we haunt Ken do you think, or is that mean?

Jonathan: Well, it does seem a bit mean, since he has written so beautifully into this space, but yes, why not, let's haunt him. Let's deaden things up a bit...

[-: I'm not sure if this is okay to write—"deaden things up"; it's definitely edgy stuff everywhere in the western world, especially from white people. We don't do dead, do we? We do hamming it up dead. Hammer-house-of-horror dead. But not dead dead. We do dying, tragedy, grief and mourning for a bit. But not for long. And then we move on. That's why it's okay for me to carry on writing about my dad to keep him alive... to keep his memory alive, but it's not okay to keep talking to him when he's thoroughly dead. Worst still when both of us are dead.

'Beloved'[1] was dead of course and she had a lot to say for herse
was an African American woman. I'm not sure if white Britisii people,
especially men, even men without skin, are allowed to take this definitely
dead stance. I think we are supposed to rot away like the British Empire,
not lurk and linger about like its after-effects…]

Jane: And yet here we are, two, possibly three dead white people
talking to each other and maybe that's just the point. We are not just
talking to each other, for each other… and we are not writing to keep your
father or my brother or Ken's mother alive… we are writing them,
stitching them into our simultaneity of selves, we are becoming them…
just like Sethe, who was alive still, but knew more than us and could say:

> "I am Beloved and she is mine. I see her take flowers away from leaves she
> puts them in a round basket the leaves are not for her she fills the basket
> she opens the grass I would help her but the clouds are in the way how can
> I say things that are pictures I am not separate from her there is no place
> where I stop her face is my own and I want to be there in the place where
> her face is." (Morrison, 2005, p.248)

Ken

I keep coming back to this cold place; I know that it is in between but I
am caught with all that Deleuzian stuff; this line of flight (from life to
death?) has me here, on a plane of immanence. There is a consistency
here. I am so aware of my feelings. Here on this plane, life is so acute; I
am drawn into a web of intensity, I know it is Jane and Jonathan that I am
connected with but I am disturbed by their words, their presence here.
They are drifting in and out… sometimes it feels as if Jane is giving
Jonathan words. I am beginning to feel more and more like someone in a
Bacon painting, sitting here on a cold wooden chair, like a naked piece of
meat, in anguish, my hands covering my face.

I found Jane's writing, on that scrap of paper, just a few minutes ago
and now I find myself being drawn into the ethereal existence of those
ghosts. That funny idea of ghost writing! I can't think why ghosts would
want to write and yet I can't resist the insistence of the image of my
friends, wispy and indistinct in writerly poses, writing. What are they
writing? I feel written about. What is this? I'm running scared; I am
beginning to lose my sense of whose writing is whose. At first I didn't

[handwritten margin note: Book title.]

---

[1] A haunting character in Toni Morrison's (1988) novel.

believe those obituaries; first Jane and then Jonathan. And now I find this
dialogue, on this piece of paper, they are talking with each other, about
me: what's this all about? Is it because they have been in this in-between
world longer than me and can talk the talk? I am not so sure about this
palace of limbo anymore, I am tuning into a sense of presence that is
disarming me.

Tuning? Tunes, music, that's it, it's so quiet here, how can I draw
myself into listening? How can I live in this in between place without
music? I remember those people, they were playing music at my funeral; it
was as if they had read my will, they were playing music that I loved;
there were knowing smiles on their faces. I remember drinking and
dancing in those mad shebeens in the 80s, wildly tranced out at those
totally insane all night raves in the late 90s, all part of the soundtrack of
my life. I must have written those tracks down somewhere and someone
must have dug them up and played them as part of some mad elegiac
chorus. I just hope that everyone danced. That's all.

I have a soundtrack, now, what is it? It's different, quieter... it's
Dylan. The insistent effect of this living hegemony is wrapping me up, it is
not just his words that are written upon my soul, there is a living affect
within the spirit of these words that wells up in me and wraps itself around
me. It happens so often; I find myself singing these words to myself, they
fit the moment that I am in, they are part of the haecceity, and it is only
later when I stop, reflect and sing the words over and over again that they
gain some kind of conceptual sense, born anew outside the womb of affect
and percept.

> Pointed threats, they bluff with scorn
> Suicide remarks are torn
> From the fool's gold mouthpiece
> The hollow horn plays wasted words
> Proves to warn
> That he not busy being born
> Is busy dying.[2]

Oh my god, of all the verses in that amazing song, from an album that
was a soundtrack to my life when I was only 18 years old, it is that one
that comes back to me. Why? Why? I keep feeling bounced back to Jane's
words in that dialogue, with Jonathan, on that scrap of paper...

---

[2] 'It's alright, ma (I'm only bleeding)', Bob Dylan from the 1965 album, 'Bringing
it All Back Home', produced by Tom Wilson, CBS.

Why did I say that?
Jane's words?
Are they?
Jane's words, not Jane's and Jonathan's words!
Is Jane ghost-writing Jonathan?
I am intrigued by this and captivated too. I want to challenge Dylan's words at the end of that stanza. I can remember when I was alive, well, you know, alive in that other place, in that other 'splace' (I must check out Badiou too, is he alive? Maybe I can conjure him up as well; I was always troubled, writing down there about how to work to bring together and perhaps to differentiate, 'space' and 'place') how I came to terms with the idea of being "busy dying".

In her conversation with Jonathan it is as if Jane is offering up something new when she says:
"We are not just talking to each other, for each other... and we are not writing to keep your father or my brother or Ken's mother alive... we are writing them, stitching them into our simultaneity of selves, we are becoming them..."
And yet here we are, two, possibly three dead white people talking to each other and maybe that's just the point.

I love that. That seems to be so affirming. I know that I don't want to become my mother or my father or anyone else in a molar sense; I don't think that Jane is being that literal (why change the habits of a lifetime!) I sense that she is presenting something molecular that is similar to Deleuze and Guattari when they talk about 'becoming-woman' or 'becoming-animal' or 'becoming-child' in 'A Thousand Plateaus':

"Yes, all becomings are molecular: the animal, flower, or stone one becomes are molecular collectivities, haecceities, not molar subjects, objects, or form that we know from the outside and recognise from experience, through science, or by habit." (1988, p.275)

I am so glad that I came across that piece of paper but I wish I had been in on the conversation that Jane and Jonathan were having there. Somehow it seems to me that this dying business is helping in discovering, or perhaps it is recovering, something new. Yes, so maybe it is worth trying to re-phrase Dylan, maybe, through this writing, it's not about being busy dying but about being busy being born.

I wonder what those others are talking about now.

[Aside *(Jonathan)*: I intervened earlier to voice my questions about how this writing will be received and to wonder about our cultural discourse about death. Now I have to step in again. Ghost-writing. Ghosts writing: Jane giving Jonathan words; Jane and Ken writing themselves as ghosts; Jane and Jonathan writing their obituaries from beyond the grave and ascribing their authorship, respectively, to Jonathan and Ken and Mildred the post-structural Camel; Ken feeling written about, confused about whose writing is whose, "tuning into a sense of presence that is disarming (him)".

What is this "ghost-writing"? In the land of the living—though this 'land' feels alive enough to me—a sport star 'writes' a column in a newspaper or an 'autobiography', both of which, explicitly acknowledged or not, s/he might well not have written. In that world, ghost-writing is pretence, though the best ghost-writers are at pains to represent fairly and authentically the 'living' person. (There/here, that world/this world, alive/dead—those binaries abound but they don't seem to work here/there.) In this space—wherever and whenever it is—there is, shall we say, authorial confusion and conflation but not pretence.

And who is this writing now? This other voice, another ghost, here, this 'editor'? Who am I?

Jane says to Jonathan:

> "We are not just talking to each other, for each other…and we are not writing to keep your father or my brother or Ken's mother alive… we are writing them, stitching them into our simultaneity of selves, we are becoming them…"

Yes, we—or is it 'they', Ken, Jane and Jonathan?—are becoming-others and becoming-each-other. Is that what they are aspiring to here, in the Deleuzian molecular sense of which Ken writes? Is that what they are doing? To become ghosts so that they can become themselves? So that Ken can fly without fear, so they can lose themselves in the ecstasy of letting go, free themselves from the constraints that 'individuality' places upon them? Are they seeking an individuation of the Jane/Ken/Jonathan assemblage?

Let's return to where they were: Jane and Jonathan conversing over on cloud nine, Ken wishing he was with them, in on their conversation.

I am reluctant to hand back the text to their voices, though it concerns me that Ken is anxious about where he is and why he is not with Jane and Jonathan. I do not like to see Ken anxious. I could step back and allow Jonathan—with whichever persona he decides to inhabit—to summon Ken over. That's all it would need: a call from Jane and Jonathan to Ken to come over and join them. But I can't let go. This editor's voice feels strong and powerful. I can see the scene in front of me as it has frozen, paused, whilst I am writing: Jonathan and Jane in conversation over there, as Jane described it, on that cloud a little to the left, overlooking the one which Ken is flying around.

But if I, as editor, can see them from where I am, then where am I? And who am I? And what am I? Am I too on a cloud? Am I becoming-dead? Like Jane says, we are all born dying, so even if I am not as far gone as they are then I am on my way towards them.

I am, of course, Jonathan's internal voice; just one of the many, mind. I'm a place that he's found in this story. He is picking up on the writing that Ken and Jane have both recently sent, to which he feels under pressure to respond. He's late and struggling and I am whom he has found. I am freeing him to write. He is becoming-me, becoming-editor. He doesn't feel he can step back in because Jane has his voice—she's welcome to it, don't get me wrong, but hearing her pen/speak his voice means that he no longer has to do so. He doesn't have to be preoccupied with received notions of authenticity and truth, which they all are undermining, enacting a distrust of any straightforward notion of 'voice'. Theirs—ours—is "a hermeneutics of refusal" (Jackson & Mazzei, 2008, p.314) in order, I think, to find, paradoxically, more—or new—voices: ghosts that will speak from the depths of their beating hearts.]

PART III

SPACE AND PLACE

CHAPTER NINE

PROLOGUE TO PART III

SUE PORTER

We, the prologue writers, are writing at Ammerdown. It's now Sunday afternoon, 4.30pm, and we're all in the John Todd room, mostly silent, writing.

Today, we've written and read to each other about this space—the room, the courtyard outside, the rain that fell this morning. In this book, authors write at various points about Ammerdown's aliveness to us. (It *is* alive, so it's more accurate to say we write about how its aliveness comes to our awareness while we are here; the place makes itself known to us.)

The aliveness of the land, imagined and real (does the distinction exist? does it matter?), speaks through the pieces in this section. It is collaborative writing about landscape; it is writing that collaborates with landscape. Rilke writes:

> "Were it possible for us to see further than our knowledge reaches, and yet a little way beyond the outworks of our divining, perhaps we would endure our sadnesses with greater confidence than our joys. For they are the moments when something new has entered into us, something unknown; our feelings grow mute in shy perplexity, everything in us withdraws, a stillness comes, and the new, which no one knows, stands in the midst of it and is silent." (Rilke, 2004, p.48)

He is talking about creativity: in these chapters, the land is the creative unknown, the "something new", the moment that enters and renders us still.

Landscape, as 'Lurking in Landscapes' shows, can also be unsettling, a provocation, something that questions assumptions, something to rub up against:

> "What we are left with is our interdependence a kind of suspended constantly-being-made interdependence, human and beyond human.

Maybe this is, or could be, one of the potentials of landscape as a provocation?" (Massey, 2006, p.33)

CHAPTER TEN

GATECRASHING THE OASIS?
A JOINT DOCTORAL DISSERTATION PLAY[1]

KEN GALE, JANE SPEEDY
AND JONATHAN WYATT

Scene 1: Back story—Narrator

Ken Gale and Jonathan Wyatt submitted their joint EdD dissertation ('Between the Two: A Nomadic Inquiry into Collaborative Writing') for examination on 11 April 2008. Joint dissertations within social science and humanities are rare, but not unknown (e.g. Huber & Whelan, 2000). Theirs was certainly the first within this particular department.

Successful completion would grant each of them access to the 'oasis', the community of academia. Their *viva voce* with their examiners, the oasis's "gatekeepers" (e.g. see Jackson & Tinkler, 2000; Morley et al., 2002) was set for 25 June, eleven weeks later.

On that handing-in Friday in April, the two 'nomads' met at 10.30am at the Boston Tea Party (BTP) café, towards the top of Park Street, just along from the university precinct. They talked for a while, on occasions pausing to gaze at the cardboard boxes containing the six soft-backed dissertation copies, plus appendices, by their side. At midday, they carried them around the corner to the department, up the lift to the first floor, handed over all six (three for Ken, three for Jonathan), and politely insisted that they each be given a receipt. After, they sat on a bench in the gardens opposite. Ken felt faint. They did not see Jane Speedy, their supervisor, who was out of town that day. Later, the nomads separated, Ken towards Plymouth, Jonathan to Oxford.

---

[1] A version of this chapter was previously published in 2010 in the journal 'Qualitative Inquiry', Vol.16, No.1, pp.21-28.

Within the week, copies of their dissertation were sent by the department to the university's examinations office and from there to the oasis's 'guardians'—those who check that all is in order and that a dissertation can be examined by the gatekeepers.

It was at this point that the wind got up and the sand began to swirl.

Scene 1: Viva minus 10 weeks— at the oasis's administration

The guardians talk. They can't be seen. Only snippets of their conversations[2] can be heard over the sound of the increasing gales:
..."I was informed today that we have two identical EdD theses, *deliberately* submitted jointly, same title, identical work, same examiners. There is concern that this might be in breach of the university's regulations—joint submission that is, while collaboration as such is not."

…"Submission could be legitimate providing the independent examination of each candidate is handled appropriately. Their *viva voce* is only weeks away and the gatekeepers have not yet been sent copies..."

…"The dissertation has been through the appropriate departmental channels"

..."It will be helpful to know about the approval processes the students underwent prior to embarking on the work."

Scene 2: Viva minus 8 weeks— at the oasis's administration

Dr Speedy stands before the guardians to deliver her report, "The history of the joint dissertation trajectory for Jonathan Wyatt and Kenneth Gale". Occasional sounds of 'humph', 'yes, yes', 'indeed, indeed' and 'preposterous' can be heard from her audience.

"The possibility of a joint dissertation was mooted during the academic year, 2005/6. This was raised by myself, Dr Jane Speedy, and discussed informally with the then director of programmes, who supported the project. The idea, in principle, was subsequently raised with the then Graduate Dean who advised that there was no specific or explicit obstacle to joint dissertations within the regulations for doctoral degrees, but that the regulations were designed with the implicit assumption that doctoral

---

[2] These snippets are based upon fictionalised/anonymised extracts from emails.

dissertations were single-authored works. If a joint dissertation were to be produced, it would therefore need to be thoroughly justified as it would be subject to rigorous scrutiny. It would need to be double the word length of the EdD dissertation requirements."

She pauses to drink water before continuing.

"There would need to be a clear indication of individual responsibility and authorship within the dissertation and sound academic and methodological arguments would have to be presented justifying the joint submission. Each candidate's submission would need to fulfil all the regulations and requirements. The examinations office had no specific guidelines to offer on joint viva examinations, but made it clear that *all* higher degree candidates would need to be examined and comply with *all* regulations and suggested that any viva arrangements included individual as well as joint examination. We concluded from this that examiners would need to examine the candidates individually as well as jointly to determine whether each had met the requirements or not."

She finishes. The guardians exit amongst nods and mutterings, leaving Dr Speedy alone. She turns to speak to the audience:

"It was a seminar on auto-ethnography. I didn't realise it at the time, but introducing Jonathan as one half of "Gale and Wyatt" somehow sealed their fate. After that there was no going back. And when the request came from them to produce a joint dissertation I was somehow expecting it, even though I hadn't thought about it at all. This narrative doctorate[3] seemed to just keep writing itself into the next space... I definitely wanted to be in on this. I remember thinking that I'd be really fed up if they chose another dissertation supervisor."

"Before we all got carried away, I decided to check with the guardians and discovered that I was pushing at an open door. The requirements and criteria were to be the same, but this dissertation needed to be twice the length and the authorship of each aspect needed to be clearly identifiable. This all seemed straightforward although the latter criterion came to seem more and more absurd as time, space and identities passed and by-passed each other and folded in on themselves."

"I was off with two nomads, or, at least, they were off and I was watching from an open door. I was standing on the threshold and could see both ways—down the dark corridors behind, lined with shelves of scholarly texts and manuscripts, and out into the sand and wind beyond—

---

[3] The 'Narrative and Life Story' strand of the university's Doctor of Education programme.

brightly lit, but hazy and uncharted."

"Dust storms. I anticipated dust storms from the outset."

Scene 4: Reflection—Ken, alone in the early hours

And in these dreams… is it three in the morning? God!… I remember the desert, the darkness and the emerging pin-pricks of light appearing then receding in the intense swirling.

I remember the lurching of the camel, the dusky shadows of the palms diminishing into the fast approaching desert night, as the lights of the souk gradually grew, became strong and transformed our vista. As night took over from day, I remember becoming aware of people, new faces, moving into the crowded spaces, the smell of mint tea, the taste of strong, sweet coffee and the rich fragrance of exotic perfumes intoxicating the excited traveller. Nomads moving in space-time consciousness, following lines of flight, unsure of direction and indulging in the pressure of the force fields of uncertainty.

In those intense moments, I became unaware of the dust storm swirling around the tent outside; a million grains of sand stinging the taut tarpaulin of warmth surrounding us in the heady, vibrant atmosphere of the souk.

Exterior, interior, folding in, unfolding; conjuror's words...

I slowly move into consciousness and the pain in my temple insists on keeping me awake. The night is still dark but I can hear the birds. The blackbird is singing and clicking, sharp and resonant, noisy and busy in the garden just below my window; the strident song of a thrush rings from the top of the tall ash in the field behind the house. I turn over with the covers over my head but I know I am awake; in these anxious moments, night gives way to day. I shudder. Turning on the bedside lamp is an admission of defeat and I seek solace in my book. It has been there with me for days, waiting to be read. I know that it is waiting to be read. I know that I should follow its linear, writerly path but my ability to concentrate has been shredded by deadlines, sour tastes and a million words constantly rearranging themselves in my head. Picking it up and opening it, seemingly at random, is the cue for a story; perhaps the path of the nomad invites serendipity but at the same time surprise.

"The desert landscape is always at its best in the half-light of dawn or dusk. The sense of distance lacks: a ridge nearby can be a far-off mountain range, each small detail can take on the importance of a major variant on the countryside's repetitive theme. The coming of day promises a change; it is only when the day has fully arrived that the watcher suspects it is the same day returned once again—the same day he has been living for a long

time, over and over, still blindingly bright and untarnished by time."
(Bowles, 2006, p.240)

Where am I? This is absurd. I remember what Jane said... where is it?
I printed it off. What did she say? Jane our voyeur; Jane watching us,
watching *with* us, watching over us. Jane watching, yet being so much a
part of what we are doing, our writing, so wrapped up in ourselves, yet so
wrapped up in Jane's awareness of that writing. Jane, what did you say?
A mess of jumbled papers on the floor, the NME gig guide; the
Observer Review unread; scribbled over, photo-copied journal articles just
managing to stay in page number order and last night's emails printed off
for the last rites of work, before unexpected unconsciousness took over.

> "I was off with two nomads, or at least, they were off and I was watching
> from an open door. I was standing on the threshold and could see both
> ways—down the, dark corridors behind, lined with shelves of scholarly
> texts and manuscripts, and out into the sand and wind beyond- brightly lit,
> but hazy and uncharted. Dust storms. I anticipated dust storms from the
> outset."

God, I am so tired but I need to write. Paper, where is the paper? A
pen. Right, write. Jonathan. Jane. Those words, that swirling dust storm of
words:

> I remember
> those words
> conjuror's words
> in these dreams
> "the watcher suspects
> it is the same day returned once again"
> I anticipated dust storms from the outset.

Scene 5: Viva minus 7 weeks—
at the oasis's administration

The guardians' anxious conversation is heard above the hubbub.
...."It may breach university expectations about examining an
individual as such..."
..."concerned about a number of issues in relation to the *viva voce*
examination and the implications if this should go to appeal..."
..."there will be many eyebrows raised at the very least, even if the
regulations do not preclude joint submission..."

..."I need to talk about this as a matter of urgency..."

Scene 6: Viva minus 7 weeks—Jane, at the oasis

As it happens, for the moment, the guardians were not taking much notice of me. They were all far too intent on watching out for the nomads on the horizon and in guarding and preserving their oasis and its ancient laws. For centuries now, only one man (or more recently woman) had been permitted to drink at these fountains at any one time. This had not always been how things were but rather how things had got themselves somehow fixed. Indeed, the ancient scholars had always worked together on their illuminations. This individualised cult of the oasis was more recent and, thus, aroused strong passions amongst followers. The nomads had at first stumbled on, then articulated and now actively sought to extend the possibilities at the oasis. And they were coming. Coming to claim their right to drink here together.

The faint dust cloud on the horizon had been moving nearer for some time. I could just make out two camels and riders. They were heading this way quite fast and even, perhaps, quite eagerly. I could think of no way of warning them without revealing my own identity.

On they came, the nomads. They were unarmed and, I suspected, had been looking forward to reaching this oasis. It was my map they were following into this trap. They would not be expecting this. What was I going to do? I had not been expecting this. Suddenly it came to me that what we needed to do was to slip away, to lose our footing, to come adrift and get completely lost. We had always been expecting dust storms and now we were going to need one to wrap ourselves up into. We needed to get lost, sharpish, partly as an act of philosophical ethnography (Lather, 2007), partly not so much to exclude the oasis and its dwellers, as to overturn and overthrow its received idea (Derrida, 1994), partly to redraw the landscapes of space and time in ways which allowed for more generous, reparative and perhaps even slip-slidy readings of the oasis dwellers than we could currently envisage (Sedgwick, 1997), but mostly to avoid ambush.

Scene 7: Viva minus 4 weeks—at the gates of the oasis

The gatekeepers and guardians anxiety levels are rising.
..."This situation does sound tricky!"
..."Given the atypical nature of the submission... I gather the whole issue was thrashed out prior to the submission..."

..."Any assistance you can give me on this would be helpful. Without help it seems a daunting responsibility."

Scene 8: Viva minus 3 weeks—narrator

Jane stands outside the oasis's gates, looking out for the nomads' approach.

Watching them approach, Jane realized that although the oasis had once seemed like their destination, it was now more like a passing place on some bigger journey. They were (all of them) already en route somewhere else, indeed, the oasis was already behind them, part of a trajectory that was eclipsed. Even now, as she watched them coming, she saw that they were not moving in a linear way but were also zig-zagging, disappearing and then re-emerging somewhere else along the horizon. It was hard to keep a grip on them. The slip-slidiness had already begun.

And as she slid away into a reverie of her own—a kind of re-membering of their lives—she drifted back to their beginnings together, at that first doctoral class:

Jonathan a bit aloof, or shy perhaps, she couldn't decide. He wove her some connections, a research conference (and she did vaguely remember the tall, lanky figure in the doorway) and Carolyn in Adelaide, a mutual connection, which made her think of those plastic tree frogs Australian kids always have in the bath and of coffees on Hutt Street in the sun... She held the ends of the threads between them lightly, head on one side, not sure where this was going...

Ken was bubbling over with it all. He came up at the end of the class and thanked her, she remembered, and she realised that he was a teacher at heart, someone who knew what it all cost in human terms, knew how much it all mattered to her. She had warmed to him then, when he hugged her, warmed to him more really to start with (it was later, through the writing, that she had fallen so completely for the other one). Yes, Ken had been her first love really.

And they had singled each other out quite quickly she remembered, the nomads, settling in together in her office. They had rooted each other out, those bright, sharp, edgy ones, in record time, she noticed... and off they'd gone with the ball, full tilt. They were glorious.

And at some point she noticed that they'd noticed each other. She couldn't remember when exactly, but she knows that she'd noticed them noticing the different energies, the different writings. The 'Writing as Inquiry' class stood out for her for some reason, that dreary room. That first afternoon, with Ken in his stride, tripping over himself with <u>ideas,</u>

concepts, song lyrics and nomadic moments. He was eloquent, clever, excited, funny... and she caught hold of Jonathan, watching Ken in the moment: "Clever bastard", she thought she saw Jonathan thinking.

Next day was the poetry-writing workshop and Jonathan blew her away... blew her right across the landscape with the story of his life in 50 words.

(Jonathan's voice)

"Born. Kenya.
Sifted smarties dropped into damp soil.
Baboons.
Mum, dad, brother, sister.
Trains, tears, sport: school
Bully. Bullied.
God, no sex.

Trains, sport, studies: university.
God, no sex.

Excitement. Existentialism. Liverpool teenagers.
Guildford, home, more teenagers.
Despair.
God, no sex.

Teacher. Teenagers. Tyneside.
Tessa, Tessa, Tessa.
Sex, no God."

She laughed, along with the rest, but there were also tears in her eyes... and she caught hold of Ken, his eyes flickering between her face and Jonathan's, back and forth, back and forth: "Clever bastard" , she thought she saw him thinking.

Leaning against that tree in the desert it came to her, not for the first time, that they could so easily have become each other's rivals, these two men: terrorists within each other's landscapes even, had they not chosen a more nomadic life. It had not been by chance their love and friendship, or so it had seemed to her then looking back. It had come about through a mutual determination to trouble and unpick each other's edges and seams instead of ruffling and scuffing up against differences. Once nomads of course, they depended on each other for survival. Once nomads, it was collaboration or death.

It had had something to do with vulnerability, she thought, but then

memories can shift their shape according to the refractions of the
remembering moment… rather like the false shimmerings or mirages in
the desert…

Scene 9: Viva minus 2 weeks—
camel-riding on Park Street—Jonathan

The ride is no longer comfortable. Other than during that period of
early unfamiliarity I have scarcely noticed, but suddenly I am sore. My
camel, I realise, is reluctant; he tips markedly from one side to the other
and I wonder if he is intentionally attempting to sling me off. I hold on,
but barely. It is a long way to the ground.

The terrain has changed. We have been in wild and desolate regions.
Others have been warm and inviting and still others cool and harsh, but
they have always been unfamiliar, disorientating places. Ken and I have
been together through them all. At times we have been aware of a third
traveller alongside us, looking, behind her disguise (a disguise that, in
truth, we have chosen to drape over her) much like the Jane that we meet
at our regular but infrequent rendezvous. Now, suddenly, we seem to be
on familiar but strange territory, and nearing our destination. Cars pass,
slowing as curious drivers peer unnerved at the strange sight, like film
characters at a spaceship.

We see Jane ahead, outside the BTP, which will be our last opportunity
for refreshments. We will tie our unlikely steeds to the lamp-posts,
dismount, and drink coffee as we make final preparations for our attempt
to be admitted to the oasis. Jane has seen us coming and will give us sound
advice. We have come to trust her implicitly.

We are close but not quite there. She, BTP and the oasis seem some
way off still. I look at my companion: he also seems tired, but content, still
full of life and vibrancy and energy even after this arduous trip. We long
to reach the oasis to engage with its gatekeepers and, with luck, win them
over. I long to be there, but as we make our approach I am feeling pulled
away, distracted by other pressures, other competing forces from back
home. These heighten my awareness of this journey's preciousness. If, and
when, we get to the oasis—and it's not a certainty even now—I am
determined to stay, or, at least, to take it with me. I am in love with these
travels (see Lee, 2005). I am in love with our nomadic existence. I may not
love my camel just at this moment but I am deeply grateful for where he
has taken me.

I am full of wonder at the beauty and richness that we have
experienced. And I wonder how we come to be here, how we started, how

I started. I glance again at Ken, who is rolling with it, waving enthusiastically at Jane a few hundred yards away. In his excited gesturing he disturbs the concentration of the cyclist hurtling down the hill towards us at great speed. She wobbles worryingly.

I remember so clearly that first encounter with them both, Ken and Jane, up there at the top of the hill. Ken, sitting at the back of the open rectangle of tables, facing Jane, sharing his picture of his parents, mentioning guinea pigs, and later—though not too much later—his first reference to Deleuze as he asks a question. Jane, at the front. I'm pleased we made our brief Adelaide connection. A few months previously at a conference, I had been drawn to her session on auto-ethnography, knowing nothing about either her or it. I didn't introduce myself. Downstairs, later, I collected a leaflet about the Bristol narrative doctoral programme, and, back at Oxford, chased her by phone during the summer, leaving message after message, calling and calling until we talked. Then I was hooked.

As I watch her now, up there ahead leaning against the café frontage, I reflect that it's her edginess (she refers to herself as 'mad' sometimes; Ken writes about his 'madness' too) that I love, that I've been drawn to all this time; that sense of wildness, her passion, her willingness to live dangerously (as I see it). I trust these experiences of her, and trust her. I find that she cares, for me, for us, for the work (see Acker et al., 1994).

I feel a little wary, though. It's because I feel staid beside her, and beside both of them. Beside Jane and Ken I feel, well, a little colourless. A girl I liked once watched me play rugby, a game I've hardly ever played. She told me afterwards that she worried for me because I looked like I might snap. (That rugby game was the end of her interest.) Alongside these two, I sometimes feel brittle though I have another knowing, which is that they seem to recognise a *daimon* (Cavarero, 2000) that they appreciate. By definition, I don't quite get what they see, but I trust their knowings.

Yes, it's Ken's *colour* that is part of the attraction; I was drawn to it during that first experience of sharing our writing, with Chris, in Jane's room, with Jane's paper about her late brother (Speedy et al., 2005). A connection. The beginning of our travels, though we did not know it then. Wandering around with Jane we were, even at that point. Sometimes, when Ken and I have been wandering we have believed that we have been alone: immersed in our surroundings, we have written as if it were only us. Jane has been there as our reader, our guide, our politically-adept ambassador. Our collaborative writing, Ken and me, has always in truth been a *ménage à trois*.

The camels struggle upwards, unused to the smooth, slippery tarmac and steep upward angle. We glance up to the top of the hill towards the Wills Building[4], a symbol of the oasis. My optimism rises.

Scene 10: Viva minus 3 weeks— crisis at the gates of the oasis

Another hubbub. Another dust storm. The gatekeepers and Jane are in urgent, frantic conversation. There's a newly-discovered viva-day diary clash.

..."I am really sorry, but I need to ask if you can either re-arrange the timing of the viva... I realise that this is very inconvenient..."

..."Well, if you think the candidates would be OK to wait until July, which is the earliest date I could possibly do it..."

... "I think we should go with the date we've set and find someone else. I don't think it's fair on them to have to wait..."

... "I wasn't aware that you were not free. There are complexities about this viva that make it important that we get this right..."

... "I suggest we stick to 25th June no matter what. These candidates have been through enough already..."

... "I am out of office for several days..."

... "I am in Berlin can you deal with this?"

... "Have to leave for meeting in London. Will ring from the train. Blimey, what a palaver..."

... "I could do earlier but not later, which would probably mean leaving the viva by 11.30—we might be hard pressed to fit it in by then..."

... "Off air now until this evening..."

... "Okay, it seems we could start really, really early..."

... "Brilliant, brilliant..."

Scene 11: Viva day—Jonathan

The camels are watered and fed, and so are we. I sit outside our tent at an ugly rectangular table, its fixed benches too far way to sit at comfortably. The morning is overcast but warm. I think that I've probably made the right call in wearing a long-sleeved shirt. What to wear has been a question for me this morning. How formal should one be for gatekeepers? No tie, white shirt, black trousers. Formal enough. Ken, who

---

[4] The Wills Memorial Building at the top of Park Street, Bristol, a university landmark.

is still inside the tent settling up, is also in black. The Nomads in Black.

It's nearly 8.00am. We're meeting Jane at BTP and then it'll be time to meet the gatekeepers. We're nearly there, I think to myself. Nearly there. We've made it to the oasis, the arrangements are in place and there have been no last minute emergencies. Just.

Last night, over dinner, Ken and I talked about today, our writing and more besides. Families, relationships—the stuff of our writing. By then, we had begun to relax, to feel here, to realise that we nearly belonged. We talked about our anticipation of today.

But before dinner, on our way from the tent to our first watering hole, Ken had asked, as we walked through the heart of the oasis, "After all the fuss, like changing the time, what could possibly go wrong now?" We speculated: we could eat something dodgy, and one or both of us could wake up feeling ill. Or, maybe, one of us would get into a fight (preferably not both of us, and definitely not with each other) and end up in hospital. A few moments later, waiting to be served at the bar and continuing to talk, immersed in more optimistic thoughts about where our collaborations might take us next, the barman asked, "Who's next?" Ken, instinctively and without looking around, replied, "Yes, please." The man to Ken's left immediately responded, "Actually, I thought it was me", which the big, bullet-headed man to *his* left, glaring down the line at Ken, supported with "Yes, it's him next, then me, and then you."

The worst looked like it might happen.

I told Ken that I was going to sit down and, like a good friend does, left him to resolve this alone.

Scene 12: Viva day—Jonathan

We're in a room on the top floor. It's light but institutional. The gatekeepers sit across the table. They begin:

"Well, firstly, we want to say that this is a strong piece of work. We'd like to see this as an opportunity for a scholarly discussion."

And I begin to believe that we really are in.

Scene 13: Viva day—Ken

Jonathan describes "a room on the top floor (that is) light but institutional". I see the gatekeepers, the bright light and the extensive view across Bristol behind them, and wonder, somewhat irrationally, if this is intentional. I think of old black and white war movies, the Gestapo and the interrogation room; it was always light in the agonised prisoner's faces,

with the questioner's faces always sinister and half hidden in shadow.
I shiver:
I can hardly see their faces.
One, off to the left, seems quiet and reserved:
Oh no, I hope this is not a good cop, bad cop.
For me this is viva as *haecceity* (Deleuze & Guattari, 1988).
What was that question?
What did he mean by that?
Jonathan seems cool: what did he say?
God Ken, forget the view, get focused, try to be in the moment.

Jonathan and a gatekeeper are having a conversation. What are they talking about? They are bound to draw me into this in a moment: what the hell are they talking about?

I wonder, in which direction are the docks? It must be to the west. Ah yes, over there, where the clouds are. Goodness, its raining. I knew I should have brought my jacket this morning, what am I going to look like in a soggy black t-shirt after this is over?

Concentrate. Concentrate. Come on, you have only one crack at this. A question. Come on, you can take this one.

"You don't think that your works suffers from an over emphasis on the work of Deleuze? He is a central figure in your work; would it be fair to say that his presence in your dissertation is somewhat obsessive. What do you think?"

He's looking at me, come on, now's your chance, get in there, you can do it.

"No, I don't think so. We talk a good deal about the 'inhabitants' of our work and these people and the conversations we have about them help to constitute the 'habits' of our writing. Yes, I think you are right to say that Deleuze plays a central role but I don't think we are obsessive in our use of his work. For myself, throughout my life, I have been drawn to philosophies of rebellion and resistance. They have attracted me and helped to mobilise my idealism; my thoughts and actions. So my thinking, feeling and writing in this dissertation have been charged by the writing of Marx, of Foucault and now, most recently, by Deleuze. These are my ancestors! But, as I say explicitly in the writing, there have been many others: without effort I think of Sartre and de Beauvoir, Kerouac and Ginsberg and Irigaray and Butler but, if I think of a history, a chronology, then it is those former three that seem to signify important stages in my life. I find it fascinating that whilst each gradually over time has displaced the other in terms of my thinking, sentiment still draws me back, from time to time, to their historical predecessor. So, yes, Deleuze *is* important, very important, but I want to stress the importance of looking at the way in which he resides with the other inhabitants of our work."

They are smiling. Jane is writing furiously and grinning. I hope she shows us what she has written; I'll never remember all this. She'll have to type it up, otherwise I'll never understand her writing. Stop drifting off, stay with it dude, you're on course now, stay focused. That's what all the footie coaches say.

Another question now: it's about "projective identification" (Klein, 1984). I have a spin on that but it's philosophical rather than the psychoanalytic approach that will show that I understand what Klein was talking about when she used the concept. Jonathan is looking really confident. This is his domain. He is going to take this one.

Scene 14: Degree day—Narrator

Jane is waiting in her specially tidied office. She imagines that they probably won't recognise it without any piles of papers on the floor and is worried that she'll never find anything again. The champagne is in the fridge and she has set out glasses and nibbles on the coffee table. They are due. They're having their photos taken. All Ken's children are here and Tessa has come down with Jonathan. They both looked glorious this afternoon in the Great Hall in all the gear.

Whilst she waits, she decides just to catch up on the emails. Oh, great, she says to herself, there's one from the Bluestockings group:

"As long as all five of us write thirty-five thousand words, is it okay to present our doctoral dissertation as a feminist collective biography?"

"Yikes," she thinks.

Looking out across the square, she can see Ken and Jonathan and their entourage heading up the hill towards her, still in their gowns. Behind them, in the distance, there seem to be dust storms gathering over the Senate House building.

CHAPTER ELEVEN

LURKING IN LANDSCAPES

CHRISTINE BELL, MIKE GALLANT, CINDY GOWEN, YING LIN HUNG, VIV MARTIN, ANNE O'CONNOR, SUE PORTER, JANE REECE, ARTEMI SAKELLARIADIS AND JANE SPEEDY

Landscapes are not just physical or geographical; they are external and internal, immediate and remembered or imagined. As writers we respond to many aspects of our environment. These responses are often about our search for particular and personal meaning, whether individually or shared. Through exploration in words and pictures, we hope to demonstrate the delights (and sometimes pains) of different ways of lurking in real and imaginary landscapes. Our different—unnamed—voices are indicated by double line gaps:

Out on the headland the familiar shapes of the old quarry buildings hold out firmly against the skyline. A landscape shaped from and by my childhood.

I remember going back along this path by myself one summer's evening. Maybe I was twelve or thirteen, and we had been reading our books in the sunshine out on the flat rocks, near where they had once mined for slate. I had left something, perhaps my sketchbook, and had run back along the grassy path of the old railway track, just as the soft white mists rolled in across the rocks onto the headland.

I walked back, stiff with fear, not wanting to make any sound that might draw attention to my presence. And it was in that silence that I heard the men's voices: the voices of the many men who had worked the quarries, shouting to each other against the wind.

In writing about and in landscapes, the spaces we inhabit as writers, the spaces and landscapes we write about and into—our landscapes, I notice once again, also write us.

I am reminded both of Davies's body/landscape (1990), both constitutive and constituted by its inhabitants, and also of Bachelard's 'Poetics of Space' (1964). For even as we try desperately to limit ourselves to our outer geographies, as if grasping at some last bastion of essentialist reality, intertextuality intervenes and we are over-run with our own inner geographies, wherein escarpments turn to metaphor and rivers to drowning, not waving (Smith, 1975, p.167). Space, Massey (2000, p.4) tells us, is a "simultaneity of stories thus far" but perhaps we can extend her metaphor and include in that simultaneity the stories scarcely imagined and not yet told beyond the dimly lit side corridors of our dreams. "The great function of poetry", according to Bachelard (1964, p.15), "is to give us back the situations of our dreams" and my own reading of this takes me out beyond Freeman's (1998) chronological, and even auto-biographical, times into mythical futures as well as parallel presents.

Odd companions, I sit quietly beside him, pretending that I am watching the toboggans and not admitting, especially to myself, that I am overweight and out of breath from the short uphill walk. He makes no judgement, just sits and waits quietly.

We chat, or rather I witter on about this and that and he nods. Imperceptibly.

Then it suddenly occurs to me that I might have got this wrong and I start to mumble something vaguely apologetic about not being exactly sure about his gender. Immediately, I realise that I am touching a raw nerve; that this is a sensitive area and that I have offended him.

His eyes fill with dark sorrow and his arm slides sadly off onto the ground. I am ashamed.

I get up and start to walk away quickly, embarrassed, but then I turn to say something else, to try and explain that I did not mean to cause offence and that I would be glad to sit and listen to his side of this story.

But he has already shuffled off.

Condensation and grime
blur the snowy view from my window miles above the earth
with satellite clarity invisible snowbound dots write of landscapes inherent in bodies
and souls

On the Hill:
Standing on the hill
Watching me zoom by on the freeway
In my cute yellow car
The sun rises behind you—new
light shows off
your gnarled trunk
and warped branches Amazing me with your
deforming knots and limbs
Moulded to the hill by wind a bending of
broken places forming mostly a flawed
but perfect silhouette
These scars make you
beautiful,
glorious in my eyes
Tangible survival
hardly perfection
in arbor perception
An entrance ramp
for my misshapen existence
valuing the twists and turns,
bumps and potholes driving
us to embrace reality

Dorset Seascape:
a dream journey through dark grey mist
a voyage limited by time and tide
they turn for no-one tossed by icy waves in finite significance ashes to
ashes
eerily ethereally return to the landscape

I walk at the edge of the land next to the boiling sea
Images, memories
layering of past and present
Drawn back
held here still looking

December in 2004, Imperial War Museum in London WWII
exhibition:
Along the dark, silent, endless corridor,
A transparent wall stood on my right.
Inside of it,
thousands of men's black boots,
lady's black gloves,
and baby's white hats
squeezed against the transparent screen.
Every object sounded as if
they were shrieking for freedom.
There was only dead silence.

I turned to the left,
The white walls were carpeted
with layers and layers of letters.
Smile faded away
Tears faded away
Words were left.

Wandering down the corridor,
into the basement,
two black walls stood almost parallel
in the white room
I was drawn,
by the screeching sound,
up in the air of this room,
to look through the crack
between two black walls.
It was wide enough
to clearly see the long train,
fully loaded with people,
heading towards concentration camp
SILENTLY

January in 2010, The Downs in Bristol, a few days after heavy snow:
The white carpet has gradually
Been replaced by charcoal grey slush.
Icy roads disrupted the traffic,
but excited children.

People were happy
skating,
sledging,
skiing.
Children shrieked with excitement. Young people thrilled to it.
Adults rested at home with joy.

They slipped and
fell over.
They swore and
carried on.
Or maybe,
They laughed
and carried on.

Artwork can be seen
everywhere,
snowmen,
snow angels,
snow animals,
snow people,
even igloos.

I saw smiles
in this snow scene.

It is the landscape, either real or fake, bringing us into different worlds
in which our embodied selves in landscape, vocally, visually and even
silently, represent different emotions, memories, and stories.

Looking intently at the shadow along the water's edge, I imagined a
winding road—and this led me to recall how even the most banal road (the
M5 in Gloucestershire) can serve up treats for those prepared to receive...
and how edges mostly lead somewhere:
This winding road along the edge this shadowed sandscape
held in the setting sun
this place too small to hide and to hold

If
if time stands still
and mountain ranges hold in place
just for one moment
the grains solid as concrete epitaphs
the breaking foam
aspic
waits for them all to pass then
then will the little creatures of the beaches ride up and down in tin cans
conversing with others by measuring their wealth in plankton bank
notes
and their meanings in rhetorised semantics
trusting that the waves will never break on them and miss
miss the moments and the edges and the places and the spaces and
create their own non-places?

In my own tin pot world last week held on
a tar macadam super highway
(we need to be able to travel to keep the economy moving)
in super modernity
my car in a jigsaw puzzle going nowhere
slotting into an Escher graphic
myself expecting
expecting to agitate for mountain movement and true grit and salt to
rub in the wounds
expecting to feel the edgy adrenaline and tapping fingers on the wheel
instead
instead I turned and smiled
and acceptance smiled back

Oh ok, I'll cut the crap because this really was real—and there I was in
the outside lane of the M5, going nowhere fast, and feeling all this
agitation coming on, and then I just said to myself (mindful-like), "sod
it—enjoy the time you have—no pressure—nothing I can do"—so I turned
to the car in the middle lane next to me and noticed a real person at the
steering wheel, who turned to me and we smiled acknowledgement to each
other—and then I smiled to myself—
And the queue moved a little and I turned and smiled again—and yes,
another smile came back, and another (yes, and one or two stony faces of
agitation never met my eyes I admit, but so many contented faces did...)
and this non-place of super-modernity, that appeared to have no real story

since its construction, was alive with being, and...

This was no dream—the world did truly stand still at 9:11 am, and non-place became our
    our place too
    to be
This winding road in Gloucestershire this shadowed landscape
held in the rising light this motorway retreat

Sarbin (2005, p.205) posits that:

> "... the built and natural environments provide a multiplicity of stages upon which people engage each other in dramatic interactions. Such engagements are the raw materials for building life-narratives from which identities are formed."

Yes; but is this true of all places at all times? Are there some constructed landscapes that militate against the construction of human identities? Augé (1995) describes non-places as geographical places that, in the context of what he calls supermodernity, lack direct cultural identity (the most obvious examples are connected with transportation: airport lounges, motorways, bus stations...). They may signpost the passer-through to places with identity—in this way they become threshold places, spaces of liminality. In the context of this story, even these spaces without cultural identity can be a shared stage for the construction of shared narratives:

> "At first everyone will seek for himself what seems to him the best path. But the fact that such a path has been used once is likely to make it easier to traverse and therefore more likely to be used again; and thus gradually more and more clearly defined tracks arise and come to be used to the exclusion of other possible ways. Human movements through the region come to conform to a definite pattern which, although the result of deliberate decisions of many people, has yet not been consciously designed by anyone." (Hayek, 1952, pp.70-1, quoted in Smith, 1998, p.160)

A collaborative writing group like no other:
We chose to know our journey through hindsight,
to create no need for rule books,
ascribe no currency to convention,
no value to conformity.

Look closely at the path
and you will see

it contains
part of what lines it.

Grandeur may be appealing
to those who seek it
but we recognize it
as socially constructed and transient.

Drifting:
Snow is piling again now against the doorstep, leaving me feeling hemmed in, abandoned. I want to abandon the snow, too, leaving instead to sit, as I once did, in the garden watching lizards and weaver birds play hide and seek on the bougainvillea that almost hurt my eyes with its clashing purples and pinks.

I want to walk along The Avenues, long, straight and lined with trees, the purple jacaranda clashing with more fierce pink bougainvillea hedges, making sure I move to the shaded side of the road, smelling the sharp clean eucalyptus of the blue gum trees and stepping over lemons, limes and avocados, bruised and squashed as they'd rotted and dropped from overhanging trees onto the red dirt tracks that form the sidewalks. Then, as I reach the artery road of Prince Edward Street inhale the fragrance of the rose and cream blossoms of the syringia trees that line it, so strongly, it makes me gasp.

 I sit instead, ignoring the piled-up snow, moving back and forth between then and now, giving myself little talks about not living in the past, concentrating on the tyranny of emails and papers and proposals and answers to the initial emails and watch myself move like a hamster on a wheel labelled 'Work'.

I thought that I liked winter, its excuse for hiding, growing, learning, re-membering, be-coming, wise and ready for a new start. That hasn't happened.

The philosopher, Alain de Botton writes, "If our lives are dominated by a search for happiness, then perhaps few activities reveal as much about the dynamics of this quest—in all its ardour and paradoxes—than travel" (de Botton, 2003, p.9), referring to travel as contributing to an understanding of the Greek "eudaimonia" or "human flourishing" (ibid.). Through travel, he observes, we anticipate change and renewal.

De Botton claims it is the concept of travel that we want, the association we have with that country, describing his attraction to the interior of an apartment from an Amsterdam street:

"I could see an apartment with three large windows and no curtains. The walls were painted white and decorated with a single large painting covered with small blue and red dots. There was an oak desk against a wall, a large bookshelf and an armchair. I wanted the life that this space implied." (de Botton, 2003, p.76)

And offering further explanation that mirrors something similar to my own feelings about England in:

"My enthusiasms in Amsterdam were connected to my dissatisfactions with my own country, with its lack of modernity and aesthetic simplicity, with its resistance to urban life and its net-curtained mentality." (ibid, p.78)

Later:

The snow has finally melted in dirty puddles of mush but I'm not complaining—the pavements are relatively clear and I can walk now without anxiety. I go to the greengrocers and in my attempt to recreate something else, somewhere else here, I buy some apricots: lovely, dusky pink on peachy tones. Back home, I create a little ritual of making tea and washing the apricots. I settle down to eat them and a first bite gives me the flavour of the paper bag the greengrocer placed them in. And I remember someone else's words—an unnamed journalist who cannot be identified in the 'Global Post': "Jacaranda time in Zimbabwe: Purple blooms in Harare mask the rot in Mugabe's capital."

Nowhere is perfect.

(http://www.globalpost.com/dispatch/zimbabwe/091015/jacaranda-time-zimbabwe)

Hibernation:

October 2009, and my Writing Selves decide—en masse—to hibernate in my attic. What can I do? I line some cardboard boxes with straw, check the insulation and place them, with great care, on the joists.

They do not see the Dublin landscapes smothered in the thickest snow for fifty years. They miss the latest news of salt and grit and sand shortages, school closures, ecstatic children and burst pipes. I am sorry they do not see the huge white lumps of ice bobbing around on the Liffey.

Despite some gentle nudges, they don't budge. I check their breathing and leave them to rest.

I get up and start to walk away quickly, embarrassed, but then I turn to say something else; to try and explain that I did not mean to cause offence and that I would be glad to sit and listen to her side of the story.

THESESCARSMAKEYOU
BEAUTIFUL.GLORIOUS
IN MYEYES
TANGIBLESURVIVAL
HARDLYPERFECTION
INARBORPERCEPTION

Grandeur may be appealing to those who seek it but we recognize it as socially constructed and transient.

ARTWORK CAN BE
SEEN EVERYWHERE
SNOWMEN,
SNOW ANGELS,
SNOW ANIMALS,
SNOW PEOPLE, EVEN
IGLOO.

I TURNED TO THE LEFT
THE WHITE WALLS
WERE CARPETED WITH
LAYERS AND LAYERS OF
LETTERS.
SMILE FADED AWAY
TEARS FADED AWAY
WORDS WERE LEFT.

I walk at the edge of the land
next to the boiling sea
Images, memories,
layering of past and present
Drawn back
held here
still looking

It is the landscape, either
real or fake, bringing us into
different worlds in which our
embodied selves in landscape,
vocally, visually and even
silently, represent different
emotions, memories, and
stories.

OUT ON THE
HEADLAND THE
FAMILIAR SHAPES
OF THE OLD QUARRY
BUILDINGS HOLD OUT
FIRMLY AGAINST THE
SKYLINE. A LANDSCAPE
SHAPED FROM AND BY
CHILDHOOD.

what coffee does to me
the rush of feeling in love with this
BLIMEY
rave

CHAPTER TWELVE

DOING COLLECTIVE BIOGRAPHY AROUND SHIFTING IDENTITIES

YING LIN HUNG

Theories and methodologies based on people's experiences and observations are designed to help those who wish to grasp the meaning of significant episodes that happen in their daily lives to make sense of themselves and their lives; to turn some dim light upon a meaningful moment; to stir up the existing doctrines and ideas of the everyday; to deconstruct taken-for-granted knowledge.

Collective biography[1], previously called collective memory-work, originated with Frigga Haug (1987) and a group of women in Germany collectively working on sexuality by means of telling their stories from memory. Haug suggests that this particular methodology uses memory of everyday experience—the empirical element of their research—as the basis of knowledge to work themselves into the social structure, and also "offers some insight into the ways in which individuals construct themselves into existing relations, thereby themselves reproducing a social formation" (1987, pp.33-35). Crawford et al. (1992) became interested in the way that Frigga Haug and her research team retrieved memories of their daily experience in the study of female sexualisation. They posit this as a successful method for working with gender and emotion because memory work offers opportunities to deconstruct the process of constructing emotions. Past events to a large extent construct identity and form future actions but, with this particular method, the written memories of past events transgress the boundaries of past and present and bring a social constructionist perspective to understandings of individuality (Crawford et

---

[1] Davies and Gannon's work on collective biography has influenced us all. See also this volume, Chapter 6 (Speedy) and Chapter 7 (Porter & Rippin).

al., 1992; Haug, 1987).

Developing Haug's work further, Davies & Gannon (2006) coined the term "collective biography", which juxtaposed two contradictory notions —the collective and the individual, creating and highlighting the space in between them. Hence the contradictions of the phrase make the method itself explicit as well as mysterious. Gannon (2001) pointed out that "the oxymoronic implication of the phrase foregrounds the tension between the individual and the collective that is both the crux of the method and the source of its dilemmas" (p.788). Collective memory-work started off as a feminist project in which Haug and her fellow writers traced their memories of relationships with bodies to reconstruct female socialisations and female sexualisation (Haug, 1987). They also inspected power, sexuality, subjectivity and the most ambiguous topic—memory (ibid). Davies and Gannon (Davies & Gannon, 2005, 2006; Gannon, 2004) expanded Haug's method of weaving with collective memory to work on various topics and scrutinise power, agency, discourse, subject and subjectivity in ways that had led collective biography towards an explicitly feminist post-structuralist method.

In a collective biography workshop, people talk of memories of certain topics and then all stop to write stories. Each person then reads out their own writing, followed by collective discussion of each piece of writing. I adopted this method to examine how language and culture make impacts on Taiwanese people's shifting identities when they come to the UK. I am concerned more with the way in which people ideologically construct their identities and grow themselves into the structure of society (Haug, 1987) than whether their subjective experiences produce 'real' identities and thence I have not been at all concerned with validating true/false accounts.

Doing research with a group is not unusual, but to gain insights into the collectivity as well as to express the individualities that exist within a group is another matter. Collective biography not only provided an opportunity for participants to speak out, it also required them to write in/up/out. Writing is the main focus of this method, which is supplemented with group discussions where all of us (my participants and I) worked together in four workshops to talk/discuss/think/write about our memories of and in the UK. We comfortably wrote our stories from a first-person position, rather than the third-person position that Haug (1987) suggested. After reading through our writing, however, I found that the obvious commonality within our writings was hard to ignore. Thus, apart from retaining our individuality, I also create a 's/he', instead of using 'we', to represent the collectivity of our group. One of the reasons is that 'we' just represents people without referring to any specific characteristics and might be mixed up with the general pronoun 'we'. In our group, 's/he' foregrounds the particular elements of the collective character.

Memory is the most unreliable and slippery material to research, but nonetheless it is the major factor in how we construct our lives and identities (King, 2000). When people talk of or write about their memory, the event that their memory reconstructs becomes real to them, however 'inaccurate' it might be (Crawford et al., 1992; Rosen, 1998). Memory-work allows us to re-experience those events in the present (Davies & Gannon, 2006). "The meanings of then become the meanings of now, the feelings of then become the feelings of now" (Rosen, 1998, p.102). That is to say, memory is a continuous process (King, 2000) constructing the self through the discourse of deconstructing and reconstructing past events along with the subsequent emotions, feelings, meanings, beliefs and reflections of then. "Reflection is at the heart of memory-work. But although reflection is an individual process, in memory-work it is made public within the collective" (Crawford et al., 1992, p.52). Memory is not just individually, but also socially constructed through reflection (Onyx & Small, 2001). Collective biography workshops record people's individual memories, thus we are not investigating collective events but collective elements from a group of people's individual memories.

In this project, we were seeking out the commonality that existed in our individual memories of living in a foreign culture and land and using a foreign language, which may have changed our individual identities. We, in common with other Taiwanese people, share our original culture, language, problems and difficulties, but our lived experiences have varied according to our different roles in UK society. In our workshops participants felt awkward about reading out their own writing, so they chose to 'talk' about their writing. That is to say, there was more written and unwritten information interwoven within our discussions than is usual in collective biography work.

One of the purposes of our group's work was to (collectively) bring together our individual memories/stories (biography) through writing and discussion. We enquired into identity transformations throughout our lifetimes in the UK. It is this writing within a collective biography group that most specifically differentiated between us. Thus, talking and writing about our memories of living abroad and the impact that this made on us gave rise to sharp contrasts between individuality and collectivity.

As facilitator in our workshops, I left it up to the participants to decide whether they wanted to talk and write in Chinese (Mandarin) or English. Their view on this was consonant with each other—everybody wanted to speak and write in our mother tongue, Chinese, in order to avoid the stammering in our thoughts and words that we knew would arise from our lack of English vocabulary and that would quite possibly result in an incomplete (re)presentation of our thoughts and feelings. To some degree, each of our Chinese writings in the course of these workshops was inevitably mixed up with a few English expressions. Hence we, a group of Taiwanese people who were neither English speakers nor professional social-science researchers, were pioneering the eastern use of a western methodology, collective biography, which was initiated in German, developed in English, and now being employed in Chinese!

One of the Japanese participants wrote in a letter to Davies, in a collective biography conducted in Australia, "it was very difficult to tell you my ideas in appropriate English... this session was very helpful to develop my English and also my behaviour as a Japanese person" (Davies, 2000, p.108). Telling one's story or memory in the context of one's own culture in 'another' language seems foreign to the nature of story or memory itself. On the one hand, the meaning and the spirit of our culture may be missing in the process of telling indigenous memories in a foreign language. On the other hand, the process of speaking our stories in imperfect English might help us to be aware of the unconscious part of our Taiwanese selves and how our identities might have changed. I believe that the space in the gap between speaking and thinking enables people to reflect on themselves, and at the same time the 'said' is rescued from the 'saying' by writing the words down. Unlike the Japanese students above (in Davies, 2000) retrieving their memories of Japanese childhoods and speaking/writing about them in English, we retrieved our memories of living in the UK and spoke/wrote them down in Chinese. The workshops caused contradictions and conflicts that were not simply in language but, rather, were contradictions and conflicts from our lives that sharpened our perception through language (Haug, 1987).

We were using this method cross-culturally in two ways: in terms of both culture and language. 'Group work' is, in a sense, a phenomenon that has been generated from a western worldview. 'Group work' is, however, scarcely an option for us in terms of ways of working (this might be my personal stereotype of western and eastern culture!). Bringing a new western-invented methodology derived from western philosophy into a wholly East-Asian group is an adventurous, bold and, in this case, tentatively implemented practice, not least by way of the 'double translated' information that all the participants received. I wonder, now the project has finished, whether this specialised method works for us in the way that it works for western scholars, and whether we are able to produce spectacular thoughts in the way that western scholars seem to have done and shed light on darkened areas of our minds. I hope this study will not be 'lost in translation'.

Language proficiency and identity shifting (the collective s/he starts)

Language is indeed constitutive of and constituted by identity (Norton, 1997, 2000). The relationship between language and identity has been widely investigated, the theories of which have also been developed over time and across various disciplines. Linguistics is the major field, but this is divided into many subfields from different perspectives, many of which go into too much detail for me about language itself (see Kiely, 2006; Mills, 2001; Reyes & Lo, 2009; Riley, 2007; Seeba, 1996). Linguistics is actually out of my field of study here. I am more interested in language in relationship with emotion and attitude (Hannerz, 1973), for "the subject has human agency" (Norton, 1997, p.411).

In social settings, taking a post-structuralist stance on language and identity, language is, as Butler insists (Salih, 2002), performative, and identity complex, contradictory, multifaceted, dynamic across time and space, and discursive-performative (Barker & Galasinski, 2001; Norton, 1997). Despite language, a context-specific tool, acting as the means and medium of delivery for the multiple narratives of the self and self-awareness, language also constructs and constrains the self, the subject of language. Language must be placed in social contexts in order for us to be made constantly aware of the changes (or lack of changes) of a 'coherent' self or the (in)consistency of a 'fractured' self in different languages.

第一次
在教授面前
被要求打電話訂實驗儀器
當時心裏最在意的
其實是教授的反應
這是一種對"說英文"
自信心不足的表現
那時覺得講出100%"正確"的英文
才是"speaking English"
但太在乎別人對自己講英文的反應
反而使自己無法表達清楚目的為何
因為總是花時間在思考"用字"

而非對談的內容
自己很累
對方很
For the first time,
I was asked to make a phone call
in front of my supervisor
to order equipment.
The thing I cared about the most then was
my supervisor's reaction.
This was caused by my lack of confidence
in "speaking English"
I thought speaking 100% 'accurate' English was really "speaking
English".
Caring too much about people's reactions
made me not able to clearly express myself.
Because I always spent time to 'choose words'
rather than to think of the content of our conversation.
I felt tired and
people were confused, I guess.

工作上最困難的是
與病人的電話對談
曾有不客氣的病人
因為我的口音
知道我不是當地人
直接說不要跟我講話
要找其他人
這些打擊
有時會讓我好想逃避
但只是短暫
面對它克服它才是必要
在新的環境裡
跟當地人要打成一片是不簡單的事
當同事在聊生活銷（瑣）事時
也不是太能打入她（們）的話題中
花了有一年多時間
才能夠很自然的打／接電話
或是與其他人輕鬆閒聊

The most difficult thing at work was
having a conversation with patients on the phone.
Some impolite patients
heard my accent and
realised I am not local,
they refused to talk to me on the phone and
asked for other staff.
Such a blow
made me want to escape,
but it's just temporary.
Facing and overcoming it is a necessity.
In a new environment,
It's not easy to get involved locally.
When my colleagues were chatting,
I felt difficult about joining them.
Not until one year later,
I could pick up/make the phone calls naturally
or comfortably chatted with others.

S/he lacked confidence in speaking English; to be precise, speaking 'correct' English. Whether s/he was a student or a non-student, s/he had come across certain embarrassing moments in which s/he was challenged by people and her/is own worries. S/he indeed spoke English. Perhaps s/he was not speaking perfectly, even with a strange accent that English speakers did not understand, but surely her/is English was sufficient to allow her/im to live an everyday life in the UK? S/he had experienced a number of dreadful moments that took her/is heart away from the spirit of the UK, and moreover, these experiences broke her/im down from time to time. In addition to people's unfriendly reactions, her/is own thought of having to be correct and perfect was one of the factors that shattered her/is confidence. This led to various negative emotions, such as, feelings of pressure, depression and withdrawal. The emotional strain may cause interference, suggests Luzio-Lockett (1998, p.215), "as emotions take over the control of one's linguistic utterances". All the above suggests that assimilating into a different language and culture always causes a lot of frustration, even for her/is own free will. S/he was in fact not fulfilled with an aimless life in the UK, and surprisingly s/he was not put off by the low confidence with English and those embarrassing experiences. S/he could have chosen an easy way to live within a Taiwanese (or even Chinese) community in the UK, but s/he squared up to the challenging life. I am wondering what kept her/im trying. Let me take Heller's words as an example of what s/he insisted on doing:

> "Thus the first principle of ethnic identity formation is participation in ethnic social networks, and therefore in activities controlled by ethnic group members. Language is important here as a means by which access to networks is regulated: If you do not speak the right language, you do not have access to forming relationships with certain people, or to participating in certain activities." (Norton, 2000, p.12)

Being a part of the composition of 'her/im', I can see her/is and longing for acceptance into the English community and, to some extent, self-realisation in language assimilation. In spite of unpleasant experiences, the enhancement of English and improvement in assimilating into an English community strengthened her/im. Her/is stories may be unique to 'the group of her/im', but the common element that I extract from her/is writings here was by no means unfamiliar to many other second language learners (for more stories and examples, see Norton, 2000).

Cultural influence and identity shifting

Living in two different cultures, her/is own native culture within her/imself and the host culture in her/is surroundings, provokes reflection on her/is spontaneous changes in identity. The act of changing may be foreseen, but the change per se remained ambiguous, even unknown to us. Cultural identity (Gone et al., 1999; Hall, 1990) is not said to be the centre of attention here; rather, how cultures play a part in our shifting identity is the focus of attention. I cannot ignore the fact that cultural identity is indeed part of the identity I am looking at, because "cultural identities are the points of identification... which are made within the discourses of history and culture" (Hall, 1990, p.226). Culture, as Gone et al. (1999, p.372) argued, is "understood to be a public... and reproduced symbolic set of practices", which are shared and available for human meaning-making. Cultures do not tell people what to follow or when to conform. From an anthropological perspective, culture is said to be the "complex whole which includes knowledge, belief, art, morals, law, customs, and any other capabilities and habits" (Baldwin et al., 2004, p.6).

在台灣大家吃的都是中國菜
即使吃西餐
也是改良過符合台灣人口味的西餐
但在英國待了這幾年

雖然大多數時候我還是煮中餐
但對西餐的接受度是越來越高
也因為西餐做法簡易
所以我現在煮西餐的次數是越來越多
現在吃完飯一定要吃點甜食來結尾
這當然是英國飲食的引(影)響啦

People eat Chinese dishes in Taiwan.
The food is adjusted to be in tune with Taiwanese tastes,
even though it's called western cuisine.
Throughout these years in the UK,
I cooked Chinese food most of the time,
but I accepted western food better than before.
Because western cuisine is easy,
now I frequently make western meals.
Now I must finish a meal with pudding.
This is the impact of English diet.

我覺得這句話是個問句
有問就要有答才有禮貌
然而，英國人自己不一定這麼認為
就好像以前台灣人問"假爸味"
另一方並不用把他剛吃飽的那頓有什麼好料統統向人家報告一下
可是我也沒辦法像大部份英國人
把這句話當耳邊風完全不理會
但是回答"Fine, thank you, how are you doing today"又似乎太囉嗦
人家應該也不期望會得到回應吧？！

"How are you doing today?"
is a question I think.
We must answer to show courtesy.
However, British people may not think so.
It's just like Taiwanese people asking, "Have you eaten yet?"
One will not tell the other whatever they have eaten.
I can't be like most of the British people
taking this question as an invisible one,
but giving an answer like, "Fine, thank you, how are you doing today"
seems too much.
People may not expect to hear any response?!

"Cultures do not talk to each other; individuals do" commented Sealey (2004, p.139) and what we are coming across in this project is not only encounters between individuals with their own meanings and embodied cultural concepts, but also encounters between different cultures within individuals. There is no doubt at all that people who are experiencing a multi-cultural milieu will have part of their identity changed (un)willingly. Identity shifting does not stop at a certain point on its way across the spectrum from separation to assimilation. People may shift back and forth (in psychological, political and geographical senses) over time without even noticing the changes that are taking place in them. Their identity sways to and fro and is always on the move. This identity shifting is a mixture of general cultural assimilation and experiences of specific significant events, as people shift from one phase of life to another with the passage of time. The notion of what is appropriate and conventional behaviour at a certain age is always shaped by cultural ideas (Baldwin et al., 2004). This mixed and complex circumstance makes it even harder for diasporas/immigrants to identify whether certain types of change are affected by culture specifically or by the process of aging. It is not possible to cleanly separate each of these threads in people's lives, and, it seems inappropriate, given the complexity of people's lives, to ascribe certain changes to one single factor.

Tentative but particular findings

Identity can be understood as a process, as 'being' or 'becoming', which is why it is difficult to identify oneself (Jenkins, 1996; Sarup, 1996). The process of 'becoming' or 'being', without an end, could be described as 'identity shifting'. By engaging with collective biography, I have placed an emphasis on the collective symbol of her/im, which represents the collectivity of our encounters with language and culture. The project was constructed to draw our experiences together and to interrogate the collective changes that we have gone/are going through. Whoever we were respectively, the similar experiences we had had in the UK had diverted our individual changes in the same direction.

Learning a second language is unlikely in a short time to subvert the logics and ideologies that have become implanted in our minds. Feeling constrained while expressing ourselves in our second language, not only do we lose our self-confidence, but also we start to sense the split 'selves' within. Insufficient language proficiency shakes our self-confidence but has not really deconstructed our identities. It is easy to confuse the shattering of confidence with identity deconstruction, because we lost some sense of ourselves whilst losing our confidence. Being used as a vehicle for our daily life, language indeed possesses the power to shape some of our identity shifting, and yet it was not language but other factors that had a the long-term effect. Language was never simply the language itself, but a powerful culturally embedded device. It is the cultural meanings/explication/implication that language (Stuart, 1998) carried affecting our attitudes, values, social interactions and, therefore, changing our identities. Culture, in this sense, is a far more influential factor than language in identity shifting.

The process of identity shifting opened our minds wide in the ways that those different attitudes and values struck a blow against our original beliefs, but also created new possibilities for us. On the one hand, these differences brought out possibilities, but on the other, s/he started losing her/is self-respect. The process helped her/im to stand on her/is dignity wherein s/he mentally and unconsciously stripped out everything s/he owned to make her/im feel inferior. Not until s/he got the beliefs and values of British culture firmly under her/is belt, did s/he start appreciating her/is own beliefs and values. At this point her/is sense of inferiority stopped. S/he lost some sense of self-worth in the beginning of her/is stay in the UK, and thus the process of identity shifting helped her/im to win back her/is self-respect.

Writing and reflexivity

One of the particularities of collective biography is the interim stage in which individual writings are woven together by the researcher into a collective text. As a group, we collectively worked on each individual's memories and explored both what was said and not said. We did not produce 'collective writing' but collectively wrote individual memories around shared themes during our workshops. The contradictions, similarities and the multiplicities that group members conveyed enabled me to produce a reflexive final text. It was clear that whichever of us produced this final writing would produce a different text, given the same resources. In this case, the final text of our collective biography stayed invisible to me until I put my thoughts, and all our words, on paper, next to each other, bit by bit. In other words, collective biography involves two processes of writing as inquiry, one by the group and another by the nominated collector/researcher(s) (see Davies & Gannon, 2006). The final text included not only a process of tracking our group writings and discussions, but also my own thinking as I was affected by the language I heard; the books I read; the people I talked to; the things I saw; the food I tasted and smelt, and the life I lived. "What I write today on these matters may be different from what I might have written yesterday or will write tomorrow" (Etherington, 2004, p.27). Borrowing from Etherington, this is writing of its time. I have no idea what will occur when I write. Sometimes a little turning in my mind will take the writing into a different focus at the end of each piece. In this text, for instance, I am reflexively exploring the process I have undergone—a practice of writing as inquiry about writing.

Talking from different positions takes reflexivity to a new horizon. I cannot discern which voice is whose in our collective biography anymore. Our multi-voiced accounts, like our identities, are intertwined: some are retained; some are altered; some muffled; some twisted; some outspoken and yet others have disappeared. This final voice/text moves in between the collective s/he and each individual of her/im. The outcome is a body of reflexive knowledge, which provides "insight on the workings of the social world and insight on how that knowledge came into existence" (Hertz, 1997, p.viii). Throughout this study, my own perceptions of the participants greatly affected my writing and how I was perceived, in turn, affected how I understood myself (Reinharz, 1997). "To regard reflexivities as invitations towards liminality and towards constructing our identities not as 'nouns' and thus fixed, albeit open to change, but as 'verbs' and as discursive process may lead us into more creative (and messier) research conversations" (Speedy, 2008, p. 42).

Is collective biography a promising methodology for Taiwanese people in the future?

Being a black sheep is, perhaps, a respected position in the contemporary UK. Taiwanese people have not been attuned to accepting relatively 'odd people out'. In collective biography, we may be required to ask/challenge things about other peoples' memories. The association between challenging and being aggressive seems fairly strongly held for Taiwanese people, as we have been brought up to value the importance of harmony and concord above all. Even though over years s/he had managed to learn from British people/culture to keep our criticisms impersonal, I could sense that s/he avoided challenging each other during the workshops. Is it that Taiwanese people cannot face challenge/criticism calmly? Or is it that they feel awkward about it, which creates insecurity? Or is it that Taiwanese people always pursue harmony and concord? Each individual in our group will have different answers to these questions. We have not been taught how to deal wisely with conflict and discord in a group, but again, who has?

From my point of view, the practice of collective biography fits for Taiwanese people for researching light topics. By light, I mean those topics that do not make people feel pressurised and emotion-laden and yet still have their interest aroused. It could take discussions on such topics further than people expect initially. Making a commitment to a group, which pays no mind to the material world, requires either a tremendous drive of self-exploration and self-fulfilment, or great curiosity about human beings and related issues. The most distinctive feature of collective biography is that it is a practice of writing, so that it suits those who are willing to write and/or those who are fascinated by writing. The flexibility of the method opens the space for people from different cultures, different backgrounds and different ideologies to cross boundaries, to transgress familiar milieu, to challenge/support each other, and to make a close bond between each other. As Linnell et al. (2008) suggest, this method does not provide a solution but, rather, raises more questions and opens more possibilities. I do not envisage a popular take up of this practice in Taiwan or other areas in South East Asia in the near future, but, as time goes by, I predict that the practice of collective biography will grow and grow because of its emphasis on writing practices and its surprisingly therapeutic effects. Watch this space!

PART IV

EMBODIED WRITING

CHAPTER THIRTEEN

PROLOGUE TO PART IV

SUE PORTER

I notice love gets in here again, and that seems appropriate, as one way of thinking of collaboration is as a striving for an expression of faith in love. And love being pretty embodied. Anderson reminds us of the value to be gained from embodied writing in this post-Cartesian moment (Anderson, 2001), stressing how we are "viscerally and perceptually part and parcel of the world in which we live" (p.84) and so able to tune into it and its "sensuous enactments" (p.84).

All three of these chapters deal with a sense of being, and being-with in a physical as well as companionable way. They also refer to place and significance of connections to place, as experienced through our bodies rather than our minds alone, as a temporal-spatial event (Massey, 2005). Gale and Gallant specifically reject the Cartesian concept of the disembodied mind, this earthy corporeality often grounded in these chapters by food, and a sense of place, the ways that place is occupied and evoked as space, through memory and other spectral traces, understanding space and place as realms of becoming; employing a postmodernist, rhizomatic construction of space as a "meshwork of paths" (Ingold, 2008, 1808).

All these chapters therefore attend to aspects of bodies, embodiment, being. And the issues arising, which give opportunities to question our assumptions about being human: including memory and forgetting; how we locate ourselves, and the relationship between identity and our physical capacity (childbearing) and impairment (brain damage).

Last night (23 June 2013), Jane reminded us of the 1970s TV play 'The Stone Tape'[1], in which walls had both ears and voices: the emotional past

---

[1] A television play written by Nigel Kneal and directed by Peter Sasdy, starring Michael Bryant, Jane Asher, Michael Bates and Iain Cuthbertson, broadcast on BBC Two as a Christmas ghost story in 1972.

was embedded in the solid and seemingly inert body of rock and stone, to be released on contact with more lived emotion, with the bodies passing close full of feeling and enacting the present.

It seems that our to-ing and fro-ing of writing both collects the embodied experience, and feeds into it the lived experiences of another, others, as the collaboration cycles around a writing group. We tell stories, and feelings are sparked into life, to create another telling, to ourselves and maybe to others. Layers, accumulated, felted into a close union through the repetition: a body of narratives.

The ways in which writing can take us into and out of our bodies (Gale & Gallant, Chapter 16), stimulating memories and obliging us to make conscious choices about sharing and withholding. And the ways those choices open up more choices, and on and on as writing to and with gets under our skin. Withholding, allowing withholding, raging against a silence and forgetting (BCWG, 'Remembering and Forgetting with Sue', Chapter 15). What's written on the body? The body of the group—binding and tearing it. Feeling each other's pain (BCWG, Chapter 15; Porter, Rippin & Speedy, Chapter 14), sitting with that pain and the feelings evoked as an act of commitment. In the case of Porter, Rippin and Speedy in 'Places Inscribing Bodies', we eavesdrop on leaky and broken bodies speaking/writing to each other on different occasions and across time, culminating in a reflective, and appropriately partial, messy and inconclusive sense making. Food and drink appears in this writing, where it calms, soothes, nourishes, possibly most significant when the writing and the writing-together gets hard and painful.

Writing this, I find myself referring to the writing 'groups' whilst also questioning whether I should say group. The we-ness, the between-us-ness, what one writer describes as appearing in the space between us, invisible but knowable, always in negotiation, under construction (and at times feeling like under deconstruction).

Writing together or apart—where are our bodies when we write to and fro, to and fro? These chapters point to: the significance of proximity and of place; traces of what's been (as in 'Places Inscribing Bodies', Chapter 14, where hoped-for babies birthed too soon and were lost). These three pieces move between places, which themselves become significant, occupied by the bodies and the becoming of the writing groups. Traces are left in that place by the members and the assemblage of writers, itself a body.

Gale and Gallant (Chapter 16) display energy in debating the impact of the stance that we have become disembodied and share an exploration of alternative theorising. The contrasts between messiness and a sharper, crisper, to-ing and fro-ing over theory, crossing swords over theory, even when the words say "peace" the sense is of taking up arms, of offence. The body IS—not always relaxed, not always loving.

In 'Remembering and Forgetting with Sue' (Chapter 16), the collaborators use their relationship, developed through years of rounds of writing, to bear up a member who has received the body blow of a diagnosis of dementia. Pain, love and the lending of memories shared seek to cushion the shock, to accompany the forgetter. The web of writing catching memories and the need for a sensitivity of practice that did not transgress an individual's boundaries, an enacted extension of the desire not to assume knowledge of what should be in the other's mind and on their lips, akin to resisting the pull to finish the sentence of the stutterer.

As Mike Gallant says "I wouldn't do this alone". These chapters show that we seem to need accompanying bodies to travel to some places. Thank heavens for collaborations.

CHAPTER FOURTEEN

PLACES INSCRIBING BODIES; BODIES CIRCUMSCRIBING IDENTITIES; IDENTITIES SHAPING HISTORIES OVER TIME

SUE PORTER, ANN RIPPIN AND JANE SPEEDY

The female body has long been a site of contention (Laqueur, 1992). Historically constructed as a pale imitation of the male, an Other to the masculine norm, it has been seen as a faulty version of the perfect male body, inverted, leaky and fugitive, abject (Halberstam, 1998; Kristeva, 1984; Laqueur, 1992). In this chapter, we, as three women, write from the experience of living within imperfect human bodies, which are coded feminine, and the place the writing emerges from and inscribes is that of the bodies doing the writing. Our collaborative writing, a mixture of 'call and response' email exchanges[1] and face-to-face meetings when we sat and wrote together around shared themes, epitomises what Clandinin et al. (2007) would call the "narrative inquiry space" of relational, contextual and temporal dimensions.

This circular collaborative writing cycle between three women moves from place to place over time, both the 'real' time taken to write and the remembered autobiographical and mythical times that emerge in the writing. This emphasis on embodied times, spaces and relationships is emphasised by the use of voice, but also pause and silence as this text circumnavigates things that have been left unsaid and were, erstwhile, unsayable, but have nonetheless been written on these bodies in invisible ink. Here, patches of visible and invisible writing are tacked loosely and then quilted together with seams left raw and jagged edges showing; this fraying technique of 'putting together' allowing solitary threads of story to splay out at the joins.

---

[1] See Chapter 4.

Bumping and bundling into each other

We said when we met in the Lido café, in Bristol, England (December 2012) that we would write this chapter as a chronological narrative in four parts. This is the conventional academic structure: to lay out what will come next with clarity and certainty, and a precision that results from the perfection of hindsight. But what did we imagine we were doing: what are the four parts amidst all these segments and snatches of writing? And what about this perfectly seamed voice of We. When did we become a 'we'? Did the 'we-ness' happen all at once, or in a series of different yet cumulative pairings? To talk about we-ness is to disappear the other groups to which we belong and have belonged to, which brought us to the point of sitting in that cafe together. Those stitches attaching us to other groups start to pull apart as the thread frays when we move off into other configurations. We had started writing together as part of a collective biography group at the University of Bristol writing about love. At some point, which we explore, a new triad emerged out of the larger group in order to bring to life other writing, which we felt compelled to make happen.

Hello both,

I have written some additions to Jane's start, which may or may not be on-track. I have also added a next-section that starts to explore the time that our writing started to burst the boundaries of the group, focused by Jane's Sunday writing from Hawkwood[2]. To do this I have added in 3 sections that follow a temporal thread, just to mark the timescale:

1. In the garden at Hawkwood;

2. After the Hawkwood weekend;

3. Reflecting together: Llanishen[3]—2 reflections; Lido.

I have then loaded into these sections my writing from those stages. The writings are complete, and I'm happy to edit down when we need this.

See what you think.

---

[2] Hawkwood College is a residential centre set in the countryside of Gloucestershire. The authors use Hawkwood for writing retreats. www.hawkwoodcollege.co.uk

[3] Llanishen is the Welsh village in which Sue lives and where we have met to write, eat and talk.

But to say that our writing began in a collective biography group looking at love is to simplify to the point of ridiculousness. Myriad interactions brought us together, so many that perhaps the writing we consider here became inevitable.

Sticking with historical/autobiographical chronological time, we should start with all the many crossings and inter-weavings of our lives, since we have been interconnecting with and interrupting each other for the last twenty-five-odd years of living in the South West of England. We could start in 1989, when Jane and Sue both tried to buy 'The Heavens', a house in the Stroud valleys in the Cotswolds, which Sue and Glenn eventually lived in for nearly 20 years; or we could start in that same year, with the phone call that Ann made to the Counselling programme at the University of Bristol, asking to speak to a 'Jane'. She had wanted to speak to quite another Jane, whose introductory workshops she had attended a while back. We, Ann and Sue, met on the doorstep of the Graduate School of Education (GSoE), when starting the doctorate, but more of that later. I suppose what did connect Ann and Sue before our meeting through the EdD (Doctorate in Education) was a body of theory and practice, called 'Management'. Sue had joined the School of Management at the University of Bath in 1996, when she signed up for a part-time PhD at the Centre for Action Research in Professional Practice (CARPP). She was attracted by action research, its emphasis on reflection *and* action, on participation and emancipatory practice.

Moving on to instrumental/chronological time spent together, we should start considerably later, in 2007, when Sue and Ann joined the Narrative Inquiry doctoral programme that Jane taught in the GSoE.

This was fateful, and we know important to Ann and Sue. Sue writes:

I remember it all started for me with a meeting with an interesting woman at a party over the Christmas period 2006. She had an interest in narrative, and I was still buzzing with how much I'd enjoyed writing-up my PhD, particularly weaving autoethnography into the text. I offered to send her some contacts and references, and we exchanged email addresses. While looking up narrative programmes to send to her, I discovered the EdD and Jane. Or should I say, I tried and retried to discover Jane, who didn't answer my emails or calls and whom I eventually tracked down in her office late one evening by ringing her direct number, yet again. During this conversation, and in answer to my questions as to whether this might be a suitable programme for me, Jane mentioned another prospective student with a similar background to mine, and eventually gave me Ann's number. I had not met Ann before bumping into her on the threshold of 35 Berkeley Square on the first day of the EdD. Yet somehow we recognised each other, and it's taken off from there. Admiration for each other's writing, encouragement, inspiration, no doubt irritation, tried patience and understanding, and love. Love of writing, love of each other, love of Jane.

For the purposes of this narrative, however, we will start in literary/mythological autobiographical time, with the advent of the three authors being and writing together in a women's collective biography group in November 2008. This introduction is being written in January 2013, thus chronicling and curating aspects of a four-year collaborative academic writing relationship that included the detritus of many other relationships, connections, histories and contexts. It was as if all manner of traces of each other had been floating around in the same geographical/ chronological/autobiographical/ disciplinary spaces and had finally bumped into each other within the same silted up corner of the academy. This chapter, as Philip Pullman (Pullman, 2003, p.i) might say:

> "Contains a story and several other things. The other things might be connected with the story, or they might not; they might be connected to stories that haven't appeared yet. It's not easy to tell. It's easy to imagine how they might have turned up though. The world is full of things like that: old post cards, theatre programmes, leaflets about bomb-proofing your *cellar*... All these tattered old bits and pieces have a history and a meaning. A group of them together can seem like traces."

But what of the mystery of how this ephemera, these scraps and threads, eventually come together in a written text. The image so often used is of woven cloth with its warp and weft, but that implies a structure and a logic. Our writings, like our relationships, are more like felt— separate fibres laid over each other, sometimes in clumps, sometimes in wisps, felted and fullered together, not laid over and under in a regular pattern, and the stronger for it. Felted fibres are locked together. Strips are hard to pull off. And what then is the felting process?

Collaborative writing strands

Writing inquiries include at least two distinct kinds of writing: writing about the chosen topic or theme of the moment—content stories; and writing about the process of writing—writing stories (Richardson, 2000, 2001), which write about the geographies, histories, psychologies and other spaces that exist betwixt and between the writers themselves and other agents in the stories that are being told, such as landscapes inhabited, and objects and materials that shape and are shaped by events. In different narrative genres and disciplinary contexts, various strands may remain unsaid or even unsayable, but what was remarkable about the work of these three authors, or more accurately, what attracted them to each other's work, was that they were all intent on giving multi-layered accounts of their worlds that paid attention to all these dimensions of their narrative inquiries. This chapter, then, is *both* an example of this multi-stranded collaborative writing that also owes much to the scholarship of Carol Rambo Ronai and her method, which could be a description of the felting process, of giving "layered accounts" (Rambo Ronai, 1995, 1999) switching seamlessly between layers of personal, theoretical and empirical writing, *and* an exploration of the 'bundling and bumping' process of being, talking and accumulating social/relational and even culinary capital together that precedes and leads up to and sustains that very writing process, described by Diversi and Moreira in 'Betweener Talk' (2009, pp.14-19) as crossing paths, building bridges and "things we talk about as we sit at the curb".

The latter type of writing (writing stories) is conjured out of the relationship between the writers, and between the writers and the topic. It acts to make visible what may otherwise be unknown, unspoken or unspeakable, even to the author. Acting like a Chinese magician attempting to make a spirit visible by throwing soot or flour into the air where she senses it to be; the fine powder making visible the shape of the demon, so giving form to the creature for those previously unable to perceive it.

The collective biography group worked together over two years, at first meeting for an intensive three days, then meeting up for a day every couple of months, and taking a weekend away to write together at Hawkwood. Over this stretch of time some group members withdrew, others became less regular attenders because of other pressures—marriage, death in the family and failed relationships (bodies and break-ups). But a core of writers kept writing. Writing out of commitment to the group; out of interest in the method, collective biography; and out of the sheer excitement of seeing where the writing would take us.

Our chosen topic, 'love', meant that it was not surprising that 'bodies' were often present in our texts: romantic love; familial love; love of friends and love of food all appeared, circulated and provoked reflections and responses. Key 'moments' in the group's collaborations became marked by significant places and meals: mushroom soup and Malteaser ice cream at Llanishen; lemon pudding and a missed paella in Stroud; an out-of-season Christmas pudding on a second visit to Llanishen; and now bread and olives at the Lido. This collaboration, academic as it is, has been nothing if not embodied in its themes, and its expression. However, it can also be understood by the limits to its ability to contain some aspects of bodies, or rather the ways that the container of the collective biography group became split into subgroups in order to allow and contain the messier, transgressive bodies that appeared in our writing.

As we have stated, our love of writing and our love of writing together, drew us towards each other, but it is possible that it was our desire to write from our own bodies about their dysfunctions and limitations and disappointments that seemed to catalyse us out of the wider collective. We had a desire and a willingness to explore the pain and sadness that our own bodies had provided us with that made us want to write together and, to a point, to retreat from the larger group. We explore this now, the place where the seams start to give, the patches to pull apart.

The environmental campaigner and scholar activist Joanna Macy (Macy & Brown,1998) has a saying, "the heart that is broken can contain the whole world", emphasising the need to move beyond the usual limits of our holding power in response to the enormity of a need, and acknowledging the emotional pain involved in doing this. When barren and broken bodies emerged in our writing then we had, as a group, to develop an awareness and a range of responses to the abject, the unspeakable. Our disciplines and ethics as a group were tested and developed through noticing our responses, including when the writing group, as a container, was unable to contain these (our) bloody, leaky bodies as topics arose which transgressed the unwritten (unconscious) boundaries of the group (Shildrick, 1997).

We have written elsewhere in this volume (Ann and Sue's Chapter 7) about the writing disciplines and extended vocabulary developed in collective writing groups, which enables members to navigate choices about disclosure in the group. Here we explore an example of 'splitting' within a writing group. Collective biography groups have, historically, (Haug, 1987; Davies & Gannon, 2006) held the tensions between writers by focussing on the writing task, rather than exploring the interpersonal dynamics between the writers themselves and in investigating the literatures of collective biography we find ourselves alone in this experience of inhabiting breakaway bodies or bodies in flight. Other groups seem to have experienced immense difficulty even simply ending, let alone splitting or dividing. It is as if moving in different directions, or being moved differently by the writing, evokes a sense of betrayal or, at the very least, of not having played by the rules (see Chapter 22).

In sitting down to write this chapter together, we have asked ourselves what we learnt from our sense of this transgressing/over taxing of writing-group boundaries, and what enabled us, as a subgroup of three—the leftovers, still continuing to write, from the 'Love' collective biography group—to respond to each other, continuing to write together, and to examine our writing practice after the group was dissolved.

In the garden at Hawkwood

It was the last session of our last Hawkwood weekend together as a whole group (as with comments made as we turned the handle on the door of the therapy room?). Collective biography groups are different from, and consciously seek to avoid engaging in therapeutic activity, although in retrospect it may be helpful to borrow some of the language of therapeutic activity: Jane's pain, however, was not 'held' by the group, who found themselves overwhelmed by it, disrupting the collective and atomising it into individual biographies.

We were sitting together on the benches underneath the canopy in the garden. We had all been writing, somewhere in the garden and then, as was our wont, one by one we read our writing aloud to each other.

Jane read out:

"Sitting here in Stroud I am so far away from myself that I cannot even find my own skin, let alone inhabit it. Skinless in Stroud. I write into the wind, shards, fragments, incomprehensible sentences. Obscure unconnected slices that are hard to follow, that even I cannot fathom as I read them back. I am not here, I am far, far away from myself.

If, to quote the BDM (the 'Beloved Doreen Massey' (2000), patron saint and goddess of feminist geographers), space is made up of the "simultaneity of stories available thus far" (p.130), then finding a place to sit and write inscriptions on and from the body in Stroud might well elude us for ever. It has so far.

It all looks so idyllic on the surface, all that crumbling yellow stone just waiting for the sun to shine on it and a branch of ageing wisteria to trail across.

Five dramatically steep valleys all converging into a space that opens out onto transcendent views of Abergavenny and Sugarloaf beyond, all tinged with a mill-town seediness that now lends a bohemian affordability and accessibility. Alternative Stroud. The arsehole of the Cotswolds. And then, of course, there are the midnight spinach pickers. Let us not underestimate the power of the moon.

I hate Stroud. Bloody Stroud. Five deep gulleys running with blood. The blood of a much loved brother and of five unborn babies, one dead baby per valley, running down into the rusty blood-filled network of rivers and silted up canals. The wreckage of a once loving and tender relationship left unravelling and abandoned as we fled, one after the other, down the M4 without looking back.

Space, place, memory, nachteraglichkeit, afterwardsness; the aftermath is a misplaced, immature, unreconstructed hatred of Stroud and Stroudiness.

"I've found us some space at Hawkwood college", Sue had ventured helpfully.
"Oh, bloody great," thought Jane. "Hawkwood College, my favourite.
Still, I'll just pretend I'm somewhere else, no need to go into town, no need to reopen old wounds."
"The only problem is Saturday", Sue said. "But I've booked us a room in the Shambles and…"
"Oh, bloody great," thought Jane. "Still, I'm a grown up, it'll be all right, I won't be a bloody shambles, not in bloody Stroud. It'll be fine…"

I hate bloody Stroud. I hated Stroud.

I hated the loneliness, the isolation and the smell of death. I hated the way we turned in on ourselves, I hated the ways our hopefulness curdled and soured and I hated the way the sun shone on and on and on the bloody yellow stone walls leaving larger and larger patches of ice, of ice beneath our skins as we closed further and further down and turned away from each other.

But I loved Michelina, the sainted Michelina who loved us and hugged us and cried with us and held us tight and eventually, even after the birth of our child had not saved us from ourselves, suggested that we sold the cottage and moved away before we destroyed each other.

An interesting diagnosis that (all on the National Health you understand). But then Michelina was not your average GP.

I don't know if Michelina ever picked spinach at midnight, but sitting here in our group, two medics in our midst, talking a lot about the NHS, I am reminded of those hours spent with Michelina, and of her many impromptu visits to our cottage. I can see her now, walking up the steps to the cottage, just after the fifth baby disintegrated five months in; big doctor's handbag slung behind her back and a golden retriever puppy clutched under each arm. She placed one puppy in each of our laps and sat down uninvited.

"You don't have to have them, but I think they'll help," she'd said. And they did. Not your average diagnosis, but then she was not your average GP.

I hated bloody Stroud. I still do. Even now I cannot forgive this place for the loneliness, bitterness and havoc still stored up in its yellow stone walls.

And yet sitting in Stroud, writing about love, I find myself writing a love letter to our doctor: a doctor who practised through and with love and who loved us as we loved her and reminded us over and over again that given time and a different place we might learn once again to love each other. A doctor who prescribed puppies and departures and could see how to salvage all that was precious between us when all we could see was cold sunlight on crumbling yellow stone."

After Jane's Sunday morning writing, Sue noticed and paid attention to the group and to how we wove between us the ever-evolving container for the sharings we did. Sue wrote:

"In my mind I see a basket, made of many disparate fibres, coloured and natural, varying thicknesses. The basket rises up from a narrow base, expanding like a horn, a cornucopia, turning from the upright as it spreads its open lips for us to tip our writing into. The basket's threads largely composed of our talk, our readings, but also this place, this time, the sun, the hand on the shoulder[4].

Ah, the hand on the shoulder. What a tempered experience that is. At first I found myself appreciating the warmth of the touch, the Friday touch. I could smell her, a mix of kitchen smells and warm skin, soap and fresh sweat. A touch of the moment, two moments, yet rich in detail. I looked up at her, into her smile, her delight—a lovely open face. I smiled too.

We talked about that touch, which I'd noticed and you'd noticed. We talked about the lemon curdy pudding, and her delight in our delight. Proud cook, generous with her secrets; "It's Jamie Oliver's lemon curdy pudding". We seemed to leave it at that, in our talk.

Not that I did. My responses confused by my (fleeting) desire to touch her back, place my hand on hers, test its floury warmth. My kind of woman? Writing this now I'm reminded, for the third time this weekend, of Dora, school friend and child of the Whiteway colony. The only girl who got

---

[4] On at least two occasions across the weekend Sue, and we all, had noticed that the Hawkwood cooks had placed their hands on her shoulder while talking to her and/or us.

better marks than I did in English: I remember how much I loved you then, sitting next to you on the bus to Cheltenham to explore the second-hand bookshops. Finding Mervyn Peake and Goethe—my shame at mispronouncing his name when I pulled the volume of Penguin philosophers off that carousel in the bookshop at the end of the Promenade. Slowly replacing it as I listened to your gentle "is that how you pronounce it?", nothing in your delivery could have moderated my sense of gaucheness, of being caught out aping what I wasn't (clever, well read, a participant in the sorts of conversations where philosophers' names were mentioned)—how could I have known better?

We cruised the new Habitat in the Prom, the Stephen Thursfield in the Lower High Street. Seldom able to afford to buy, but drinking in the colours and shapes, and the places evoked (Provence, Tuscany) by what was then so chic. You introduced me to the Black Tulip, an upstairs café, bistro-style with proper coffee. I sat there glowing, excited, in love but not speaking of love. I have no idea what I contributed to our conversation; politics I guess, a safer sort of passion.

I hitched miles to meet you, to spend that time together—you caught the bus mainly. Yet, at school, we could have had longer together; time snatched between lessons, long lunch breaks, seeing you off on the bus. But I don't remember the school-you in the same way. Not in the way evoked by that warm floury touch, that soft, brown hair, blue eyes and golden skin."

And, much later, Ann wrote:

"What I wanted to write, or didn't want to write and couldn't:

Following on from Jane's writing about Stroud, I knew I couldn't write. It was Sunday morning, lunch was fast approaching with a crowded dining room and the necessity of small or not quite so small talk. Then some planning, then home. I didn't want to be upset. Didn't want to hear the sound catch in my own throat. Didn't want to be red and blotchy over a Sunday roast and a car trip home. Didn't want to feel all my sinuses clogged and heavy, and my body dehydrated from weeping, from all those fast flowing tears coursing down my face. The need for a stiff drink to make it all go away. And I knew that I would feel this because I have felt it all before, and I will feel it again. I feel it regularly. I feel it at least once a month. I feel it in the street, on a bus, listening to the latest news report of a domestic atrocity, and despite years of the talking cure, and making baby dolls, and writing to them and talking to them, it still hurts like hell. And despite the bravery of others, the jumping off the cliff that others will hold their nose and do, I just couldn't do it. Was just too wearily certain of what would happen if I did, to be prepared to make that mighty step not into the unknown, but into the all too familiar arms of my very old friend, an all-knowing, all-embracing, ever-ready grief.

I went for a walk down to the sacred spring, sat by the sketched-out labyrinth in the grass, tried to anaesthetise myself enough to write, but I knew that I couldn't. I knew that self-preservation would kick in. I had seen others cry, on this weekend and before. Had cried myself before when confronting squarely my feelings of unworthiness in the face of my husband's consistent love, eros and caritas. I just didn't want to. I wasn't scared of the reception I would get. I wasn't embarrassed as I have spent hours sobbing my heart out to my therapist, unable to speak through tears so primal that there are no words, a pain so bodily and rhizomatic that it is before words, before language. I know this old friend. And I am slightly weary of its company. I was too tired of walking round it and seeing how it was looking to want to bring it to this company. I had had enough.

When Jane read her beautiful, elegiac, measured hymn to Stroud and her lost babies, I desperately wanted it to stop. I knew then that my old friend was at my shoulder, about to claim its place at a sun-bathed table in an English country garden. I was glad I had my dark glasses on. With them I could just about hold it back and in. Had we been inside it would have been much harder. I kept waiting for Jane's piece to end. If I could just hold it for another few seconds surely it would be over and I would be safe. But just as I thought it had ended it started again. Please, just bloody stop. A small panic welling up. You have to write about this. If you don't you are wimping out and cheating the process. You have to engage. You have to hold hands with your old friend. You have to stand face-to-face. You have to eyeball that old friend. You have to. You have to. You have to.

But that long therapy has given me at least one thing: self-defence. Protecting myself no longer feels like wimping out. Endangering myself no longer seems like the only ethical option. And so I protected myself. I drew a picture. I kept the mood light before lunchtime. I colluded with the sunshine."

And Jane replied, but did not send:

"Ever had one of those dreams about wandering the shopping mall naked when everybody else is fully clothed? Yes? Well that's how I felt that day, when we left Stroud. I felt cheated in the company of Doras, straddled and saddled with pictures of 'scapulas' and the like. Laughed out of court in my pain and blood and guts and misery by your miserliness and lack of honesty. I called and you did not respond. Intimacy matched with distance; grief with humour. Gale et al. (2011) show us "how writing touches" and declare themselves "forgers of a loving space" (2011, p.1) in their collaborations, but clearly my offerings forged no such space with you."

Instead she sent this:

"And did they grow?

I had some sense of what Ann might write, having read something a while back about these unborn babies, but this apprehension did not do justice to the sheer bloody understated power and momentum of what emerged.

And I was left, immediately and vividly with the question "and did they grow"… or did they stay as unborn babies in her mind's eye?

For what Ann's writing evoked in me was a familiar and stark staring ravingly discombobulating awareness that one of them, and the only one that I am ashamed about, the one whose loss to this world is somehow my 'fault', has continued to grow and grow. Each time I think of him, the aborted Tom, he gets older in my mind's eye.

I was nineteen when he seemed so inconvenient, so in need of being got rid of, but he never went away. I have no real evidence he was a boy. In 'reality' he was called a foetus and we never 'met'. And yet Tom has always been there in the shadows, growing up and quietly observing my life as it has unravelled before him. He was 18 when my child was born, watching noncommittally from the background gloom he inhabits. I cannot really see him, so much as discern his presence. A sudden onset of lankiness, of maleness, of awkwardness and occasional outright hostility from the back-shadows and stories of the room heralds his entrance into my life and then suddenly, intensely, now aged 35 and beginning to grey at the temples, he is there alongside me, giving my current life-space his tight-lipped once-over. He sometimes smiles, as if to himself, and sometimes even laughs out loud, but he has never looked at me directly— even after all these years I could not tell you the colour or shape of his eyes.

He knows that I did not want him, or at least that I did not even think about what it might have meant to want him at the time, but he is still there, softly observing me across all these years. And he has always, quite simply, wanted me."

After the Hawkwood weekend

"A Soliloquy in Cinquains:

Peggy's.
You gather there
I am at my dad's house

surrounded by a lack of his
presence

You eat
together and
tell each other tales that
sustain your connectedness each
to each

I am
on my own here
and sustaining but not
sustained. That is just how it is.
has been

Do not
misunderstand
I do need to be here
Not joining you in the writing
was right

Whist here
I do not think
of you at all, absorbed
as I am by these tasks, this house
his death

It's just
a bit weird that
last time you met to write
together I was on my way
here too

He'd died
that monday and
I was on my way back
with fresh dark clothes and lists of things
to do

This time
my list is new
my wicked stepmother
is older, frailer, more confused
and sad

alone

we two avoid
the dining room where his
last rasping gasping image is
too fresh

we eat
in the kitchen
which he always scorned and
then polish off his Cote Ventouse
at night

she's cleaned
his cupboards out
the smell of him soon gone
I steal away his fountain pen
and ink

I want
to move slowly
to cherish last fragments
but she needs to swiftly move on
with life

Later
ruminating
on the long journey home
I remember the writing group
meeting

And think
of the rawness
of grief and how fortune
has decreed that I should write this
alone"

Sue wrote to Jane:

"Your last, blank page:

I read your writing, cooled now as it's been posted for days. I read it
through feeling guilty, sad and a bit cross. I notice that there is a blank
page at the end of the piece called 'A Soliloquy in Cinquains', I want to
write on that page. Out of respect I write here instead, after all how would I
feel if I'd written about my hurt and my anger and my father, and you'd
written an afterwards? Not sure.

I notice the complexity of feelings in my response to you. And wonder if it all feels so complex because I'm so crap at this (being such an introvert), or because it's really complex? I don't know. I realise that I don't know how to share my feelings without the accompanying fear of blowing it all, of not being able to get back, not being let back in. I wonder whether I want to take the risk... I notice you did, take the risk I mean. You said at least some of what you wanted to say, took the risk of having the door shut in your face. Not that we would, no.

I wonder where the thread starts? Was it at Marietta's? Probably not. A dead and yet unburied father provides a clear reason not to be there in body. But you were there. We all talked of our time together at Hawkwood, the last rounds of writing, the discussions about baskets and weaving and all that gentle theorising together about what we'd been doing. What it brought up for us and how it related to us as a writing collective. And I couldn't let go of the pain of hearing you read your writing about the babies and the puppies and the memories of Stroud. I wanted to talk about how it felt, and I needed to write about the memories of losses of my own that your writing raised from a cleft inside me. Memories of that terrible time when deaths came one strike after another, blows falling on already bruised flesh, shredding whatever scar tissue had accumulated and driving it deep into previously intact places. I needed to speak about not wanting to take from you the space of response and empathy by tipping out my own memories evoked by yours, so there had been a subdued quietening round of writing at the end of that last day.

I needed to speak about being silenced by an unreasonable feeling of responsibility for drawing you back to Stroud. I felt like a small child who had tried to make something lovely as a present, but had unwittingly bound in the poisonous plant, the rosehip's itchy core, the piece of shit. I felt like a small child who thinks she caused the sky to fall in, when really it was just thunder. (And here's the scary bit; I was reminded how much I care for you. Not in that crush-on-your-teacher, substitute mother, or for-tonight-I'll-be-queer way, but as a friend, as another woman. And I don't know how to say it; I'm afraid the naming will cause the ending. That it will embarrass you, that I will be an embarrassment).

So we spoke, and we wrote, joining our writing to the hanging thread of all our Hawkwood writing, and so moving into the next cycle.

So not at Marietta's house then, the start of the thread. But we did make a new time to meet then, as we did this time. Is it too disingenuous to say we did so because we knew how hard it is to get a shared date? That time, I think we made a date and waited to see if you could make it. I remember asking, and you saying you could make it, but saying it in amongst talk of a thousand other things. Did 'we' get lost in a thousand other things?

This time it felt different, as if we felt (however unreasonably) a little abandoned by you, as if we needed to make a date to keep a place, to be a placeholder for a group already feeling shaky (no Anita, no Jane and for most of the day no Louisa). You start to feel excluded, we start to feel abandoned, and we all start to spin out of connection. Time to take care of the group, as well as each member—is that the rub? As we listen to one speak of her vigil with her dying sister, of another's troubled love, another's grief, do we become a speaking support group rather than a writing collective? Are we losing a sense of 'we'? I notice how we get into theorising our writing more easily than into writing. The reading, responding, writing balance goes.

For the past several years I have worn at least one of three white gold rings, made for us by our friend Diana Porter. Glenn has one, bigger ring; I have two smaller ones. Mine each have a tiny diamond tucked into the empty heart of a letter. When the three rings are held together the letters spell out 'the feeling of we'. Despite the rings being different sizes and different widths the writing still joins up. The 'we' still appears.

I wonder how typical this falling together and falling apart motion is in such writing groups. Group process points to similar patterns, why should we be different? Taking the risk of exposing your emotional response to the way the group is behaving seems to me a way to stay in-relationship. In writing this I am responding, despite not having heard you read, conflating the spoken response with the writing, maybe.

I'm going to set up a meet-o-matic for the 'Love' group. I will mind very much if you don't come."

Jane wrote:

"My thoughts on Sue's thoughts re: process and other comments re: distinctiveness and some adjacent to this process, process thoughts of my own…:

I have an immediate response, is immediate me-too? I had an immediate response to Ann too, was that me too? I think not…

I think conceptually we are beginners here at collective biography… we write together but our voices are distinctive or words to that effect… Could we shift that, unravel that a bit… move from anonymity to somewhere slightly beyond, behind, underneath subjectivity?

We are still very individualistic—something to do with staying with particularly boundaried senses of 'me' and therefore that shadowy 'old chestnut' of me-tooness. I don't have answers to Sue's questions; she wasn't expecting any, but I do wonder what will happen when we begin to lose that distinctiveness and what impact that has on the 'created me's and senses of me too-ness that might abound here. We probably don't have enough writing yet between us or enough time lapsed to lose sight of our own distinctive voices… but I hope we get to that point and then I think 'me' as response, me as me-too… might shift and become 'the writing', the collaboration becoming almost molecular…

Which will bring other process issues and concerns…

The other day when I went to read Ann's writing I was almost tempted, nearly created mayhem probably, to start to unravel the individual writings and weave them into a patchwork piece… bits here and there, threads flying… a "felting" as I think Deleuze would say (Wyatt et al., 2010), but I controlled this urge to bugger about, decided to wait a while until we had aired these possibilities as a group…"

Reflecting together

Llanishen writing

Sue wrote:

"One of the things we know and value about this methodology is the way each other's writing helps us to find new access to our own material, how it can deepen and inspire our writing. However, I'd like to name some consequences or shadows of this call-and-response process.

One was surfaced for me after hearing Jane's moving writing on Sunday morning. It was a desire to write about my own painful associations with the place, yet I was also, for the first time in this group, afraid of sounding like I was writing a me-too piece. On reflection, I think that this was less about wanting to give Jane's writing a respectful amount of space and more about wanting to protect myself. I stopped myself from going deeper into painful memories.

I'm left wondering what I am really clear about (or at least clear enough to write about) how to work and facilitate this move to share generatively, or at least consciously. How do we keep me-too as a response to others writing, rather than competitive chest-baring? (Heavens, getting a bit close to Breasts Akimbo here!)

At two points during this last piece of writing I really wanted to write something else; one a piece about a series of bereavements I experienced shortly after moving back to Stroud, and another that explored why/how people feel free to touch me. But here we were, sitting outside in the sunshine, writing for what would be the last round before we parted. And I couldn't introduce this note, didn't want to feel the discomfort myself, didn't want to discomfort you all. So I wrote myself a couple of notes on the blank back of the pages I did write on about being reminded of Dora by the floury touch of the cook.

I include my notes to myself:

"I note also wanting to speak/write about my losses here[5]: Ken and Chris[6], Rob[7], Geoff[8], and my cats, my cats[9]".

"I started off the piece about the touch thinking I'd write about ablebodiedness and those touches, but didn't."

In process terms, it seems important to me to include some trace of the unwritten and unspoken, as well as the shared material. There appear to be many reasons for this unshared material. I'm aware of Ann's careful choicefulness, which included timing and self-protection. I shared what I think are similar feelings of not wanting to expose myself to the results of revisiting my grief, and for me this also included the experience of hearing my bitterness and anger spoken out-loud.

There is something else in what Ann has written that interests me: she writes of feeling a pressure to disclose, and this rings warning bells for me about the ways in which we can feel coerced, and indeed coerce ourselves into self-disclosure, possibly feeling it's the only way to be authentic. Ann wrote of: "A small panic welling up. You have to write about this. If you don't you are wimping out and cheating the process. You have to engage."

I'm curious about how we can come to speak about and value these conscious choices not to engage, as well as noticing our less conscious ones. After all, they are often well founded, and they speak of our experience of our place in the world just as much as our gorgeous, vulnerable writing. As professionals, and maybe particularly as academics

---

[5] In the two and a half years after moving to Stroud.
[6] Both good friends who committed suicide.
[7] A close colleague who died in a road accident, a father of five children all under twelve.
[8] Another friend, who died of an HIV/AIDS related infection on St. Valentine's day, having stood next to me at Rob's funeral only a year before.
[9] Three of whom died of feline infectious peritonitis, and each of whom I nursed to their last natural breath.

with the expectation on us that we will write and publish, there may be things we don't wish to be known for writing, don't want to expose to dissection by 'colleagues'.

It also seems to me to be important to track these feelings that we must engage with the process, this seeming loss of autonomy. Is it because we have entered into a collective that we feel guilty about holding some things back? Is this intensified because we are all women, and there is a sense of writing to support each other's exploration in our project? Is it made still more difficult to 'hold out' on each other because we are writing of love (and with love)? I don't know the answers to these questions, but want to raise them as my curiosity about the process we are engaged in.

So, having revisited our writing, we seem to hover on the edge of something. Shocked by the power of our words to evoke. That place, those memories evoked. The way Jane's writing; the tumbling, bursting forth of it, broke open, broke into those contained, protected places.

I continued to live in Stroud, despite the feeling that all around me my friends were dying, leaving things unsaid, and all the potential of our days together, what we might/would have had. I remember feeling somehow it was me; that I had been, to paraphrase Wilde, careless enough to have lost four friends in quick succession. Four friends and four cats.

So, I separated the place from the time and the incidents, and held the feeling and the responsibility and the grief to myself. Was it the process of trying to write as a collective biography group that made some space to re-connect the place and the happenings? Was there a particular space created by us as a group of women, there, then?

In our proposal, we wrote of embodied writing, and things silenced, written on the body in invisible ink. And now I want to know how we came to expose it, to warm the milk, the onion juice. It's as if we allowed ourselves a space to story.

This speaking is fugitive. Then (Hawkwood) we listened to Jane, offering respectful silences and comforting proximity, to soothe the rawness of the words and the emotion behind them. When we returned to writing (that last cycle of writing in the garden at Hawkwood on that Sunday morning) I feel I turned away, and I hear that Ann turned away too, choosing different strategies to cover our wateriness and the pains evoked.

I chose not to write about my dead friends; at the time it felt like being in a slow-motion battle where people were felled by HIV instead of bullets and the noose instead of the arrow; when disease descended on our house, distilled out of the air (very much the place actually, as a neighbour lost her dear cats too).

I chose not to write about the painful and contested edge—my body and its accessibility to others, boundaries shifted or not by my impairment. Instead, I note that I noted down the thoughts, the ideas to come back to, and moved on to write about my love for Dora.

So, I wonder, does this tell us something about a leakiness around the collective biography group, where our memory work, embarked upon in service of the group inquiry, puts out tendrils, air roots that move on and out beyond the group setting (time and place), but keep the work going? After all, I notice that we did keep writing, and we did share the writing between us, kept turning the mixture and allowing the air in.

I'm finding it hard to write this, not knowing where it's going and feeling I'm turning, and in turning look for a place that's either comfortable or moving, and not finding much purchase if I'm honest. I feel content that there is stuff to work with here, that it's possible to find the loose thread, or to rub the surface long enough for the image below the over-painting to start to emerge and offer that 'seen through another medium' glimpse into a certain type of fugitive sense.

Pentimento: one story thinning the skin that had been grown over the raw stuff, making a one thing of multiple things, pulling things out of time back into a shared place.

A pentimento of the place (Stroud) and the space (the Love Group) where our single lives have come and been threaded together through the collective biography process, the place working on us and through us. The emotional identities of the place emerging as we allowed ourselves an emotional identity of the group, the space, supported there by the place, extending out from that earthed point into a virtual space of considered sharing and withholding of moves towards each other and retreats away—but actually getting more open and ever closer despite the gaps of time and the lack of physical proximity.

It seems we had tapped into a rich seam of what bell hooks (2009, p.1) would term "the geographies of the heart", thence charting the "wilderness of spirit, the everyday anguish that shapes the habits of being for those who are lost, wandering, searching".

We have built a different understanding of the collective biography group, as is embodied by/in us and mediated by points of memory and opportunity to share (the shared realisation at Ammerdown of what might be in these exchanges that we could mine about the spaces between the three of us; the contextual, temporal, relational). We have continued with the labour, started in the original collective biography group, ploughing it sometimes overtly, sometimes more tacitly. Occasionally a glint breaks the surface (Ammerdown) at other times we dig together (now)."

Jane wrote:

"Here we are. The three sisters. Returning to the space where much was plotted two years ago. Subsequently a father, a sister and whole writing group have died and we have twice been to Hawkwood for different kinds of writing moments. We, all three of us, write a lot. We write both to save and savour our lives, and we also write for a livelihood. We write alone and we write with others, but we three have become a kind of unacknowledged kernel of the Bristol writers. Maybe that is what this meeting is for? The meeting of the unacknowledged kernel. There are many others who both write and facilitate writing. There are many poets and storytellers and workshoppers and there are multifarious others who write with us and circumstances in which we write in different pairings with each other.

I think this might be the first time we have sat, the three of us, and written together in the same space and place at the same time… and even though this is Sue's house, where she and Glenn and animals various, some invited and others probably uninvited, actually live… I think of it very much as one of our writing spaces. I think of this place with a certain air of aesthetic entitlement that would have little legality in court but that you'd find it hard to budge me from. I wander around this place, as I do Ammerdown, Hawkwood, and 35 Berkley Square, opening fridges to see what's nibblable and chatting to passing ferrets as if we are on intimate terms, with an air of quiet ease and authority. I am at home with these women, the Christmas pudding bubbling away, the view hanging mistily from the balcony. And together we are writing. I am with the poets on this."

Ann wrote:

"Somewhere in my workroom is a grey shoebox. I suspect it's under the chair where the flotsam and jetsam wash up. In the box are three dolls. Three strange totemic dolls. Three dolls, which might have got me burnt in any half-decently run witch-craze. Wrapped up in tissue. Silent.

I made the dolls from rolled-up cloth. They are heavy. They have a solidity. Not soft and filled with kapok or the newer polyester stuffing. Not like a rag doll with woollen plaits and felt eyes. These dolls are bound in swaddling. They could be hung up on the wall like sixteenth-century infants strapped to boards and pegged up out of harm's way or to make their limbs grow straight. You wouldn't hang these glowering presences on your wall. I considered briefly putting them in a box frame, but the thought of the look on the framer's face when the lid came off the box and there under the tissue paper were three mummified foetuses, like three long-dead Egyptian cats, gave me pause. That, and saying, "Pete, darling, I'd like to hang my three unborn children on the wall or pop them on the mantelpiece", made me think again.

Jane asks if they grew. And did they grow? Or did they stay as unborn babies in the mind's eye? They did stay unborn for years. They stayed swimming gently in some amniotic fluid in the 80% of the brain that goes unused. Floating in my own private psychic limbo, doing a lazy backstroke, round and round for thirty years with all the care in the world of a magic goldfish, old beyond its years but ever young, strong and moving.

But the babies were biding their time. They swam easily, gently at my body temperature, round and round, gathering a tiny bit of strength on each rotation, waiting and watching until I and they were ready in body, spirit and mind.

Just as I learned from catechism class that the Lord never tempts you beyond endurance, beyond your power to resist, and, as the art therapists tell us, your psyche never throws up images to harm you, so the babies waited until I was ready. I have to say that their estimation of readiness and mine might not have been in synch, but despite being glittering fish in a somatic pool they had a native wit. They knew that, to get to swim up and out into the light, up through the lightening shades of blue to the palest shade where the daylight hit the water, they would have to swim hard for the surface when I wasn't looking. They waited in the deep, circled a few more times, and then, when my mind was elsewhere, worrying about my work, or fretting over something trivial, they kicked hard and swam straight, vertically, powerfully and broke the surface.

I remember sitting at that worktable looking at those three cat mummies, those three bound foetuses, and wondering what the hell they were. What in God's name possessed me? The dolls I had been copying were a bit odd, but they were recognisably mannequins, people who sat on little specially carved wooden chairs and crossed their elegant legs and dangled their fingers and exuded languid airs. I had three fat slugs of babies, bound in the most gorgeous silk I could find, decked with jewels and ribbons and bits of mohair. And they weighed a ton.

I found them an anonymous grey shoebox with its tissue paper still intact. I put them to bed. I knew instinctively not to show them to Pete. Bury them a second time.

I took them out only to write to them or to take them to my therapist. I showed her my writing. She read it. She asked to keep a copy. I never printed another one. I talked to the black doll, a funny inverse black madonna in that writing. Talked to it, loved it, pleaded with it. And then put it back into its box. With the other two. The one with the sinister plastic kewpie doll face and the little one who perhaps would not have made its fifth birthday. And I put the lid on.

Now I cannot tell you where they are. I can tell you roughly where they are. I could go and have a look under the chair. But they seem to have melted away again, job done, back to their own private limbo, their own psychic pool.

So, they didn't grow up. They remain only potential. They may in some string-theory parallel universe have a life and history and children of their own. In some of the many worlds, I may be a grandmother making dress-up dolls for my granddaughters. But no faces and no names."

Lido thoughts (Jane)

Meandering in and out of intimacies in our writings and our lives, it seemed that there was much time spent "sitting on the curb talking", as Diversi & Moreira (2009) would say, and not enough time inscribing our bodies. Yet I came home from those sessions tattooed all over with the markings of invisible inks.

What we all experienced from and with each other in Stroud was an ethical transgression, followed by a leaking out over the boundaries, a 'running away together', splitting off our writings and writing times from the rest of the group. There had to be somewhere to go with those broken, barren bodies of ours: bodies too freaky and leaky for public display. Under the canopy, you were given opportunities to stare and to play. You looked away, but took my hand and promised to play later. As Butler says: "Laughter in the face of serious categories is indispensable for feminism" (Butler, 1990, p.ix), and I think she means playfulness, clowning, full-bellied laughter here, not coy girlishness or giggles. I waited on our return from Hawkwood. Exposed. I was waiting for a full-throated, deep-bellied response from the two of you, and when it came, I both laughed and wept. So you had heard and seen my offering, my writing from the guts, for the leaky, damaged gift it was. Later, much later, there was a response to my call. Sometimes there is just silence. Our calls are like those lone, faraway calls of herons in the night. This intimacy is not instant, but sometimes there is a passing of time, fairy-tale time perhaps, digital time-keeping,

perhaps, between call and response in our writing. I am with the poets on
this:

"See when it all unravels—
The entire project
reduced to threads of
moss fleeing a nor'—
wester;
d'you ever imagine
chasing just one strand, letting it lead
you
to an unsung cleft in a
rock, a place you could
take to,
dig yourself in—but
what are the chances of that?" (Jamie, 2012, p.50)

CHAPTER FIFTEEN

REMEMBERING AND FORGETTING WITH SUE:
SOME STORIES OF HANGING ON IN THERE

BRISTOL COLLABORATIVE WRITING GROUP[1]

This chapter is constructed from writing and reflection within the Bristol Collaborative Writing Group (BCWG) over the last few months of 2009. We have been meeting and writing together since 2004, and our aim has been to narrate landscapes of memory and identity through collaborative writing processes. Over that period, we have developed relationships and patterns of writing where trust, acceptance and creativity are increasingly present and singular subjectivities are increasingly troubled. The chapter focuses on a brief period of writing and reflection on issues of memory and 'forgettory': writing which emerged in response to our friend and colleague, Sue, who had recently been diagnosed with memory problems.

Since 2004, our intention has been to explore questions of identity through writing together. Our writing together has evolved over time and has emerged from different processes. Often one of us will 'call' through a written or spoken story. We will respond to that person, and into the space s/he has created, in different ways, sometimes with our own stories, thoughts, or ideas about the world. We have been nurtured by the

---

[1] The Bristol Collaborative Writing Group (BCWG), originally a mixed staff and postgraduate student community, has been active within the Graduate School of Education, University of Bristol, since 2004. All the group's writing is generated through the collaborative endeavours of its members: Sue Wilson, Susan Williams, Jane Speedy, Artemi Sakellariadis, Viv Martin, Tony Brown, Laurinda Brown, Nell Epona Bridges and Dave Bainton. Each of its publications has been produced through a different means of bringing these writings together. In this case, the principal author of the paper was Viv Martin and it was refined into a finished product by the rest of the team acting as an editorial group.

relationships within the group, but also by relationships with landscapes, ancestors, animals (domestic and wild), people (living and dead), ideas, and writings of many who have gone before. As such our sense of self as subject has become both more than and different from singularly and essentially human. A rich resource in our writing conversations has been the work of Davies & Gannon (2006), Gannon (2001) and other Australian feminists, such as Onyx & Small (2001), in collective biography and memory work, and also of White (1995, 2000), Myerhoff (1980, 1982, 1986) and Speedy (2004, 2008), which invite us to position ourselves as witnesses to each other's stories.

Our work together has been principally about the accounts we might give and the theories we might generate about relationships between identity and memory. To which end, we have developed a form of collaborative writing as inquiry (see Richardson & St Pierre, 2005) that allows us to listen intently from within this fluid constantly shifting space, but to also listen out for the irreducibility of our constantly moving selves to their constituting conditions. In this respect, our collaborative and overlapping accounts of our selves have become both singular and plural (Butler, 2005). Our writing rarely finishes itself, but is woven together from traces, lacunae, fragments, debris and bits and pieces.

The fragments that follow were principally written during, and in response to, two meetings. Our friend and colleague Sue had been having some problems with her memory. At the first of the two meetings, Sue talked of the diagnosis she had recently received. We then wrote in response. As is usually the case when we meet, we read out our writings. Following the meeting, we sent our writings and re-writings to each other. We met again a few weeks later and continued to write into the space created by our stories of remembering and forgetting. This chapter has been woven from those texts and subsequent reflections.

rrreemmeemmbbbeerrriiiinnngggffffoorrrggeeetttiiinnggrreemmbbrrng

Last night I dreamed that I was in the holocaust, walking along with others, in the ice and snow, feeling frozen, with a phrase going through my head when I woke: "It was a lie—Arbeit Macht Frei".

At the beginning I was anxious, wary of joining this writing group. I had never thought of myself as someone who could write. I had been a biology teacher for years and then retrained as a counsellor. But writing? That was not me, not my identity.

We have been meeting now for years—talking, telling our stories, and writing about them. And the group has shrunk as people came and went;

some left complaining of the lack of achievement; others had to finish MScs, PhDs... and didn't have the time.

One died.

Few of us understood what the point was.

Yet a process of slowly recognising that the group was one of steady acceptance enabled me to trust that I was becoming part of something important, and I felt committed to it. There was little of the usual pressure: to perform, to succeed, to achieve and outdo others.

But there was a combination of acceptance, patience and creativity. And then, sometimes, there was a feeling, an atmosphere, a way of being that we simply called "Gerald"; and when "Gerald"[2] was around, his/her ways of being seemed to enable almost any mystery to evolve and develop, through the simple process of being heard and of listening to others' stories.

rrreemmeemmbbbeerrriiiinnngggffffoorrrggeeetttiiinnggrreemmbbrrng

I read with the prickles of tears in my eyes that overflowed when I stopped reading—not the angsty tears of rage or unresolvedness but that acceptance of how it is—moving into the story of remembering and forgetting...

rrreemmeemmbbbeerrriiiinnngggffffoorrrggeeetttiiinnggrreemmbbrrng

Where the hell did I put it?

The thing I put down and now can't find.

The memories I can no longer remember.

The memories built into my identity.

My memories of being me.

They are still there—aren't they? Can I remember if I have forgotten them?

Good memories and bad. Does forgetfulness distinguish them? Or are they simply ticked off in some particular order that has no meaning to me?

And here I am, still wondering. Is there peace in forgetting? Or is there frustration and fear; the fear of other's responses to that slowing down of capability? Just like when I was a child and afraid of not being able to do anything right. Now the same fears of being stupid, being dim, being forgetful. All the anxiety of 'failure' in a world that only measures

---

[2] See Speedy et al. (2010)

success. If I were free of the judgments of others, then maybe slowing down into a place of gentle forgetting would not be so bad.

Now, every other Saturday, we drive over to the home where my father now lives, and I try to make sense of his words that seem like gibberish. And when, now and then, I understand a word or phrase he is trying to speak, he changes, he seems alive again, smiling, perhaps nodding at an old photo, and talking, sometimes in strange phrases. But he is reaching out again, and sometimes there is sense there. And the frustration when we can't understand is palpable. He needs to be understood.

We sit and listen, then we write…

For years… Sue came and spoke and witnessed and was intensely part of us, but never wrote. Only when she had subversively given up on the master's degree project, only when she no longer had to write in order to cross rivers, jump hurdles, did she begin to write. She has written consistently, but infrequently, and tenderly to and about us and about herself. Perhaps most powerfully in my memory, she has written to and about being a step-mum, and to and about never wanting to give birth or to inflict the experience of parenting she had had on others. I await more writing from Sue, writing from her memory and forgettory and wonder what collaboration means if we are not able, between us, to fill in the sentences for our dear friend, if the ends of them should in time fall from her shelf. She talks of her garden and not getting here and I wonder how we are going to get to her garden. Also, perhaps, how difficult it might be to have to stop us—to say—enough is enough of you lot, I want to garden in my garden and leave my sentences to unravel themselves. I do not want you all coming and trampling over the peonies and adding adverbs where no words at all are needed.

"It's a pain", she says.

"At least it doesn't hurt", she says.

rrreemmeemmbbbeerrriiiinnngggffffoorrrggeeetttiiinnggrreemmbbrrng

"It's not that you're forgetful, you know, it's just the sheer amount of – things you're trying to remember."

So said a student last year—I had forgotten to do something I had promised to do and this was the response. And also part of the problem. As a child and growing adult I simply knew things—when I was a teacher I did not use a diary and had the reputation of being efficient—I wasn't trying to remember anything—it simply happened.

I try to put the things I need to do listed in my diary like a colleague does—then I lose the diary and the list, having been downloaded from my brain, ceases to exist. Another student says that I taught him to "put it in your diary so you don't have to put it in your mind". I was surprised by this. I wonder if I am doing this to myself—I don't have strategies for this world of not memory. I am also aware that I lose the interconnectedness of all those things—plotting a route across Bristol to deliver and pick up from many schools and observe lessons and have meetings and still no diary. Now I don't automatically see the connections and everything seems to get harder as I pass from random job to random job, lacking flow.

What is memory for? Short term, long term? Photographs of long ago—being the mother in the frame—1930s—what gets recreated through looking at a photograph of myself long ago? What is memory for? Locating us in a permanent past present with new stories capable of being told with new awarenesses.

I make a memory box for you, Sue, of things that fill my mind when I think of you –

rrreemmeemmbbbeerrriiiinnngggffffoorrrggeeetttiiinnggrreemmbbrrng

Over the years we have tangled with ideas and concepts of 'memory' as well as evoking, catalysing and creating memories. Eva Brann (1991) regards memory as imaginative and creative:

> "Imaginative memory not only stores for us the passing moments of perception; it also transfigures, distances, vivifies, defangs—reshapes formed impressions, turns oppressive immediacies into wide vistas… loosens the rigid grip of an acute desire and transforms it into a fertile design." (cited by Sacks, 1995, p.167)

rrreemmeemmbbbeerrriiiinnngggffffoorrrggeeetttiiinnggrreemmbbrrng

We had a conversation a while ago. Probably on one of our journeys. The detail of the journey doesn't stay with me, nor really the context, but the feeling does. I wanted to protect you from having to face that feeling, but clearly you are facing it, or something like it, now, in your life.

Now, having stopped writing for a second or two, I find myself wanting to check what I have heard. I took my hearing aids out a little while ago—I often do that after a period of concentrated listening. It's like going off duty. So I went off duty before I came in here and now I'm regretting it. I want to be 'on duty' for you (strange choice of words, I know).

But the issue is, did I hear right?

I heard something about brain, about checks, and I know your family background, and I know your fear (see, I did say that word after all, I did name that feeling).

But did I hear right? Did I hear enough? Are there checks still to do?

And you look so calm, serene even. I wonder what journey you have taken to this point.

The visual part of my mind fills with a picture of your house, your garden, and the lane outside, and the cattle grid and the choice of paths; left to Town Brook and Rectory Wood or right to Carding Mill Valley. And I realise how much I want to share those places with you, all special places to me and now your home. How much I want to walk those paths with you, and chat and drink tea in the National Trust Tea Shop while it fills up with the evaporation of wet walkers and the windows mist so that we can just make out the ashes the other side of the stream. And I want to show you that mistletoe, the furthest north mistletoe.

I've wanted to do these things for a long time and yet I haven't made the space to do them. I want to do them more now.

rrreemmeemmbbbeerrriiiinnngggffffoorrrggeeetttiiinnggrreemmbbrrng

I'm wondering about
Imagining myself into a space
where the things by which we
locate ourselves
the reference points by which
I locate myself
are no longer available to me

I remember a world which
had shrunk
drifting in and out
of consciousness
noticing smells
drifting in and out
of consciousness
sounds
distant voices
drifting in and out of consciousness
trying to locate myself

and wondering how we can be
your reference points
if there is something
we can offer
which will help
you to locate yourself
which will keep your lucid presence
which will hold the you
that you want to be
for as long as you want to be held

rrreemmeemmbbbeerrriiiinnngggffffoorrrggeeetttiiinnggrreemmbbrrng

Heart thumping...
How loud can it thump without others hearing?
Heart thumping...
How hard can it thump without catapulting itself across the room?
Heart thumping...
How close can it get to bursting without streaming down my face?

Time I *think* for a long pause...
Time I *feel* for a long pause...
Time I *know*... for a long pause...

No time here for levity, frivolity, brevity,
no time here for future, for plans, for certainty and security
no time here for me in control...

Heart thumping…
No time for silence…
How come this group moves so easily, so willingly, so deeply into a
significance that is so often unacknowledged?
How come our 'we' always unearths a part of me, the heart thumping,
unspoken me.

So how can I tell my story? Will it detract from the other more
significant stories? What if I could quieten my heart so that it behaved, so
that... But no.

*"You have significant damage in your brain. This is most unusual. No,
I can't yet say if it is degenerative. No, I can't yet say how much you can*

recover. Yes, it will feel that you have lost your sense of self. Yes, you have lost hearing, co-ordination, memory. Yes, you will find writing up your PhD very difficult..."

And overnight who I am tumbles into a dark, insecure, confusing and fragile world. What if... how come... should... if only I had...

Can you hear my thumping heart?
Can you feel the slip-stream of my catapult?
Will there be a day when no-one will notice?
Or will I be a me who no longer notices?

rrreemmeemmbbbeerrriiiinnngggffffoorrrggeeetttiiinnggrreemmbbrrng

They'll come to me one day and I won't know who they are.
Not in the way that I get their names mixed up all the time now.
No, no. Not mistaking one for the other, but in the eerie way of not recognising them as my flesh and blood. In the eerie way that grandma didn't know who mum was.
My sister says it will come to us all because it's in our genes[3]
She is quite sure. She knows this. Maybe one day she will forget this too. Will she? Will I?
Will it happen?
Will there come a day when my daughter brings me a glass of water and I thank a stranger for their kindness?
Will I, one day, bump into someone in the street and, like Grace said to me, have to squint and say "what a kind face but where do I know you from?"
Maybe if I have more turmeric[4]...
Or maybe I should simply carry on creating the stories my girls will one day take turns to keep me company with: remember when you made us go to Velvet Bottom?[5] Remember the time you lost my passport? Remember when you forgot parents' evening? Remember when you forgot? You forgot to remember, remember? Remember mum? Mum???

---

[3] See Fox, 2009; Hsiung & Sadovnik, 2007, for an introduction to the relationship between dementia and genetics.

[4] Turmeric has been proven to improve problems with memory loss, see Ringman, et al., 2005.

[5] Velvet Bottom is a local beauty spot, just outside Bristol, at the top of Cheddar Gorge in Somerset, UK.

They'll come to me one day and I won't know who they are.
rrreemmeemmbbbeerrriiiinnngggffffoorrrggeeetttiiinnggrreemmbbrrng

The five-minute dementia test that took me ages…

What day is it today?[6]
Today is the first day after Sue announced to us that she may not be able to keep coming to the writing group; that she is beginning to develop memory problems, lose the plot… that her brain is shrinking. That is what stuck in my mind. That is what I thought about today when I woke up.
What is today's date? (Tell me the day, month and year.)
It is the 3rd of Cheshvan, 5770… although in some parts of the world it is still the 2nd. This means, of course, it is October 21st, 2009 to the dominant (domineering?) culture. Interesting stuff all this isn't it?… All this stuff about time and how we choose to break it up into little manageable bits. Time is so tricky, isn't it? What day is it today, you asked me (before—have drifted back to your original question). Well, in autobiographical time I suppose today is a good day, thus far, but you want me to answer you in chronological time (see Freeman, 2006), which draws me towards mythical time—towards the common cultural myth that as the days draw towards All Souls' night the membranes between the worlds get thinner and thinner.
How old are you?
Today I am quite old and tired and cross. I am fifty-four and I was born in 1954. This, my Chinese student said, was to be a lucky year for me, so why has it been so hard? Why am I stretched so thinly (like the waning autumn days above) between the older and younger generations of my family?
Some days it feels as though I will snap. Today I am a lot older than I should be.
Can you repeat the sentence, "Good citizens always wear stout shoes"?
Yes, but this is rubbish, or at least, it is total rubbish in Papua New Guinea (for instance) where good citizens hardly ever wear shoes and find them uncomfortable. Why can't I repeat a sentence that I believe in instead like, "A woman needs a man like a fish needs a bicycle".
Who is the prime minister?

---

[6] This text, devised by Rose (2009), is the latest version of those delivered routinely (and repeatedly) in UK health centres to people at risk of dementia/ memory loss.

Sir Peter Mandelson,[7] although we did not elect him.

In what year did the First World War start?

Well, interesting question, I have a first degree in history, you know. In many ways, the origins of the First World War date back to the early 1890s (and before that even) with all the tensions around the European 'scramble for Africa'... I suppose once it was obvious that Germany had lost out on the possibility of an Empire to equal that of Britain, or even France, the countdown to a European bust-up (which given their super-power status at the time meant things were going to get pretty global) was inevitable. Certainly events were well underway in both the Balkans and North Africa by the turn of the century and this was going to make the outbreak of a big war fairly inevitable. I suppose you want me to say 1914 because that's when people started declaring war left right and centre, but in some ways the declaration is not the start—it is perhaps the middle, or maybe even quite near the end.

What is twenty take away four?

The age of consent in the UK for all, regardless of sex, race, class, ability and/or sexual orientation.

What is four add fifteen take away seventeen?

I don't care. I never did and I'm certainly not going to start now.

Can you list four creatures beginning with 'S'?

Yes. Slithey toves, Satyrs, Sylphs and Spectres.

Why is a carrot like a potato?

It isn't, not to my mind. A carrot is not a famine-inducing vegetable at all and is associated with coriander and cakes with yoghurt icing and healthy carotene-packed juices that destroy cancer cells, fill the sky with sunshine and overcome economic crises in one deep orangey gulp. Carrots, whether freshly grated or honey-glazed, are never less than trendy, middle class and absolutely 'of the moment'. Potatoes are solid and reliable, even when chipped. Potatoes do not light up the sky, but equally, they will not let you down—unless you are Irish. In which case, they are iconic and painful reliquaries FILLED WITH STORIES OF OPPRESSION AND SMELLING OF DEATH. I like mine baked but boiled will do.

Why is a lion like a wolf?

---

[7] Sir Peter Mandelson, a (mostly) unelected member of the UK 'New Labour' Governments, 1997-2010, who apparently held enormous influence over Prime Ministers Blair and Brown.

In Bristol both are caged, both pace, both are sad and both have found themselves forming uneasy and inappropriately close relationships with human beings in green overalls that have been born out of desperation, loneliness and isolation. Both have lost much in the way of memory, identity and narrative (see King, 2000).

What was the sentence I asked you to remember?

A woman needs a man like a fish needs a bicycle.

rrreemmeemmbbbeerrriiiinnngggffffoorrrggeeetttiiinnggrreemmbbrrng

We meet again, a few weeks later…

The men have died—they don't live here in these spaces anymore wondering about where they've put things or being surprised at finding their glasses with the rest of the wine glasses when they give up forgetting or remembering and go for a tipple of ouzo or whiskey or…

We're left—the women—and then, last meeting, the heart-thumping revelations of more central challenges to identities—what are memories for? Short-term memory makes daily life that bit easier—now what level of the car park did I leave my car on?—an important aspect of multi-storied car-parked life (in this mechanised age I wonder why my ticket does not have where I parked cleverly displayed on it)—I don't forget this one—level 5—entrance on level 8—get the lift to work by swiping the ticket in the card reader by the lift-call buttons (took me a while to sort this one out on arrival) and I'm there ready for the get-away after the school carol concert at the Colston Hall this evening—but what if I find myself wandering around the many levels hoping to bump into my car… and later—what car?—catching the bus home oblivious… Longer term memories—they seem to last—getting stories told of childhood and young adulthood—but then this other menace—like a minor stroke and… you'll find it difficult to write up your PhD—heart-thumping…

We, the women who are left, sit around and write, five of us into computers, two by hand and yet my first memory of Susan, one of the writers by hand, is of her typing into her Mac, quickly and efficiently, the note-taker of the group—and Viv, whose book about her brain surgery I read with such awe—hand-writer—I sometimes wonder about physical memory—will I forget how to write by hand using a computer so often?

This is now a collaborative group of women and we keep to ourselves these traumas for years until they creep into our writing—I didn't know that…

rrreemmeemmbbbeerrriiiinnngggffffoorrrggeeetttiiinnggrreemmbbrrng

I am struck by intangible, illusory images
Feeling, sensing, in the mists of space and place
Out of time, out of space, and outside our selves
Where are our selves?
Who are the selves we presume ourselves to be?
The shape-shifting 'now-you-see-me-now-you-don't' selves

Feeling for reference points
Perceivable only through senses
Sensing "news of difference"
Always attuned to "news of difference" [8]

Senses distorted
Sensations no longer trustworthy
What then?
Every man is an island?

The self as constructed
Socially, linguistically, psychologically, neurologically
Constructed
Searching for reference points
in a wilderness of constructions

Reaching out
within, without
Tracing old paths, facing new paths
forging constructions

Trying to spin webs of hope and possibility
Making delicate connections from elusive, ethereal threads

rrreemmeemmbbbeerrriiiinnngggffffoorrrggeeetttiiinnggrreemmbbrrng

Those who have gone, those we have lost along the way, those we long for, the selves we try to hold on to.... perhaps we can sing them to us... connect those selves with other selves... perhaps ancestral song lines help

---

[8] Bateson, 1979, p.79

us retain and renew connections with our landscapes, our cultures, our inner and outer geographies, and our dreams... for as Voight & Drury write of Aboriginal songlines, they are "metaphysical, physical and social maps" (1997, p.84).

I recall the place of music and memory in my life: when I was revising for exams, I used to sing my notes as an aide-memoir. I had to remember not to burst into song with accounts of the Tolpuddle Martyrs during my O level history exam. And when it came to A levels—well, Vergil's Aeneid sounded great sung to the tune of 'Green Manalishi'.

Henry James (1888, p.2) expresses the complexity of first-person consciousness, or lived experience, and the difficulty in conveying it as follows:

"Experience is never limited, and it is never complete; it is an immense sensibility, a kind of huge spider web of the finest silk threads suspended in the chamber of consciousness, and catching every airborne particle in its tissue."

The social and cultural context of such 'immense sensibilities' can be captured through art and music: "The inexpressible depth of music", as Schopenhauer wrote, "so easy to understand and yet so inexplicable, is due to the fact that it reproduces all the emotions of our innermost being, but entirely without reality and remote from its pain..." (cited by Sacks, 2007, p.xi). The similarities between music and language have long been discussed (see Gardner, 1983; Storr, 1992; Sacks, 2007; Levitin, 2006). The capacity of music, with its melody, rhythm, pitch, and cadence, for capturing experience has been a source of sustenance and frivolity; it has often acted as a catalyst for our stories and the continuing construction of our selves.

Neurologist Sacks (2007) explores in detail the relationship between music and selfhood. In 'A Leg to Stand On' (1991), his account of a serious leg injury, he describes how synchronising music and movement enabled him to rediscover the spontaneity and fluidity of walking. In 'Music and the Brain', he writes:

"Beyond the repetitive motions of walking and dancing, music may allow an ability to organise, to follow intricate sequences, or to hold great volumes of information in mind—this is the narrative or mnemonic power of music." (2007, p.236)

This "narrative or mnemonic" capacity of music has been a means through which we have connected and collaborated in our explorations of identity. Music therapy, according to Sacks, "seeks to address the emotions, cognitive powers, thoughts, and memories, the surviving 'self'"... (2007, p.336). It works because, "musical perception, musical sensibility, musical emotion, and musical memory can survive long after other forms of memory have disappeared" (p.337). Within the group, we have found that music connects us to each other and to the cultures we inhabit. The collective and communal nature of music enables our collaboration to flourish through dance, song...

rrreemmeemmbbbeerrriiiinnngggffffoorrrggeeetttiiinnggrreemmbbrrng

On my first day at Oakhurst, we lost Mrs Ponsford-Jones and somehow Matron managed to make me feel as though this was my fault, although I was later to discover we lost her most days one way or another.

I was sent off down Carron Lane to find her. Eventually I gave up and, doubling back across Midhurst Common, found her wandering around the old cemetery, still in her nightie and slippers.

"Look out, the Japs are coming," she cried, clutching my arm tightly,

"In fact, they are already here. They are all over the city, I have been hiding in the cemetery until it is dark and maybe then we can creep back home and see if they have left anything in the house. I had to leave my little dogs, my beautiful little dogs behind."

The next day Mr Ponsford-Jones was visiting. They went for a walk in the gardens with their two little Shzi Tzu dogs, both named after Chinese emperors. They had met, he later told me, as children in pre-revolutionary China. Her family had stayed, stayed on throughout the revolution and during the war, with horrendous consequences. He had finally tracked her down to a Japanese internment camp after the war and brought her back to Britain where they had married and lived, but where she in particular had never settled. She had always longed for China, for the place of her birth, the place of her most vivid memories and adventures... and now, in her old age, the place where she spent most of her time.

rrreemmeemmbbbeerrriiiinnngggffffoorrrggeeetttiiinnggrreemmbbrrng

I've always had the opposite problem with my memory. Forgetting has never been my problem; with me it's always been the remembering.

My brain always seems to have been on overdrive: remembering, remembering, remembering. A kind of hyper-alertness of the past. There have been times when it has taken a huge effort to stop those memories intruding into the day-to-day living. To stop them from stopping me from being here, with whoever is in front of me, doing whatever I am doing, thinking whatever I want to be thinking.

I always know when I'm worried about something because I do nothing about it. I hide from it and I hide it from me. And this is what I did with my word losses. It was too much. Words are so important to me. Words are me. If I lose words I will lose myself. And with that realisation I stopped hiding.

The doctor was clearly concerned. Every reflex was tested. Lights were shone into my eyes. My face was touched and tapped. An appointment with a neurologist was requested.

Three months later, as we had heard nothing from the neurology department and no more words had got lost, the doctor seemed reassured. It wouldn't have stopped if there had been a problem with my brain, he told me. Had I been having a stressful time? So no need to be fearful for my brain, it seems, but my mind…

rrreemmeemmbbbeerrriiiinnngggffffoorrrggeeetttiiinnggrreemmbbrrng

Why are you holding an apple? Serenity and loss. No, memory and its opposite. What was it again? Write into this space. Followed by pizza. Why are you holding an apple? How many leaflets shall we order? How do you spell 'serenity'? How do you fit a gallon in a pint pot? How do you apologize to fellow writers? Writers. We are here to write. Write into this space. Serenity. Here. Now. Serenity is appealing, mmm… How come the lure of the spinning top always trumps it? Can one fit a gallon in a pint pot in a serene manner? Can do it in a frenzied manner; I've written the manual. But serenely? Possibly, if you are swift enough: like having the carpet pulled under your feet and keeping standing; or locking a drawer and throwing the key in; or designing a flyer and attending a collaborative writing group meeting; or chairing a school meeting and eating your lunch. "Why are you holding an apple?" Vaguely aware of only having one hand free during the meeting, I looked and was surprised to see the apple still in my other hand. "Oh, I must have meant to eat it." Did I proceed to eat my apple serenely? To tell you the truth, I cannot remember.

I remember when—no, actually I don't at this moment.

I forget quite a lot.

But the stories come back.

Stories stream behind me, born of long, quiet walks together.
I remember the stories—of a group who retreated from the world of
pressure and traffic and noise; who found laughter that melted the
pressures.
And stories that got close to something important,
All in the peace of an Ammerdown retreat.

In the quietness of winter, or in the buzzing warmth of summer, we
found the stories that excited us, and made us laugh and cry.
Stories that I now can't remember, but I know that they are there.

CHAPTER SIXTEEN

COLLABORATIVE WRITING FROM OUR BODIES: THE SCRATCHING OF THE PEN

KEN GALE AND MIKE GALLANT

An introduction

We were nine writers working with the notion of collaborative writing. We sensed our immersion in the space we describe as 'Ammerdown', a name that identifies both a real place and an immense number of significations and representations for those of us who have visited there on numerous occasions and sat together and written, spoken, eaten, laughed, cried, drunk wine, written again and so on.

On this occasion, becoming in writing together, we worked with and accepted differentiating senses of space. We worked with the notion of embodiment both to attempt to place us in (this) space and in so doing to also allow consideration of the post-human possibilities of presence and presenting in 'assemblage' (Deleuze & Guattari, 1988). In this process our collaborative writings served to act to problematise 'group' and to acknowledge the possibilities and entanglements within and between bodies in energetic space and material presence.

So, in working with ideas borrowed from Deleuze, Foucault and others, we conceive of embodied forms of collaborative writing as disengaging selves from the fixity of bodies seen as being constructed, formed in particular (and potentially unchanging) organised ways. The embodiment of the collaborative writing group can therefore be seen as an 'assemblage', where the singularity of selves exists in changing, multiple and interconnected ways, working away from a reliance upon fixed and closed phenomenological notions of self, and writing towards and into a collective, relational space, where both the organisation and the senses of self are continually re-written and where the undoing and the becoming of the self takes place in an emerging creative evolution of the not yet known. A 'not yet known' that is inclusive of space, place and person.

Alert to the close physicality of the little library room within which we sat and wrote, sensing its smells, the pervasive fustiness of its fittings and the eerie presence of its many unusual book titles, we listened to an earlier audio-recording of the sounds of our writing together in 'silence' and wrote and read to each other, and then wrote again. This piece of writing attempts to express an embodied experience of how it was, in those movements and moments of space and time, to write collaboratively with others and with that space and that time. And so, sometime later and written across the ether, in memory and reconstruction, this piece works with the wispiness of thought dreams to offer a sense of embodiment that emerged from these collaborations. It is a bricolage of edited and unedited, mediated and unmediated scratching on paper and symbolising on screen.

Ken's writing is in plain text, Mike's in italics; and Mike, from early on in the chapter, writes in text boxes alongside and between Ken's lines.

Starting with a dream

The more I listened to the scratching of the pen the less I thought about writing.

I found myself slipping into a meditative state and the emergent focus of my musing formed around me an image of Jane in a sunny studio in the south of France, oceans of light pouring in through huge windows reaching down to the floor. I couldn't resist seeing her working at an easel, sketching out great naked shapes and voluptuous line weavings. I thought of Carol Rambo's 'Sketching with Derrida' (1998) as finished sheets of paper tumbled to the cluttered studio floor, the loosely crafted images forming, being erased, shaded out and shaded in, always under erasure, always threatened by the frantic energy of the artist drawing, always drawing, not writing: drawing, sketching, shading, tracing, teasing wonderful shapes out of the madness of the moment.

I love the immediacy of the imagery of sketching shapes.

I love the ease that comes of not having to read.

I love the possibility that lives in being absorbed in the simple poetry of line, light, shade, colour and tone.

I love the change that is offered here to immerse in swimming, sensual moments where mind is forgotten and body takes over the show.

I love this image of Jane, the artist, sketching frantically and furiously in the baking light of that studio; it has taken me out of the world of thought and into the aesthetic bliss of not thinking. I can feel the warmth in the air; my eyes squint at the brightness of the light.

I love becoming dis/organised in this way.

I love the way the sketching puts thought under erasure and with desire melds it, dissolves it into a heady, embodied concoction of affect, intuition and value.

So often writing is not enough and it is in moments like these that I like to forget about it, to live, to become, immersed in feeling, soaking in the pleasures of vision, taste and smell that I do not dream in relation to thought.

Writing is insistent, insidious and stealthy. It creeps up on me, I have started to become conscious of doing it again and I begin to wonder if it is time to stop.

Time to stop?

Time to stop?

The easy way out?

The phone keeps ringing and I am finding myself back in the world of waking, conscious thought and in that world it always feels as if I experience more of a struggle; it is certainly the place where writing usually begins. In this beginning, if I am lucky the writing takes me, takes me somewhere else, out of, away from thought and into delirium where consciousness only exists as a fragment, a tenaciously persistent element in a domain of sense, value, feeling and emotion that seems to be a living that helps me to forget.

Is this the co-construction of a spark of place and person and body: together we make it true that the banana is a telephone (Leslie, 1987): embodiment is inherently collaborative, playful and constructive of shared realities? As Wackermann (2011, p.28) states: "The rediscovery of our embodied nature is a step toward a scientific, yet non-reductionist theory of human being... an initial step on a path leading away from cognitivist and cybernetic paradigms to an understanding of multiple aspects of human existence: cognitive, existential and ethical." A recognition of the significance of embodiment challenges the dualism of Socrates and Descartes and turns our backs on Theory of Mind. It privileges the body as the source of cognition, yet throws us headlong and headstrong into the thought that our mind is embodied.

Yes and what would I say of this? Where would I start? I don't know Wackermann's work so at the moment I can only respond to the words that you have provided above, to give them some consideration and to feel my way into what they seem to say and to notice their affect on my body and to sense their effect upon what I can only describe as my always emerging embodiment. And so I start with his "rediscovery of our embodied nature" and I wonder how he ever lost it. I suppose that I can see how it has become lost in a world that privileges post-Cartesian dualism and rationalist representation but then I think of the collaborative and performative worlds which we inhabit and try to write into and it surprises me that the word "rediscovery" is used at all: 'discovery' is pushing things for me.

And so it makes me feel I am not making a very good start here; taking you to task on the second word of the first quotation that you provide us with. Oh no, I can sense myself doing it again! These days I start to shiver when I read the phrase "human being". I must have called myself this in the past but I'm just not comfortable with it any more.

I suppose I have started by railing against Descartes and now I want to go a little further back and make what must be an obvious dig at Kant, or at least at the world his thinking has come to represent. I remember my early forays into so called 'postmodern' texts and becoming aware of the pervasiveness of the warnings of 'essentialism'. I have learned and have come to sense that using Kant's 'Critique of Pure Reason' (1781) does not provide me with knowledge of noumena, of things in themselves,

What I'm saying is that 'thinkers' (aka 'academics'?) have put aside the obvious reality that the world is embodied, and what have they lost in doing this? What have they created in doing this? A whole series of paradigms, a meta-paradigm if there's such a thing, that ass-u-me that the mind is a separate entity from the body. And now all that Jiří Wackermann is saying (as Head of the Department of Empirical and Analytical Pyschophysics at the Institute for Frontier Areas in Psychology in Freiburg, Germany he has much on his shoulders), all that he is saying is "wow, all us science of people people" (purposefully avoiding the possible provocation of the 'H.B.' words), "wow, we've noticed that seeing the mind as part of the body leads to much more interesting and parsimonious insights and understandings than trying to maintain the Grand Canyon between them." And I take the re-discovery bit to be that he further realises that the rest of the world never took their eye off the ball and always knew the mind and the body were one. That's all! And obviously that's enough! Quite a hornet's nest!
Oh, and now I know that you're going to pick me up on "interesting" and "parsimonious"...

it just seems to help me become quite good at using a particular form of logic. Despite this and I suppose in part because of this, these days I feel much more comfortable using, what Deleuze calls, a "logic of sense" (1990), which I find much more enabling and helpful as I become more and more aware of the shifting and always flowing movement of what I tentatively call my self. And with this usage, I find this stuttering and always morphing self more and more at odds with the notion of 'being'. 'Being' gives me that Kantian essentialism; it sets up for me a category of difference that I am never satisfied with. When I read Heidegger, at first I felt relieved to be able to live with Dasein, with that phenomenologically changing being-there or being-in-the-world that was always changing with events in the unpredictable world of phenomena but now, again, I am not so sure. 'Being' suggests to me, despite all this situational Dasein, that there is always some thing, some being, that is there, that is always changing in the world.

And now I am not so sure.

I like to work with what Deleuze describes as 'becoming'; a becoming which emerges from the always shifting nature of singularity in multiplicity, of concept, affect and percept constituting and becoming constituted by 'assemblage'. This also helps me to take to task and in so doing not to feel so comfortable with "human being"; because all this transversality and transmutation makes me feel more *post*-human than human. There is far more to my life that is full of complexity, contradiction and which I don't understand, so that my sense of having a coherent, unified, ending-at-the-skin body seems less and less plausible to me. I am so aware of forces, of becoming on what Deleuze calls "planes of immanence" and yet always having a sense of indeterminacy, of uncertainty and yet which always feels certain that change qua becoming is always taking place. Barad (2007) talks of the "entanglements" that emerge from the play between language and materiality. I understand this, even though the "entanglements" I sense I am a part of are just that. Even as I write here, questioning my being and preferring the indeterminacy of becoming, I am using 'I', 'me', 'my' and so on to make sense of sense and material embodiment in words on this page.

I wonder why there is a need to follow "a path leading away from cognitivist and cybernetic paradigms" and feel that I would want to see the paths to these paradigms and others such as those of affect, percept and concept, those that are inscribed in writing or that are used to inscribe the languages of discourse, identification and representation wound up and in play with those other forms. I feel excited by the possibilities offered when entering the entangled rhizomatic maze that presents itself when all these journeys and pathways are seen in their highly intricate processual and vectorally exchanging complexity, when we can consider the assemblage that becomes animate when vital energies come alive in the play of one with the other, with the other and so on.

And I have a feeling that an "understanding of multiple aspects of human existence" would be greatly enhanced if an understanding of multiple aspects of post-human existence were privileged in this body of thought. I have a sense that if we play with and inquire into the entanglements that live with the complex exchange between the materiality of embodiment and the way that it inscribes and is inscribed by the languages of discourse and identification, then our understanding of what we seem to

The entanglement I feel viscerally is the apparent contradiction of what I take as the bread-and-butter 'becoming', with the all-encompassing belief that I am the wholeness of what I am and what I know, and in that way I am my environment. Not that I am growing into something specified and boundaried—'becoming', for me, is an infinite process leading ever on to an unspecified future process rather than any specified place or position. I revel in the boundlessness of becoming! And I digress... When I try to draw a line between my thinking and my experiencing, I lose the "more" (Gendlin, 1997) of the relational. It's not that I want to symbolise experience without thought (that's an interesting thought though...) but to recognise the contribution of liminalities in the me:me and the me:you to the richness of experience. I nearly wrote 'understanding' there, and then became aware that I don't search so much for understanding in my 'becoming' as simply 'experiencing'. And this experiencing folds back upon itself covering and uncovering that which is already there. There is nothing new here, only the noumena yet to be symbolised. There is a potential wholeness of this becoming that I can conceptualise as the post-human that you speak of—though I'm now becoming aware that I'm drifting away from the simplicity of collaborative writing as a methodology of experience.

have to call 'me', 'you', 'them', 'us' will be greatly enhanced.

I have just jumped ahead to your next paragraph and I am excited by what I can see.

> *I love this magic of folding in our writing, so that I can jump in between your jumping in, and share a little movement in heart, a little flicker of tension in my buttocks on the chair, an eyebrow moving with an expanding eye—I'll name it **anticipatory excitelment**. OK, now that paragraph you noticed...*

What a beautiful paradox it was that we gathered in the damp and dusky chilled atmosphere of a small library of predominantly religious and spiritual books. Here we scratched and scraped with nibs, flowed with ball-points and tapped at keyboards. There is the character of encounter about embodiment, a rich diversion from the traditions of western science and psychology where the absence of the body confirms the reification of the mind. In that library, we used the art of writing, the sounds of our physical inscribing on the environment, the dying inks, the visual changes in liquid crystals on an Apple to inspire and elicit writing that acts as a methodology, to discover something 'extra' in our writing practice, what Gendlin (1997; see also Levin, 1997) might describe as that already known or the "more", an embodied alchemy of human being in space where language cannot work alone.

Embodiment can be seen as a theory, a paradigm, a perspective, a methodology, or simply a whole scientific field (Tschacher & Bergomi, 2011). For us, on this autumn day, it was a chosen perspective, a methodology for taking words out of our minds and placing them in relation to the physical process and experience of symbolising experience.

Ken, does this mean anything to you? How would you respond?

Yes, I can; I feel that what you have written here is full of richness and brings our thoughts, feelings and perceptions to do with embodiment, highly charged and onto centre stage.

Yes, I love that phrase you use to describe the traditions, discourses and enforced habits of "western science and psychology where the absence of the body confirms the reification of the mind". I have felt my way into the work we always seem to have done with our colleagues and friends, our lovely loose assemblage that we usually refer to as the Bristol Collaborative Writing Group. I am so aware of the way in which this work has always helped to break open the hardness and the fastness of the kinds of reification that you write about here. The other day I looked back at some of the early things that I wrote when I started the Doctorate with Jane in Bristol: it was all so, oh so, mind full. And now I write with memory of this writing weekend at Ammerdown and I have such strong feelings about that: I remember my tears, the laughter and I remember the dampness and fusty feelingness of sitting there with our group, in that library, writing. It is the strange materiality of that space that you talk about above that is so essential in the coming together of these words, sitting here over a year since we all first sat there and started to write. For me, this is about embodiment but it is an embodiment that I experience in multiplicity within the collective and often dispersed energies of all of us who sat there in that little room and wrote. Although I have a sense of self, it is a self that is somehow folded into the moods, textures and perfumes of our collective becoming in that space. That space that is constituted and always constituting through the pervasive infusions of bodies and chairs, pens scratching and words arriving, words read and spoken and eyes crying, brief smiles and distant noises echoing through the building, the strange contrast between the cloying dampness of the room in which we wrote together and the light airiness of the unkempt garden where I wrote, sitting alone and yet immersed in the sense of the others and the spaces that always unfolded in those always mysterious becomings.

It is this process, this interaction with the world that creates my world that comes before concepts and symbolisation. Concepts are the product of the experiencing process.
    One
    Breathing the oxygen of spirit, sculpting the paper, ripping through the stories déjà vu, uncovering new, tension held and released in a rhythmic riot.
    Sigh.
    Breathe in the yellowed library, laying a little pigment on a fresh cavern surface, representations spilling from visceral places.
    Clear the throat.
    Breathe deeply, breathe and touch the inner skin.
    From the tips of our fingers tapping, and the scratch of nibs, exudes only a human thing.
    Turn the page afresh, settle back encased in cushion, the vision falters, the presence, the now.
    Breathe.
    And again from deep remembered canyons and mixing pots of my ochre and your chrome, titanium white shines a light on the magical moment.
    Sigh.
    I feel my hand against the paper surface, clamminess against the silver

implement, my arm touching the support of the chair—and pen taking the
support of the peopled place.
    Breathe in calmly
    and out—I smile, a certain tension held for a second and then wiped
clean, muscles sinking, flaccid contentment, safe encampment, comfort
blanket of the womb
    I am
    (Breathe)
    a part

    Two
    I wouldn't do this alone—not in a month of Sundays (which
coincidentally is what it is today). So how do I write when I am apparently
alone? Only by being with you my world—only by being with you.
Whether you are here now, you are always with me my world. And I sing
out this love song, this joyous moment, I sing out my words of love for you,
my pen on paper world, my little splash of inkblot, my unmediated,
uninhibited, un-bracketed, uncovered universe of being
    a part

    Three
    Swallow swim south mouth criss cross crescent moon too soon
    a part

I can't think of what we all do together without thinking about
embodiment. I love the sense I have of this embodiment; it is not a sense
of wholeness or unity, of coherence and integrity, or organisation and
structure: it is one of frayedness around the edges, it is one of danger and
doubt and secrecy and nakedness, it is one where surprise and prediction
go hand-in-hand and where our repetitions are always different. Our
embodiment is wonderfully disorganised and beautifully purposeful; our
dishevelled ramblings produce starbursts of clarity, our bodies melt into
one another and then they disperse, sometimes they sing, often they cry
and always they write themselves into new becoming. This embodiment
makes sense for me in the way that our language is both lost and becomes
something special in the folds of our skin, the pumping purpleness of our
veins and in the way that when our words touch the point of contact is
always a new event that shatters the carapace that had protected anything
that had gone before.

    And for me, as a practising psychotherapist and educator, this collaborative writing is akin to asynchronous therapy (i.e. therapy that is not contained within a single time or place, for example conducted through a series of email exchanges), a structured co-creation of meaning, a kenning indeed (in Scots), an identity, and experience itself. There is a joy in this:

17.10.2010 Song for Jane

I don't want to start a cult—right now I don't want to write—right now I want to soak in the sun and the birdsong, the kitten squeak of Nell's electric motor. I don't want to start a cult. I insist. No, you heard me, I don't want to be... I want to be a part

[intake of breath, he realises the intensity of his passion]

I, I, I, I—methinks I do protest too much. At breakfast I questioned the nature of charisma—was single-mindedness a necessary constituent of the charismatic? Apparently not. I know I am not charismatic—I don't want to be—as I said, I want to be a part.

[he is aware of the tension in that expression—a part]

Coffee cruncher extraordinaire, the chink of cup on saucer, the shared experience far from the RCT[1] world of truth, knowledge and p-values[2]— and yet so close, so close if only... if only?... if only what? Do I want to be a part?

Like a broken record, I regurgitate the same old vinyl crackled mantra: my self is only myself in relation to my self is only myself is only myself in relation to my self is only myself in relation to my self is only myself in relation to my self is only myself in relation to my self is only myself in relation to my self is only myself in relation with others in relation with others in relation with others in relation my self is only myself in relation to my self is only myself in relation with others in relation with others in relation with others and writing clarifies this.

So now I'm clearer than I was before when, joss stick in hand, rummaging without reason, where I'm dancing and Jane straightens her locks, flicks and lifts the Dansette onto the floor hoping for more insight, more understanding. Loosening her scarf she holds it aloft—swinging her hips, turning around, the scarf flapping in my face, she is sweating and I...? I, the observer, I the unengaged.

So now, here and now, with this library of experience all around, can I place my life book on the shelf, with reverence, beside yours?

---

[1] Randomised Controlled Trial
[2] Statistical measure of probability

Ending with a song?

"At dawn my lover comes to me and tells me of her dreams/with no attempt to shovel the glimpse into the ditch of what each one means."[3]

It was Laurinda's, following on from my last writing and reading, my last plaintive call to sketch, to be in the moment of my body, to live in the movement of sense that frees me from my mind. It was that talk of flows that has brought me here, to this writing. I am so aware of flowing in the writing that I have heard read out this morning. I have felt washed by the words; I feel them taking me to worlds of great surprise. I have a full sense of my body in the sea, immersed, flashing in great heaving waves, never sure of my footing, always trusting the stroke of my arms, relishing the alone oneness of Being in the waves, always slightly scared that I might get washed away by their volume and force: lost.

Flows, flowing, allowing loss, giving over to being lost, allowing those thoughts to dissolve in the wash of the words of Other, marvelling at the words of Other, feeling a pounding, erotic charge as the notion of self and other in relational space becomes dissolved. Collaborative writing gets a meaning... this is what it is!

Is this what makes it all worthwhile?

Now I sense my self living comfortably with abandonment, living for the brief moment of catching the crest of this just curling, about to break, momentous wave. There is no existential angst here! This is the moment. You have written yourself to this point now, go with it, let it take you, relish the tumbling, searing ride that knows no boundaries of thought and that is lost in the tremendous rush of sensual body space.

As I write this now, sitting alone in the rambling feistiness of this beautiful Ammerdown garden, bathed in sunshine, wondering if I will be able to get home in time to be able to clamber down the cliff, scramble over the rocks and throw myself into the mystery of the wild sea before the autumn night cheats me of my life source, I think about desire. I struggle with the squabble that Deleuze and Foucault engaged in before the latter's death, the former claiming that desire is productive, the hedonist historian identifying its connection with lust and passion and lack. I wonder where I am positioned in all this. I wonder how my struggle with Descartes' separation of mind and body will end as my body seeks to lose itself in

---

[3] Dylan, B. (1965) 'Gates of Eden', 'Bringing it all Back Home'. Produced by Tom Wilson. New York: Columbia Records.

flows of sense, affect, intuition and feeling, yet wracks itself with thought, anxiety and worry every time the tide goes out, every time the sun goes down, every year as the autumn equinox heralds the onset of winter.

The working morning began with writing at the top of a page, 'Collaborative Writing from our Bodies'. I will add to that 'from our bodies', 'to our bodies', 'in our bodies', 'with our bodies' and I feel charmed by the possibilities that the rich, alchemical mix of these phrases is now offering me. I have been troubled by thinking, by living with pure naked thought; troubled by these thoughts that seem to live in a world of pure categorical difference, fixed, established, sanctified in some kind of abstract certainty of self. This troubling takes my thinking singularity into lonely lines of escape, of mad rushings to the sea or long walks on dark lonely moors but this morning writing into, out of, to, with and from others in this shared collaborative writing space has reminded me of the shared immediacy, the intense physicality that engaging in this work can have. I sense the changes that shift from the flows, I feel people moving; in this gorgeous multiplicity I sense connections being made, I hear an intake of breath, I see a tear quietly escaping, someone's face flush. I love living in this world of sense: I am becoming; something else, someone else, always becoming.

PART V

THE PROCESS(ES) OF COLLABORATIVE WRITING

CHAPTER SEVENTEEN

PROLOGUE TO PART V

THE AMMERDOWN PROLOGUE WRITER(S)

I've immersed myself in Part V today, read all three chapters and, notwithstanding the unavoidable digression into reminiscing, have focused my attention on the underlying theme of process. At the danger of being accused of getting carried away, I propose below a form of words to describe the collaborative writing processes that underpin the chapters in this section, then present my own memory of process in relation to the chapters I have been involved in, and finally offer some thoughts on the process of writing the section prologues for this book.

In 'Between the Four' (Chapter 18), Brown et al. talk us through their experience of producing a collaboratively written text during the course of a collective biography workshop. Readers are reminded of the authors' previous experience of collaborative writing practices, which "somehow misted over any need for leadership" and of the effect of the collaboration "opening ourselves up to a conversation to other possibilities". In 'Friend and Foe' (Chapter 20), the Bristol Collaborative Writing Group (BCWG) share their initial collective ambivalence and re-present their internal negotiations in weighing up pros and cons of engaging with electronic technologies at a time when online communication was at its infancy. From a group that formed to write and spent much of its time talking, this section moves to a group that met to talk and found itself writing. In 'All Googled out on Suicide' (Chapter 19), Jane Speedy and the 'Unassuming Geeks' share the process of reconvening a group to mourn the loss of one of its members and transforming its conversations into a text where "the edges between therapy, research and writing are blurred and troubled".

I notice that I have been involved in two out of the three chapters in this section and offer here some personal reflections on the collaborative writing process for each one. The writing with Laurinda, Ann and Jane ('Between the Four') took place in Ammerdown, in the very room where I am writing now, about three years ago. Jane, Laurinda and I had written together for years, as members of the Bristol Collaborative Writing Group; Jane and Ann had also written with one another before. I remember how the four of us worked diligently together within an egalitarian ethic not often found in academic circles, each contributing to the process of bringing together four pieces of writing which began their life as individual creations and gradually transformed into a coherent whole. My memory is of an intense energy in the writing process, which I understood to stem from our shared histories of writing together and our tacit agreement to "lead from every chair" (Zander & Zander, 2000).

The chapter on the BCWG's grappling with technology was the group's first published piece of writing, which was submitted for publication in the journal 'Qualitative Inquiry' in 2008, after more than four years of the group's existence, writing with, and initially only for, one another. I led this writing process, which to us meant drawing from a vast body of texts written and stored over the years, to produce a first draft. From then on, BCWG members who chose to get involved worked together in face-to-face meetings and online to produce the final draft. This process led to interesting insights into academic publishing, particularly as we attempted to challenge established patterns of declaring authorship, or co-authorship, in academia.

Six of us have gathered at Ammerdown to write together, intending to bring into being a prologue for each section of this book. We are working in the Todd room this time, arguably too large for the six people that are here, yet probably large enough for those present in person to spread comfortably and those present through their writing to be afforded some space too. I am sat on the floor in one corner of the room, tapping away at the keys of my laptop on my outstretched legs. I look around me. Jonathan is almost in mirror image, writing in the corner of the room diagonally across from me. Sue has been writing in the middle of the room balancing her iPad on one leg, her wheelchair now softly whirling towards the power socket on the wall. Tess, Jane and Davina are spread out utilising additional chairs as footrests, laptop tables or bookshelves. There is only one small table in the room, on which rest the recently bound 'Red Book' (see Chapter 23) and Davina's birthday flowers.

From time to time Jane asks how you spell an obscure word and gets one or two answers, usually identical, and comments that this is like having Wikipedia in the room. A question or two from Tess, a brief conversation here or there, but mostly we write in silence. We are sharing our writing with one another by regularly saving in designated shared Dropbox folders and have marvelled at the experience of constantly seeing files being updated before our very eyes. All six of us gather in a circle in the middle of the room at regular intervals, read out our most recent offerings, talk about how our new writing fits in with the body of texts that has gradually been evolving, then negotiate who will work on which section for the next slot of writing time. As we each sit and work from our separate positions in physical space, we also silently weave in and out of the virtual spaces we have chosen to share, in a collaboration that is potentially more active in the ether and regularly rekindled in the material space that we share. None of us designed this working pattern and nobody had planned it in advance; to the contrary, we had arrived expecting to work in pairs or groups of three. But, in the process of checking-in with one another and beginning to explore our respective starting points, this pattern of collaboration emerged and evolved as our preferred way of writing together. This is what we found worked for us in this space, for this time, with this configuration of contributors to the collaborative writing process.

I have just left our working room in search of a quieter space to write in and found myself in the library. It is in this room that, almost three years ago, some of us met to begin work towards bringing this book to life…

As I round off this piece of writing, I wonder how my fellow prologue writers might 'respond' to this 'call' and where this writing might take us. It will be interesting to see if or where others choose to contribute and, if a juxtaposition of voices eventually resembles a synchronous dialogue, whether others might choose to see this as 'unprocessed'.

***

Now I have internet, I have got into Part V and deleted stuff, but not added anything. I reckon this is it, and not boring… I could not add layers as it is written from a definite 'I' position by you… but I reckon you've nailed the prologue to process…

I say go for it, anyone can add, let's make this a plural 'I' and create a collaborative solo!

Collaborative solo. The shared eye. A multiplicity of 'I's. You pass the paper across, I-dentity moving from you to me to them to us. Authorship evaporates and ownership collapses. The soft contract between us hardens in the sun, like terracotta. The writing takes the lead, bumping us out of every chair. The humans are undone, their mastery ousted. The writing writes us. Rites of our lives. The agency of objects overturns us: plays us for patsies. Inhabited silences between collaborative 'I's.

We have our celebrities: the sainted Massey (2000) and the oft-quoted Ingold (2011). We've got our selves entangled with the aftershock of the blessed Barad (2007)—these are the post-post-structuralist patron saints of the new geographies, philosophies and anthropologies—we are not alone at the shrine. We have new Gods—we worship neither Zeus, nor Jehovah, nor bask in front of the mirrors of our shared humanity.

Om myaho, rengay kyo, Om, myaho, rengay kyo.

Shanti, shanti, shanti.

"these fragments I have shored
against my ruins
Why then Ile fit you. Hieronymo's mad againe.
Datta. Dayadhvam. Damyata.
Shantih, shantih, shantih" (Eliot, 2009, p.64)

What is the equivalent of a piano's right foot pedal in collaborative writing? That which sustains all parts of a polyphonic text together. I quip poorly that it is a virtual tool…

CHAPTER EIGHTEEN

BETWEEN THE FOUR

LAURINDA BROWN, ANN RIPPIN,
JANE SPEEDY AND ARTEMI SAKELLARIADIS

This chapter, narrated by the first-named author, is an example of collaborative writing produced under very particular conditions; by four people, together, in 'real' and limited time. It was written and performed on a single weekend, so that, in a sense, it observed some of the classical unities: one theme, one weekend, one group of protagonists. The four of us wrote together firstly in a wider group, then, in our four, read our work to each other, talked about samenesses and differences, what took our attention and then one of us acted as typist for a collaboratively produced text, which we performed to the larger group of fellow writers. Giving ourselves the goal of producing a finished collaborative text in a single weekend created a different kind of energy around collective writing and reflection, which could be characterised as 'speed-writing'. We do not put this forward as an exemplar of collaborative writing, but as an example of a different take on the process. In the chapter, we aim to show the original writings and how we braided them together into a whole.

Before the four

So, this voice is one of the Bristol Collaborative Writing Group's (BCWG). Two others of the four were also members. As you can read in other chapters of this book, the BCWG often meets at Ammerdown, a retreat centre, and I remember setting off for a weekend of writing, led by Bronwyn Davis and Jane Speedy, along a now familiar path to that same place. It seemed strange to be going to write with a different group, being led, as opposed to looking forward to being with an established group with practices that somehow misted over any need for leadership. What I was aware of was that Ammerdown as a space had supported my writing within a collaborative group:

"Sitting circle—letting emerge what needs to emerge—letting emerge the interactions and trust. Who is the leader in the group now? Who was the leader then at the beginning? Her wisdom was subverting the need to be productive, finding the spaces in between our working and lived lives. Those who are left, through their fingers, find meaning and questions, which, when read aloud to others, create a connection and then more writing arises teaching us what we already know in our bones and in our flesh.

We, we are family; we, we are together (Taylor, 2006). Over time, the feelings of interconnectedness that illustrate family are here. Jane is sitting Shiva, at the end of an Ammerdown, writing into the lowering sun, not wanting to leave this place and perceiving, intuiting 'Gerald' (Speedy, et al., 2010). We laugh together, sing together. Collaborative-group writing means not coming knowing what I want to write beforehand, being attached to something, but opening to what comes. (Extract from Laurinda's reflections on writing with BCWG and Jane's role in the group.)"

Driving to Ammerdown to work with Jane and Bronwyn, I thought that I did bring my past experiences with me to this group. The practices would be different but I was certainly not coming knowing what I wanted to write beforehand and I was opening up to whatever was to come. There would be new exercises, bringing new awarenesses and possibilities.

The stimulus

In one session, everyone on the weekend did indeed do an exercise and my sense of opening myself up to the possibilities was captured and inspired by the following text, which we had been given within some of Bronwyn's writing:

"Poststructuralist theory asks, through Foucault's work in particular, how, historically, the conditions of possibility for now one view of what the subject is (and should be), and then another, are formed, and with what effect (see for example the writing of Foucault in Rabinow, 1997). It asks: How is one kind of subjecthood or another made possible? How does one set of possibilities become normalised such that the subject cannot imagine itself otherwise? And most important, how can the human subject evolve beyond the current sets of actions and reactions? The creative evolution of life depends not on the accomplishment of that idealized image of the subject-of-will, but on openness to the other and the not-yet-known." (Davies, 2010, p.55)

The invitation was to write into stories that we tell ourselves and have told ourselves over our lifetimes. My image of this was of the well-rehearsed stories of their lives together told by a couple, told entertainingly over countless dinner parties, and contributing to the couple not imagining itself otherwise. We were only given a few minutes to write initially, capturing a story in words. We were sitting in a circle, each of us having written, and we then heard each other's stories. We were invited to respond to anyone's story in writing, giving another reading of their event or of our own provoked by another's story, like a call and response. At the time, I wrote the following about the new process, articulating some resistance I was feeling:

> "Autopoetics—there's been auto/biography, autoethnography and now autopoetics
> We talk, we write
> There are activities that we do and then write and then read
> I'm different, from a different academic writing tradition
> I'm here to extend and develop
> But, what am I supposed to write?
> A new person comes in the group and before reading out their writing says that they don't know if this is what they were meant to write
> I am aware that (and articulate) it's been a long time since I felt like that in BCWG..."

There is not a 'supposed' in BCWG, but here I do wonder if it's different. Although my initial image had been reified stories of coupledom told around a dinner table, what comes to the fore and begs to be written this time, and frequently for me, are stories from childhood. These are so fixed when they arise, normalized, not imagined otherwise, told and re-told and rehearsed. They are not remembered so much as heard by me, the youngest in the family, from siblings and parents. Here, in collaborative writing spaces, there is the potential to evolve beyond the fixity of the given actions and reactions.

What happened next

Here are two of my written offerings to individuals after people had read their stories aloud the first time. Each person was asked to take words spoken by another in the group (in the first piece of writing, "Othered—being othered") and write the image that came to mind:

"To Sue:
"Othered—being othered"

I'm in the library
Getting a book for my Mum
Getting a book for my Dad
Getting a book for me
Standing at the checkout desk
Hopping from foot to foot—
Crossing my legs
There's a queue
Urgency
As I manage to speak
Loo? Toilet? What to call it confusion
The hot steaming urine gushes down my legs
The librarian's face—shock/sympathetic
Don't tell my Mum…"

"To Joyce:

Lying in bed
Head aching, feeling sick, heat throbbing, woozy
Sunstroke (Mum's voice) (hot red in the face sunburnt—radiating—woozy)
The doctor arrives
Asks me what I see
I tell him
The talking mice are playing on the bedstead. They've turned green.
They're waiting for you to go.
Sunstroke he says and gives medication
Limey yellow green zzzzz—darkened room—"

I was surprised to find the writing, "To Sue", left unremembered in a folder on my laptop. The energy for transformation was given to the writing "To Joyce". We were asked to take one piece of writing with us to form a group of four who would collaborate on a text generated from our writings that we would perform to the rest of the people on the retreat. We had been asked to remove some words from the writing we would take to the group of four. I took out the double struck-through part. I also considered changing the single struck-through parts:

"Lying in bed
Head aching, feeling sick, heat throbbing, woozy
~~Sunstroke (Mum's voice) (hot red in the face sunburnt—radiating—woozy)~~

The doctor arrives
Asks me what I see
~~I tell him~~
~~The talking mice are playing on the bedstead. They've turned green.~~
~~They're waiting for you to go.~~
Sunstroke he says and gives medication
Limey yellowy green zzzzz—darkened room—"

Reflections before the meeting of the four

We were asked to do some stream of consciousness word play related to one of our stories. I wrote:

"Direct perception—evolution—veil—shamanic traditions, spiritual traditions—what science can tell us—when did the mice go? Drawing from the rhs of the brain… shamanic technology."

The work on the writing had already helped me to evolve beyond the confines of this oft-told tale to a deep awareness that, although the family of talking mice were my friends and were real, from that time on they were not to be talked about publicly. I resonated with Jane's word play, her metonymic surfing shared with the whole group, mainly because of the 'mouse':

"Mad song—a little mouse with clogs on, well I declare Ronnie Hilton (1965) singing clip-clippety-clop on the stairs—Beatrix Potter—clothed—not clothed."

However, I was also distracted by my previous history of practices of collaborative writing and story telling. From my notebook, written during the session, my attention was captured by how I work with student teachers (one-year postgraduate course):

"Interesting these exercises that are akin to my professional practice working with a group of student teachers, collectively working at issues in their practice.

Sitting listening to Bronwyn, being aware of samenesses and differences in our practices: the student teachers tell brief-but-vivid stories from their teaching practice, all locating one and then someone starts and offers their tale. The rest then let go of their original story and some tell a new one, a 'matter arising', provoked by the first tale, and then another and another and another contributes. At some stage, I say, "What are we talking about here?" No simple answers, but comments in a different place to story. We build the collective stories of our teaching lives in that group throughout the year where each story of becoming a teacher is different and yet, as with these stories today, there is a braiding of their lives and seeing their experience differently. Could I tell a brief-but-vivid story of this practice of brief-but-vivid stories?

One task for me this weekend will be to let go of these embodied practices that are so similar yet so different."

And I continued to reflect as we were being given the instructions for the next task where 4 of us would meet with our writing:

"The first drafts (see two examples above) didn't feel collective or collaborative to me because I was staying with my own writing. The word 'tweak' is a mechanism I use to not take the meaning of a word for granted. I will notice when the word 'collaborative' is used this weekend and think 'tweak' so as to be open to different interpretations. So, for me collaboration is creating together—'Women's Ways of Knowing' (Belenky et al., 1997)—that sense of not letting go of my own writing feels new.

We were doing an exercise—I don't think I see this as collaboration—but of something else? Is it co-operation? The practice is maybe linked to Bronwyn being in Australia and distances meaning participants are a long way away so that the listening is via e-mail. Practices would develop differently if there was not simultaneity of space and time."

Between the four

We each brought writing with us to the group of 4 and offered our writing to each other, reading it out. The energetic task of same/ different materialized. Our attention was taken by the 'ings' in our original pieces and in what was a relatively short period of time we had some writing. In this task, I was present, not judgemental, nor being distracted (I know this because the commentator in my notebooks left), simply being there in the actions and interactions of the group of us. All that remains is the final piece of writing, braided from our separate writings that we brought to each other. I do not want to go through a process of reconstructing what we did and what it felt like. I think we were all present in that I do not remember anyone losing energy, being worried, giving negative energy and we enjoyed presenting the work to the rest of the group.

We are not presenting this piece as a final, polished piece of writing, but simply to offer a different way of working when you are starting a new group to get people used to reading out what they have written to others in the group. After the group's writing, in conclusion, I will try to capture that brief-but-vivid story of telling brief-but-vivid stories. Firstly, this is what we came up with in an hour and a half:

> "How can the human subject evolve beyond the current sets of actions and reactions? The creative evolution of life depends not on the accomplishment of that idealized image of the subject-of-will, but on openness to the other and the not-yet-known.

There has to be a space, "a simultaneity of stories-so-far", to quote the sainted Doreen Massey (2005, p.130), but in this writing we all describe a relationship to place:

Lying in bed, head aching, feeling sick,
heat throbbing,

woozy

Our spot on the cliffs.
out on the headland,
beneath the crag –
sheltered, warm,

cosy.

Lemon walls.
Formica desk.

Next to the gents' toilets.
Fluorescent light

Gritty
Holding the ball
some of my team mates
on the other side of the court
facing the attack line

nervously

Writing as inquiry does this... how does doing this collectively make this doing it differently... individually we can only take our writing where we take ourselves, what is different in what we are doing now... what we are doing now opening ourselves up to a conversation, to other possibilities, extending the space of the possible?

In this process, those four writings have patently taken us somewhere else—it feels like we are not so attached to the original writing, maybe if we mess with our writing it will do something else. What if we put together the bits that are doing the same thing?... I don't know what it is.

This is much better than the original story, why is that? Structure? Something to do with the poetic structure, grittily, cosily, woozily, nervously. In creating this text, we are working collectively, transformed again into working grittily, cosily, woozily, nervously as the four of us.

Each story speaks to the emergence of that which was not yet known in relation to other people:

The doctor arrives asks me what I see
and I say, The talking mice
are playing on the bedstead,
they've turned green
they are waiting for you to go
talking playing waiting
talking playing waiting

I noticed the opponent team are fast retreating
Muttering "oh no it's Artemi"
In that instant another Artemi new to me
Springs out of nowhere and pushes me out of the way
Retreating springing pushing
Retreating springing pushing

It's ten o'clock. We are still at work.
Charles is spacey on adrenalin. Up to the wire.
Who wants coffee? He will pull an 'all nighter'.
My heart sinks at the prospect, but I feel only affection for him.
His joy is infectious. I resent working until late in the evening, into the night,
but he thrives on it, the caffeine,
the chocolate, the camaraderie.
Because I love him, I will sit here as long as it takes.
Working sinking loving
Working sinking loving

Dad is not needing much help with the crossword clues. He is making quick work of it all, but then I get two inter-connecting clues in quick

succession 'mean pinball' and 'PINBALL Wizard'.
He is surprised and delighted
"How the hell did you know that, Janie?" He asks.
"Easy peasy, lemon squeezy", I reply, "That's what the deaf dumb and blind kids always play"
getting surprising delighting
getting surprising delighting

Actions reactions, rituals rehearsed and comfortable repeated behaviours of the word putter inner, the ball passer, the innocent mouse conversationalist and the team member, are transcended through the relational and the proximity to the talking mice, the warm corduroy trousers, the team synergy and the love of Charles, the possibilities in the eyes of others into ritual performing of another Artemi—new subject-hood, ourselves shamanic doctor figure, the mean cross word player, the late night vigil writer.

You are not an individual, you are there to transcend self and become part of the body of Christ, the not yet known, the godhead."

Reflections

At the start I was on the outside looking in, cautious, hankering after the comfortableness of another collaborative group. And yet, what happened between our 4 was truly collaborative without any one of us being the leader. Perhaps the deadline supported the process this time. What could have been a pressure, taking us out of the present into worry about not finishing, say, became a support in letting our present attentions play in the meaning-making of patterning. It was the 'ings' that took our attention, the process of coming to know, not the fixedness of knowledge. And the story of the story is that my fixedness, as it turned out to be, on the way of working of BCWG at Ammerdown has transformed and taken flight, extending my space of the possible ways of writing in a collaborative group.

CHAPTER NINETEEN

"ALL GOOGLED OUT ON SUICIDE": MAKING COLLECTIVE BIOGRAPHIES OUT OF SILENT FRAGMENTS WITH THE UNASSUMING GEEKS

JANE SPEEDY

Prologue from the principal researcher

We originally came together to meet and write in friendship and mourning. We set out to write an obituary for a friend of ours who had died. This gathering turned into a remembering conversation[1] about/for Gregory, as well as a remembering conversation for our group. People have only gone from our lives when they are no longer remembered and spoken of. We decided to come together to remember Gregory and the 'Unassuming Geeks' and speak of them, but we found ourselves hijacked by silence. This was not the serene silence that comes with contemplative solitude, but rather the cacophonous silence of much that was unsaid and possibly unsayable. We began to write into that silence. Turning to the literature of suicide we found ourselves adrift amongst generalisable statistics (whilst we longed for particularities and specifics) and poignant, but valorised and reified voices (whilst we seemed shabbier and less coherent). Trapped uneasily in between certainty and authenticity we turned for some kind of framework for our writing to the ancient Greeks—

---

[1] Remembering conversations is a term used within the narrative therapies to describe therapeutic conversations that (re)join and (re)connect people's lives; in particular Hedtke and Winslade's (2004, p.3) work has been about establishing "connections that need not be severed by the transitions that death brings" (see also Carey et al., 2009).

amongst the earliest scholars to write about suicide and to feminists and fiction writers (habitually disruptive elements). Lest fiction unravel or encourage hubris, the Gods watched over us whether we turned to them or not.

The geeks chorus

We met as a talking group between 1999 and 2002, and again as a talking and writing group between 2003-5, with Jane as our facilitator and five (originally eight) of us, all school or university students at the time. We had first pitched up in Jane's office as the crew she had gathered as witnesses for Gregory. Gregory had been Jane's therapy client and we were the witnesses to his 'leaving ceremony', which was a celebration of his rejection of the term 'suicidal' in favour of "legitimately concerned about the world". It was a good evening. Gregory's mum was there and his sister. Afterwards we all went out to the pub, which is where, after a few pints, the idea of our group emerged. As did our name: 'the unassuming geeks'. The reason Jane had brought us along in the first place was that we'd all considered suicide at some point and had all gone through that barrier and out again to a different place (if you ever do). We had so much to talk about in the pub; it seemed logical to go on meeting. We did a lot of talking to start with and then gradually we morphed into a writing group. We wrote masses of stuff and then we published an article and wrote a play that was performed. Then we more or less went our separate ways, apart from two or three of us meeting up with Jane every now and then. Gregory, who died last year, went off to live in New Zealand and we decided to start this chapter with some of his writing: one of the many pieces of writing we had never published before.

"Once upon a time there was a boy who was nearly a man. This boy who was not yet a man was something of a worry to his mother, or so the doctors said.

"That boy has no idea what he's putting his parents through", the neighbours said.

But the boy had collected all sorts of ideas from all over the world. He had millions of enormous ideas. He had ideas bigger than the biggest idea you could ever possibly think of multiplied a million times over. He kept his ideas in a big heap in the bottom drawer of the dresser in his bedroom and he kept this drawer tight shut. Sometimes, at night, he could hear all his ideas shuffling around, scrabbling for space. He knew better than to let them out though. Some of those ideas could swallow a whole continent for breakfast, never mind one solitary boy who was still not yet quite a man. He was keeping them safe, for later. If and when he could see his way out of all this, well, then he might open the drawer a little chink.

Sometimes he had hopes for the future as well, but he kept them wrapped in silver paper and tied them close to his chest. No amount of cajoling or trickery or artful dodging would get him to untie these. And even though hidden enemies sometimes sent in ghosts and phantoms to slither under doorways and steal them away in the night, he always saw them coming and he hid beneath the covers till dawn.

He also had lots of dreams, in some of which he was a terrible worry: a big shapeless worry like a see-through maggot. He worried his mother up in one gulp. He worried his way around the house, worrying up the drains, and worrying though walls, leaving rubble and bodies and confusion everywhere. He would wake himself up by moaning out loud, only to find himself soaked in sweat and feeling exhausted from the worry of it all. But then, when he got out of bed on such mornings and looked in the mirror he was constantly surprised to see how small and solid and boyish he was. He always expected to catch a glimpse of the strange wormlike creature he had worried himself into during the night. But he never did.

And then one morning he looked into the mirror and saw that he had, indeed, become a man. Just like that. Immediately he had opened his dresser drawer and listened to the first big idea that leapt into the air.

"Why don't you go and live on the other side of the world?", it had said.

And so he did. Apparently this was something of a worry to his mother.

"That young man has no idea what he's putting his parents through", the neighbours said."

Jane says

The writing started because after each of the group meetings I would send by email what, as a narrative therapist, I might describe as a brief "therapeutic document" (see Epston, 1994; Fox, 2003; Speedy, 2005; White, 1995; White and Epston, 1990); a short poetic distillation of the conversations we had been having, sometimes just a haiku or two, such as:

"Do not mix death talk up with
Ordinary chat
And everyday humdrum stuff/
You have been spotted and named
As mad and rare and

Different from all others/
Suggestions that we all think
of our own deaths in
regular fleeting moments/

Will be ignored and erased
And manicured out
Of all records for all time/"

(Speedy, 2001)

And after a while people started replying online to these, which led to
an on-going email correspondence that outlasted the talking group. It was
Gregory who suggested, or rather, who first noticed that we had become a
writing group. And it was my suggestion that we blended our established
way of witnessing each other in the group, borrowed from Michael White
(2005) and the narrative therapies, with feminist notions of collective
biography drawn from the work of Bronwyn Davies and others (2006).
You geeks were not keen on feminist methods, I recall, until we
established the difference (via bell hooks, 2000) between feminism and
'for women', and had found some collective biographies from men (Pease,
2000a, 2000b). You became a prolific collective biography group. We
would meet and talk to a theme 'the medical profession'/ 'suicide
prevention strategies' / 'gender and suicide'/ 'holding our breath' / 'first
memories of talking about 'it'' / 'the things that doctors say'. Then you
would all read your writing out loud and I would facilitate a practice of
witnessing—of noticing what resonated, what stories from people's lives
were brought forth and so on—and then we would re-write, or write more,
or go to the pub.

You were on a mission to get published in a therapy journal (which we
did, Speedy et al., 2005) and a medical journal (which we didn't). The
words that you wrote as a play, after Shange (1975) were also the catalyst
for physical theatre performances in the UK and Hungary (Speedy &
Worth, 2007; Worth, et al., 2008) and then Gregory really did go and live
on the other side of the world and you all went off in your different
directions.

The narrator's voice/Academicus, the god of social research and lost ways of doing things

There are several layers to this account already, but let's disrupt them
quickly before we all get too settled in. We already know the research

participants made up the name 'unassuming geeks' and now have made themselves up again into a 'geeks chorus', apparently in a conversation with Jane. There were originally eight. Five are left, of whom one has died, which leaves four. There seem to be at least two of Jane, the principal researcher who wrote the prologue and the Jane in conversation with the geeks.

And then, continuing in the g(r)eek tradition, there is a narrator /god involved in the research drama, speaking now, coming in to contextualise, position and draw our attention to and away from elements. This narrator's voice could be written by the principal researcher or as a collaborative text. We have not been told. Some of these accounts are fictionalised— even those from the Gods.

Jane and the geeks chorus appear to be in 'casual conversation' and yet they are also performing in some kind of geek tragedy. Somebody has died—possibly a suicide—and yet this group seem to be playing with us and making puns, which sits awkwardly with the hushed western style of death and suicide that we have become accustomed to. There is a 'toying' here with empathy, voice and authenticity [2] and yet, according to Aristotle the life spirit of any play is its mythos: a word we might variously/simultaneously translate as story, plot, myth or act of speaking.

If these are not 'voices' but masked performances, it remains with you, the discerning audience, to sift between palpable falsehoods, for deep significance and/or life spirit. Luckily you are not alone. The myth that 'stories speak for themselves' and that the researcher team are setting them out before you and then leaving it up to you to decide is one palpable falsehood the Gods are here to direct you away from. The advice of the gods? Stay attuned. What are they saying/not saying here?'

The geeks chorus

The therapy journal article really kicked ass and was definitely worth doing. We've had loads of emails about it and even more since you expanded and re-published it. People liked the ending:

> "The men in the box marked 'other' have
> considered suicide.

---

[2] See Patti Lather (2000) and, indeed, the whole of this book, for a critical discussion of representations of 'voice' in qualitative research texts.

Collecting statistics on those who commit suicide is a bit of a dead-end job.
We have considered suicide and erred in favour of breathing in and out.
No red carpets
We just sidled in through the side entrance
We are stationed, breathing in and out, at the sign of hope.
We have not yet settled, but remain on our haunches
We are crouching in the shadows of statistics
We have not yet settled
There are dogs barking
At our heels
And loneliness threatens still
to eat away our hearts
And yet, our sweat gives off an unassuming
whiff of triumph
We are stationed, breathing in and out, at the sign of hope."

(Speedy et al., 2005, in Speedy, 2008, p.134)

But we are wondering how and where to place those words now that Gregory has taken a different turn. Now that he has stopped breathing, what does that say about where we are stationed now? What does the sign of hope mean to us all now if one of us gave up on it? No whiff of triumph here, is there? We are stumbling around now amidst the ruins of our own words. We came back together about six months after he died. We met in the pub to chat. Then we went back to Jane's office to write and now we are meeting again to try and generate something from that writing. But we've been caught out once already by believing what we wrote, or rather, by not paying attention to what we didn't write, to what was left out.

Jane says

I don't remember the chat in the pub. I remember sitting in silence for about half an hour.

Jane says

And I don't remember going up the hill to write. I remember, going back up the hill to my office and just sitting in silence.

The geeks chorus

And then you said "I wonder what was going on for us in all that silence?" And then we all started to write, without talking, which we'd never done before. And then we read out what we'd written. Nobody commented at all, we just read it out:

Man in orange writes: Remembering.
  Remembering him.
 I was remembering his wildlife passions
especially for birds—for sea birds
   Gulls, cormorants, razorbills, shearwaters
    Guillemots, curlews, sand pipers and arctic terns
and then I remember thinking –shit–
I bet the others are thinking really profound stuff
and here I am dribbling on about curlews and cormorants
like I just swallowed the 'Observer Book of British Sea Birds'.
But it was what came to mind for me
 and I carried on listing them in my mind's eye,
listing them and trying to remember what he had said about:

Puffins, kittiwakes, gannets, little egrets, oyster catchers and plovers
 But all I could really remember
   was some kind of longwinded dirty joke about seabird cities,
it was all about high-rise cities on Scottish cliffs and it ended with the punch line:

"Crested shag"
I never really got that joke.
I'm even not sure there was one.
The whole point was that we were about nineteen.

Nineteen-year-old British geeky boys are hardwired
 to laugh awkwardly
   every time somebody says "shag"[3].

So we all did.

He'd say "crested shag" and we'd all fall apart.

Ornithological stand-up. Undervalued really.

---

[3] From Cambridge dictionaries online: shag verb /ʃæg/ v [I or T] (-gg-) UK offensive to have sex with someone, retrieved from: http://dictionary.cambridge.org/dictionary/british/shag_1

Man in purple writes:

When we got to the pub, I was relieved to hear that his mum and sister weren't coming because I didn't know what to say to them. I didn't know what to say to anyone actually, but then nobody did and the silence, I thought was quite companionable.

In the silence I was thinking about silence, about what we hadn't said, well we'd said it, but what we hadn't written about, or if we had written it, we'd not chosen those pieces to be published or performed. I was listing what we had left out, left unsaid, in the previous writing. I was thinking about smoothing over silences and what we were silent on and wondering why that was.

We hadn't said, for instance, that in the early days we were literally a lifeline—that no one missed a group. Young men, aged 17 to, what, 25?— in their prime, sometimes even on a Friday night and yet nobody missed a group with Jane? A chubby middle-aged lesbian therapist, I mean c'mon!!

We never said this, but we became crucial to each other's survival and I think when we wrote our pieces[4], what we chose, the writing we chose was much pushier, much more out there, pissed off with medics, irritated with therapists and all their fear-mongering. What we wrote, or tried to write, was the angrier, catchier, rappier stuff. What we didn't write about so much was fear and vulnerability and not really knowing or understanding very much about anything.

We didn't say very much about loneliness and fear and feeling lost. We said more about/to them—the parents and doctors and nurses and teachers and therapists and less really about/to ourselves. In the group there had been more talking amongst ourselves, but we left that out. Jane wanted more of that in, about what was going through our minds sometimes, this weighing our lives in the balance. Looking back I might have wanted more about how much we needed each other in order to stay alive, how much we had an unwritten pact to keep each other talking and writing and just turning up every time. But Jane left it up to us to choose,

---

[4] See Speedy et al., 2005; Speedy, 2008; Speedy & Worth, 2007; Worth et al., 2008.

> *she was just the facilitator, and so we ignored her on principle... and then we silently, tacitly ignored the wussy stuff, the 'men as wimps and cry babies stuff'. We made ourselves more heroic perhaps, even though we were sending up 'boy's own stories'.*
>
> *In the talking group, that was kind of low-key therapy, self help with bandages, and a grown up to make sure we got home safely and remembered to look left and right before crossing the road, but what we haven't really said much about is how much of a lifeline the writing group was.*
>
> *Officially we were 'over' our individual crises—that was one of the criteria for group membership—but unofficially, we were all clinging on like rubber dinghies were going out of fashion. We never discussed this.*

A chubby, middle-aged lesbian therapist writes

Although it remained unsaid, our previous writings were propping up an invisible, unacknowledged contract that if we stuck together and kept writing we would stay alive. This was not only unsaid between us, but "unsayable" (Rogers et al., 2006). This was 'magical thinking' and it is only now by 'dreaming and writing' that we have "found out what [we] thought" (Didion, 2006, p.162). There was excellent clinical supervision of course, both for the talking and the subsequent writing group and a great deal of careful deliberation about crossing between therapy and research and about eligibility for the group (see Speedy et al., 2005). But we were all co-complicit in this silent pact, until Gregory broke the tacit agreement and we all began to whisper and then speak its name out loud. There is no wrongdoing in such a pact of course, some therapists swear by such arrangements[5], but it was interesting that this remained unacknowledged until now.

I remember discussing my sense of connection, of responsibility, of 'what if' with said supervisor when Gregory died and duly receiving professional and personal absolution. Nonetheless, his death is not an isolated personal or professional matter, but rather part of a male

---

[5] Transactional Analysts, for example, frequently make use of a technique described as "closing down escape hatches", i.e. contracting not to suicide during the course of the therapy (see Stewart, 2007).

pandemic[6] within the developed western world and, as such, seeps beyond the professional jurisdictions of the 'personal problems industries'. This death sits uneasily with us all, not only in a sense of particular issues of friendship and mourning, but in a sense of the co-implication and responsibility that surely we all must share? The death of even one young man in our society, surely speaks somehow to the rules that govern that society? In that sense there is no 'absolution' from complicity: firstly because we live and breathe and are constituted/constituting within those same regimes and, secondly, because if the vital task of giving accounts of our own lives is such a tall order, how can we ethically hold Gregory more to account than we do ourselves?

The geeks chorus

So where does this place him, us, me, the western world—and the human race—by implication?

What was going through his mind? What was he imagining about himself and his life when he died? What are we left to imagine with? It seems such a fragmented story:

Gregory wrote in a final letter to his mother on the day he died,

"I'm sorry for all the trouble that this is all going to cause".

Then again, earlier that same week he had sent one of us an e-mail saying:

"I've just come back from a few days on the west coast—fantastic scenery. We tramped for a whole day up Mount Te Kinga and back—just breathtaking. I'll take you up there when you come out!"

He had also written on a yellow Post-It note, stuck up above his desk:

"Without insects the human race would survive a few hours at most"

And we all know that just before he died—a few hours before he died—he booked himself a flight from Auckland, where he was living, to Sydney for the Mardi Gras. Unusually, he also did the washing up.

---

[6] According to the World Health Organisation, suicide increased 60% 1944-2009 and remains the largest global contemporary killer of young men 14-24, retrieved from: http://www.who.int/mental_health/prevention/suicide/suicideprevent/en/

> *Man in green writes:*
>
> *In my dream, my recurring 'middle of doing this writing' dream, we are walking backwards and forwards along a dark narrow alleyway— all of us—including Gregory.*
>
> *It is somewhere from my childhood perhaps, in Mumbai, with strong light/dark contrasts, old dwellings and the smell of decay and waste-water. There are tall, windowless buildings on either side and each of the different ends of the alley holds light and promise, but seems much the same as the other end when we get to it. This disappoints. We walk back and forth. There is sky above us, a thin line of sky, but it is a long way off. Then we get stuck in. We are halfway along the passage and we begin to dig.*

Geeks chorus

So, he had an imagined next week and an imagined future that he did not step into. He also imagined the trouble before he died, he wrote a letter and did the washing up. These are some of the jigsaw pieces and we don't know how they fit together. We have images and imaginings—not 'whole' stories but fragments. We (re)turn to the literatures of this field again. There is even more than before—the self-help books, the medical statistics, and the ethnographies and (true) life stories, but we are disappointed. We are all googled out on suicide and none the wiser. We turn instead to other shelves. These shelves house the books that speak about what it might mean to be human, and to live an ethical life. We wonder if we can learn from this event, if through all this we can uncover some of our ethical know-how[7].

---

[7] The term used by Varela (1999) to describe an ongoing, everyday and responsive ethical practice of continual, contextual, ethical becoming, as opposed to an ethical morality or set of principles, for instance.

Jane says

We are caught pacing between two ways of 'capturing' this experience. We are stuck between the proliferation of strategy documents, generalisations about prevention and statistics about occurrences and populations at one end of the alley[8] and the 'real life stories' and self-help books for 'survivors' at the other[9]. None of these genres is making the difference we want it to—our thinking is familiar, unchallenged and well worn.

We are indebted to statisticians, particularly from the World Health Organisation, for mapping the relationships between advanced capitalist societies and suicides amongst young men and to charting the ebb, flow and continuing march of what Chesnais (1981) so aptly described as "the geographies of despair"—but we are no nearer to producing/remembering Gregory.

At the other end of the bookshelves we have the qualitative personal accounts, which should surely speak to particularities? Katy's diary[10], for example, a 'real' diary interpreted through different expert lenses, a performance through which we hear her 'voice'. It has been edited into an accessible text. But what of the other inaccessible (silenced?) Katys? What did she/they not choose to write/publish? Why this selection from 200 pages of 'authentic' data? It is not that we doubt that this is Katy's authentic voice but, rather, that notions of authenticity and of this voice 'speaking for itself' amidst interpretations remain troubling.

I am uneasy with what Maggie MacLure (2008) so aptly describes as the "poetics of sincerity" that consumes qualitative research and "speaks a familiar script" (p.98) and like her would welcome a more modest, more complex and less smoothed "poetics of insufficiency". It goes a long way

---

[8] The World Health Organisation regularly produces comparative suicide statistics broken down by gender and age and there are multifarious breakdowns of these for individual countries in relation to forms of suicide and other factors (see, for example, overviews in Palmer, 2008; Hawton & Heeringen, 2002; and specific factors in Wheeler et al., 2009).

[9] There are literally thousands of contemporary contributions to the 'life story' research and self help literatures of suicide, based on diaries or letters (Etkind, 1997; Leenaars, 1988; Lester, 2004) and family members' accounts and interviews (Le Blanc, 2003; Lukacs et al., 2007; Wertheimer, 2001).

[10] Extracts from the diary of a young woman, annotated and interpreted by a group of psycho-social professionals, published and edited by David Lester in 2004.

against the contemporary grain, is taboo even, to criticise the 'life story' literatures of suicide—a genre of scholarship often hewn out of the raw pain of surviving family members—but it is not the pain we are bringing into question here, so much as the difference between the familiar knowledge this literature brings us and the messier, more difficult knowledge that we seek. Somehow the desire for a "poetics of insufficiency" seems all the more urgent in this critical research space and yet the interdisciplinary fields of writing and scholarship about suicide remain more deeply shrouded in silence, certainty and authenticity than most.

Looking back at our previous multi-storied collective texts (Speedy, 2008) we were still too sufficient and coherent. These washing up/letter writing/email fragments that we are clinging onto now are mere splinters and fragments from life spaces and we are left not knowing. We are left holding splinters. And I, for one, am reluctant to pretend (and the temptations are great) there is more coherence than there is. We are trying, against the tide, to aim for "insufficiency".

Lather (2007, p.13), citing Pitt & Britzman (2003), explains succinctly what we are grasping for here: "The former [knowledge] reinforces what we think we want from what we find, and the latter is knowledge that induces breakdowns in representing experience".

We set down some text. We leave much unsaid: excerpts from a letter; excerpts from email; excerpts from a life. How do we 'do justice' and work ethically with what is available alongside Gregory and his family, without overstating the case, without implying that heroic, noble/victimised or redemptive and familiar tales lurk? How do we resist suggesting some kind of coherence? Various geeks are reading Varela (1999) and Butler (2004a, 2005). I return again to storytellers:

> "The stories I want to tell you will light up part of my life and leave the rest in darkness. You don't need to know everything. There is no everything. The stories themselves make the meaning. The continuous narrative of existence is a lie. There is no continuous narrative, there are lit up moments and the rest is dark." (Winterson, 2004, p.134)

The narrator's voice/Synthetica, goddess of interdisciplinarity, disruption and weaving

These enlightened humans have taken to imagining that they themselves opened Pandora's Box and that this was a matter of free will, rather than a hand-me down from the wrath of the Gods. What we have allowed them to keep in the dreams we give them and in this hall of discursive mirrors that sweeps them along—and that they still have in abundance—is hope. Staying attentive to this little group of hopeful humans, digging away somewhere halfway along a dimly lit passageway, we notice an endearing sense of hope that they will find something, that they will get somewhere by digging away.

We remain attentive (not all of us all the time you understand, it just happens to be my shift) to the positions and voices that are taken up and given expression here and would draw your attention to the absent but implicit[11] spaces in between them.

In addition to Jane and the principal researcher we now have an additional voice from a "chubby, middle-aged lesbian therapist", an artful intertextual reprise after the "man in purple". This suggests an attempt by 'Jane' to distance herself from this stance and to become, perhaps, more one of the group—one of the boys, even—as indicated in her use of 'we' throughout the text above, carefully differentiating between 'we' and 'I' during explorations of her own current reading and that of the 'geeks'. Five distinct authorial voices are available here: 'I'; 'we'; Jane; "a chubby middle-aged lesbian therapist" and the "principal researcher" (it is still not clear who is responsible for the voices of the gods).

I would urge caution on the part of readers, and would recommend that you stay particularly alert to the use of 'we' (unless coming from us of course, since we are quite shamelessly developing ourselves into a multi-vocal rendition of Haraway's (1988) "voice of God" and, as such, we are well beyond dimensions of the mere 'real' and quite simply unassailable). You may recall from earlier work that the geeks were clear that 'Jane' was not one of them and had commented that:

> "This is a bit the same, but different from being all men. We are all men and sometimes forget you are even in this project, but in some way, we know you are in here and lets face it… you are my mum's age and that makes a difference to what I might write sometimes." (in Speedy, 2008, p.127)

So just watch out for sleight of text here, that's all we are saying. There is a strong and fairly explicit claim throughout this writing to be trying to "give up mastery in search of fidelity" (Haraway, 1988, p.193) and quite rightly so, since, unlike us, these authors are "not in charge of the world"

---

[11] Michael White (2000) drew upon Derrida's (1992) work on the infinite possibilities available in our expressions of life, in finding points of entry to and ways of mapping the many absent but implicit expressions/stories we have not yet told).

(ibid.). And yet, even amidst these stated desires for particularities and a "poetics of insufficiency" this generalizing, subjugating, colonising voice of 'we' emerges.

A closer reading of this deceptively 'chatty' text also reveals a shameless appropriation of the dream sequence described by the man in green. The writer even has the intertextual audacity to place the certainties and authenticities she juxtaposes at either end of the alley, as described in the dream. Enlightened humans have, of late, ascribed their dreams to their own unconscious processes, but as we gods all know, they are actually gifts and visions handed down from us. It is one thing to appropriate the words of less powerful humans, this happens all the time and a huge and successful qualitative research industry has been made out of it. It is an entirely different matter to mess with insights from the Gods. This smacks of blatant hubris. For the moment, we are just observing these tendencies, but you can see why our vigilance is required.

We are keeping an eye on those young men too; theirs are not entirely innocent writings. Do not believe for one moment, for example, that they are dressed in the colours they say. Although you cannot see them, we can, and they were all wearing blue denim jeans and assorted scruffy t-shirts (mostly white-ish with slogans) when they wrote this chapter. These colour names, again, are a reprise from their earlier writing, a dramatic device they borrowed from Ntozake Shange (1975) and have forgotten to acknowledge in this subsequent text, but we are onto them. We'll keep you posted.

Man in Brown writes

I was thinking and feeling one hundred and one different things all in such a short space of time. I was mostly feeling uncomfortable and wishing that I hadn't come, but not seeing how I could possibly leave the pub or the group or not do this writing.

And I was thinking how much older we all look, it's been a while for me, because I moved quite a way away, so I was surprised to see that we have all changed quite a bit and I wondered if that was true of Gregory too, because, like me, he was one of the youngest. Now that's odd because we are coming together to think about Gregory, but maybe the person I'm thinking about, the person Gregory has become, isn't a bit like the person I remember him as. So, if I'm remembering him as he was—which he isn't anymore—who is going to remember him as the person he had become or was becoming and what if nobody does?

The other thing that came to me during our extended silence is that we are not meeting for us, facilitated by Jane, like we used to do. In fact, I think she wants/needs/is drawn to this meeting and writing as much, if not more than us. I think she *might be in* our *project now—the tables have turned and the therapist/researcher has become one of the various writers of what she calls a messy text. Hah!*

The narrator's voice/ Poesia, the goddess of writing as inquiry and lost lines (of flight)

What is at play I wonder?
as I watch them all stumbling around
leaking excessively between therapy and research, 'I' and 'we',
friendship and discomfort, pubs and university offices
They are all slithering about,
finding the spaces and pockets
between the personal, the political and the professional,
not just small fragments, but big
congealed overlapping lumps
There is bafflement here and distress
and a commitment to taking on
the difficult ethical work of mourning
that permeates all friendships
They mourn their friend by
acknowledging their debt to his words
by searching and not being satisfied
with thinking what they already thought
by inhabiting different traditions
of giving an account of this life and this death
And by keeping the accounts and meanings
 of Gregory's life
(and by co-implication[12] their own) open

---

[12] The narrator/goddess is grateful to Bronwyn Davies for drawing her attention to conceptualisations of co-implication a) between people, environments, events, materiality and b) within people's sociological/ biological/ neurological/ psychological make-up, as posited by Wilson (2004). Jane Speedy is grateful to Bronwyn Davies for the many conversations they had during Bronwyn's visiting Benjamin Meaker Professorship at the University of Bristol (February to March 2010) all of which contributed to the final drafting of this chapter.

Jane says

I was going to end with more words from the storytellers, words that Gregory might have uttered, but that came from somewhere else:

"The most important part of a story it's the piece of it you don't know. He said that plenty. It would be no surprise if he asks for that put on his gravestone, if there is to be one. There you see. Hangs the tale, and still yet more to find out." (Kingsolver, 2009, p.496)

But I was rightly persuaded by a strolling, performing player and storyteller of some repute[13] that a few fragments from Gregory at the end of this chapter would not so much reify his voice as honour his life and death. Gregory wrote in an email to the principal author of this text in 2005:

"Considering suicide; thinking about dying;
rolling my own death around in the corners of my mind,
as if chewing on tobacco,
is not such a weird or extraordinary thing.
It forms part of a very ordinary, everyday imaginary.
It is part of us, of me, of humanity.

Perhaps if I am not shut down, but am
allowed this practice of imagining my own death
alongside my life, I will find more of a way
of living my life to the full for as long as I can.

I know that people,
some people who really care about me,
worry that I don't want to live.

But that's not it.
That's not it at all.
Here's the thing:

being fully alive—absolutely out there in the world

---

[13] The principal author would like to thank Johnny Saldaña for his useful and insightful comments as reviewer of this paper for 'Qualitative Inquiry', August 2010.

ONE HUNDRED PERCENT.
That's what I'm aiming for.
That's what I'm all about."

CHAPTER TWENTY

FRIEND AND FOE?
TECHNOLOGY IN A COLLABORATIVE
WRITING GROUP

ARTEMI SAKELLARIADIS, SAM CHROMY,
VIV MARTIN, JANE SPEEDY, SHEILA TRAHAR,
SUSAN WILLIAMS AND SUE WILSON[1]

This is a partial account of the journey undertaken by a group of academic nomads in search of collaborative writing space. Never intending to settle anywhere permanently, we chose to explore writing technologies that supported collaborative forms of engagement with our task and with each other. Along the way we took up with, and discarded, a variety of writing technologies. Reflecting teamwork and collective biography practices sustained our work and our commitments towards collaboration. Although we have not found any electronic technologies helpful in creating or maintaining our sense of community, they enabled collective ways of re-presenting our work to ourselves and, later, to others. Twenty of us set out and twelve remain on this journey. The current text includes three voices, each woven from writings and silences of many members of our group, thereby including traces of us all. The text explores our relationship with electronic technology and its role in our collaborative writing venture.

---

[1] This chapter was first published in the journal 'Qualitative Inquiry' as Sakellariadis et al. (2008). Dave Bainton, Tim Bond, Nell Bridges, Laurinda Brown and Tony Brown are all members of our writing group and were witnesses to the construction of the current text, having an opportunity to comment on the representation of our shared experience. These positions of "writer" or "witness" are lightly and not permanently held and we anticipate that, like all our practices, they will continue to shift shape.

Some of us joined this project in spring 2003, responding to an email inviting staff and students interested in a collaborative writing venture exploring identity construction. Others joined after hearing about this through word of mouth. Our initial conversations on identities and collaborative writing had, at times, a reading group character; we identified relevant readings, shared them as pdf attachments (or hard copies available from the office) and discussed them when we next met.

At 7:30am this sunny Sunday morning, Clare picked up her handwritten text from Monday's meeting, typed it up, and emailed it to Lyra in Bristol, who would be quilting all writings today. At 8:00am Lyra saw Clare's message, printed the attachment, and put it down with everybody else's writing, then settled down to work.

When I began this project, I had hardly touched a computer. I was irritable and anxious about even writing with a word processor or sending an email. It was, for me, a place of not knowing, of not understanding what to do or how, of feeling old, outdated, unsophisticated, left behind. "Why should I have to struggle with this?" was the constant complaint from my ageing brain, resenting and fearing the threat that the new (to me) technology seemed to pose to my sense of feeling competent.

I decided to join the collaborative writing project as soon as I saw that initial email. It was fascinating to see the diversity of the people originally drawn to this endeavour and the variety of perspectives they brought to our first meetings. I enjoyed the readings as well as the conversations that transpired from them. I remember the first set of readings arriving as a pdf attachment to an email. I cannot remember for sure, but I think I found it simpler to walk to the office and claim one of the readymade packs of printed articles (even now I find it much easier to read from paper copies).

I was one of the people to set up this project initially. Aware of my highly efficient technologically skilled self, I chose not to bring her to this group. I've allowed her entry when needed, to type or collate (the sound of my fingers clicking away at the keyboard is a regular feature of our meetings). But her real talent isn't invited. She feels too purposeful for a process so creative and intentionally chaotic. I don't think her sense of order and precision is welcome.

In September 2004, we had a day-long meeting and tried to arrive at a consensus as to how to move this project forward. We conducted a workshop on outsider-witness practices and held a brief introduction to collective biography. We all found this face-to-face meeting inspirational and agreed that each of us should write something on this shared experience and email it to the rest of the group.

I had my own email account by then and read the writings that the others sent. I remember a poem called 'Collaborative Solo', presumably playing with the thought that after all this talk of collaboration, we were still each writing alone.

Writing that piece and emailing it as an attachment was both terrifying and exciting. It felt very risky to be putting these words out there for everybody in the group to see.

Emailing each other wasn't a problem, we managed this and attachments worked well. Most people wrote something and emailed it to the rest of the group after that full-day meeting.

Our first real difficulty with technology was when we tried to set up a jiscmail list with an archive. A ring-fenced, academic, networked community sounded ideal: no spam, easy, secure, closed access. In the event, it proved a disaster. For some mysterious reason, the service would not recognize half our email addresses, every time we tried to log them on people fell off, communication broke down, and the creative period of the project ground to a halt.

We are simply waiting for an electronic system to link us all together, but there seem to be problems. This feels almost embarrassing, as if technology itself is deciding which one of us to keep in and who to spit out.

I felt terribly frustrated when we couldn't get jiscmail to work for us. Nobody could trust the process or knew if anybody else could hear them. This was a low point in the project; in fact the whole thing was nearly destroyed by technology. The process we had set up in the face-to-face workshops was now being undermined by technology's failure.

Eventually we realized that even if we could log everybody on one day, the archive system was unwieldy, hard to access, and hard to move into from the list and the chat and vice-versa. We abandoned jiscmail and started exploring alternatives. It was Blackboard that anchored us together for a while; its folders, set up and labelled after our declared areas of interest, acting as an electronic filing cabinet of sorts. This phase saw a number of bursts of intense writing activity, often around our meeting times, and long lulls void of any writing at all, except numerous intentions repeatedly voiced from most of us.

What helped me get past the "won't" of resentful struggling was the sharing and humour of being in this kind of group. We are a collaborative group. As I started to feel part of the group, it was as if I also began to collaborate behind the back of my own resistance, and let myself find the right technological buttons to press. Could an ageing brain develop an attitude of "technical" fun? Could I even consider technology as something desirable and enabling? I found others valuing it for what we could share, for what it could do for us. When I realized technology was enabling my participation in a real and cooperative community, I really began to enjoy it.

As time went on, I became aware and shared with others that I had some discomfort with Blackboard. I'm not sure what this was—maybe something about choosing to open an attachment, whereas with Blackboard it was just up there. Somehow it felt as if eyes would see it that I might not want to see it. It's hard to explain but it felt different. It is not like me not to do something that I've committed myself to, yet I never did put any writing on Blackboard. Perhaps for the same reason that I would not want to leave my work pinned up on a real board inside a real room, even if the room was to be locked and only

I had not come across Blackboard before, but it seemed a fabulous tool! It felt such a secure space, and I remember really looking forward to sharing this communal space with the rest of the group and engaging in personal conversations with them. My only reservation is that it does occasionally feel limiting; I remember that Cixous (2004) wrote her notebooks by hand, not on a word-processor, because she felt that technology limited her to writing one word after another. In her notebooks she included circles, drawings, colours, arrows.

people in our group
held the keys. It
somehow feels safer
if I can take my
writing away with
me at the end of
each meeting, real
or virtual.

In March 2005, we encountered a bit of a disagreement, which unfolded through a series of emails, mostly beginning with "yes, let's wait until we meet, but". Our meeting that month focused on some of our apprehensions about using electronic technology.

For me, talking round a table is not the same as emailing a group. Staying "in touch" via the net seems more distanced. It's the memory of the table talk that keeps me going through the more technical process. As I type the words on a screen, I need to feel my way back into our last meeting and anticipate our next. When I meet people again, it's real and it's a risk and I feel energised. I get motivated to write. When I get back to my computer, technology eases the way to share and try to evoke what has happened. My sense of community, of meeting, fades slowly as time passes and I

Blackboard just feels less intimate than email but I don't know why… I'm sure it has something to do with the structure we have given it and the order this imposes. Blackboard feels more like chapters, whereas email is more like a conversation. Looking at it that way, I guess it is a nice surprise how affectionately familiar this aspect of technology feels! You could say that the Victorian equivalent would be sending a postcard: It can be intimate. There is more disclosing room in an email than there is in a pub! Having been on a steep

It turned out that not everyone was excited about the possibilities virtual contact could open up. It seemed as if the minute we needed a password to enter our virtual meeting place, many of us froze. Isn't it funny how it is designed to protect, to create security, to preserve anonymity, yet it has inhibited more than facilitated our communication. What a shame, to feel real but not virtual intimacy… People in this group have greeted new technology with tentative suspicion, perhaps even recoiled from it.

begin to feel out of touch and out of energy.

electronic learning curve this year, this realisation is as interesting as it is surprising.

It feels scary to share your writing knowing there may not be a response... Then again, I have not responded to the writing of others, and this may concern them. So maybe the moral is, "Say something even if it is crap." But it takes courage. Then again, my silence is neither disapproving, nor is it disrespectful; it is simply a silent thinking of them all... I wonder what kind of silence we are experiencing from people who neither write nor come to our meetings but still have access rights to all of our documents. Who are our silent members and why are they there? Are they voyeurs? What is our collective identity and who is collaborating with whom?

When I sent that email attachment I had a sense of being exposed and quite alone... Then again, it seems I'm not the only one concerned at the silence of others. So has silence been a powerful force in this group? Who knows, maybe more than we had thought. I, for one, think that it is quite a struggle to find out what collaboration means when you don't know who is in there collaborating with you and who is not.

It is disappointing to post some of your writing on Blackboard and then not get a response from anyone... Every now and again, I wish I was a bit like those who haven't written anything; maybe I should have kept my metaphorical dufflecoat on instead of wandering off wearing nothing but a snorkel. It is sometimes easy to think that silence might be a negative judgement. And we all need approval, don't we?

We carried on writing, posting our texts on Blackboard, and sending an email round to alert others to new additions. That spring was a time of avid writing for many of us. We continued to meet once a month having decided we needed the face-to-face contact. For some of us, this meant travelling hundreds of miles to be present. We took notes during our meetings and posted them on Blackboard to make it possible for everyone to keep in touch.

During our last meeting, we had one of those conversations that could never be captured by notes… The honesty with which we discussed such powerful issues in such a supportive context and the sense of unity this generated were breathtaking… For me it felt as if those moments created an almost tangible bond between the eight of us who were there.	After discussing issues of motherhood at our last meeting, I wanted to continue our conversation over email, keeping it to just the eight of us who were there. The other seven did not think that was appropriate, which feels a shame, although I can see their point of view. It didn't stop us entirely though, and we have had a few short exchanges amongst ourselves, addressing pings of connectedness, among other things.	It was great to renew our personal contact. Now I understand why people have not responded to my writing on motherhood. Some found the subject too difficult or painful to write about honestly, particularly as it may eventually become public. Others were waiting backstage for mothers to respond first.

Our discussions included attempts to understand why we are writing less than it seems we intend. Is it lack of time or lack of focus that limits our output? Or is it the structure of the folders on Blackboard that gags us? Should we take away all folders and let them re-emerge from the way our writing takes shape? Should we engage with more traditional practices of collaborative writing and go for synchronicity? Perhaps even go away together on an intensive writing weekend? And what of our witnesses? It seems electronic technology has caused confusion between active witnesses who are contributing to our process and silent bystanders who, perhaps by default, have maintained access to our writing. We had originally expected that some of us would be "witnessing" the writing of others; this has generated some interesting comments on each other's writing but has also rendered it possible for writings not to receive a response, potentially appearing unacknowledged. Are people encouraged by feeling witnessed or inhibited by feeling watched? Do we need to think of alternative means of witnessing, other than lengthy written texts? (Some sort of virtual equivalent to a silent nod in face-to-face interactions?) We noted that in any group there are some who speak more than others. But what role would our silent members ascribe themselves? We decided to ask them. An email went out after this meeting requesting a response from everyone; four of our "bystanders" dropped out.

At the same time, we experienced an emotional earthquake of sorts, as two of our active members were disagreeing with each other via email. Complex conversations took place online and, in the end, one of them bowed out of our group.

It is important to remember and uphold the "trustworthiness, transparency and researcher integrity" that Bond (2004) wrote about. I think we mostly do this.

We have found ourselves in a bit of a mess and we must re-establish "our" ground rules, to stay on the ground.

It is important to remember and uphold the "trustworthiness, transparency and researcher integrity" that Bond (2004) wrote about. I think we mostly do this.

We have found ourselves in a bit of a mess and we must re-establish "our" ground rules, to stay on the ground.

It is important to remember and uphold the "trustworthiness,

transparency and
researcher integrity"
that Bond (2004)
wrote about. I think
we mostly do this.

I think we are stuck.
Everyone else seems
to have frozen in the
headlights.

And then, little by little, we started up again. This project's life went
on without one active member.

I felt rather shocked and experienced a sense of loss, which is a reflection of how much I had valued her contributions. And I echo the feeling that this is a change to my sense of collective identity and to our potential as a group. Talking about it as our group doesn't quite feel right now.	Whether the theme touches on missing motherhood or loss of any sort, there is bound to be some pain. But my own feeling is that any collaborative writing should be able to work creatively from pain as well as pleasure.	Above all, we need to revisit our ethical considerations in relation to each other and the emergence of social ghosts that are more than each other or indeed the sum of our parts, as Gergen (2001) said.

During our next meeting, we had to find a way to adapt our practice to
comply with data protection. We felt we had no option but to post our
writings under a pseudonym each. This would give us all permission to
talk freely about our histories while preserving anonymity. We agreed we
could continue emailing the group to announce new postings. In the event,
this was not necessary. Only one of us ever attempted to present new
writing on Blackboard again. Somebody quietly suggested that we
reverted to communicating via email so as not to let Blackboard stifle
creativity. This was greeted with a surge of support for structures that
sustain, not structures that contain, us. There followed a poem about
motherhood, emailed to the group with a note that, intimately personal as
it was, could never have gone up on Blackboard. And then summer came
and went; and with it went any commitment to Blackboard.

It has felt as if we were communicating into a space that held no immediate connections. Our virtual spaces are just store cupboards, filing cabinets, and message boards. Our use of Internet technologies, apart from the odd email flurries, has been archival and functional rather than continuous and creative. It has been a 'dead store' and notice board, not a live exploration space.

In September 2005, we planned a whole day together, starting with a writing workshop based on Goldberg's (1990) ideas. The workshop consumed most of our day and was felt to be a very constructive use of our time.

More than three months and 60 emails later we met again. In December 2005, we made a commitment to engaging with Davies's (1997) collective biography practices. After the process of talking and writing and reflective witnessing comes rewriting and then critical listening: listening for resonances, for "talk that sings" (Bird, 2004); for places where the story becomes non-specific and uses "general" language; for moments when the story becomes less vivid and cannot be imagined and for language that evokes and/or embodies memories. This seemed to represent a critical collaborative writing and editing process that built on our 'witnessing' practices (indeed, the experience swept most of us off our feet). For the first time in more than a year, detailed notes from this meeting reached us all as an email attachment.

| Something very memorable happened for me in this meeting: a sense I was part of our | As we worked together in a critical collective editing way, we found meaning in finding | I couldn't get this experience out of my mind, so I ended up penning some further thoughts on our |

increasing sense of connection and I wasn't feeling self-conscious. This was a kind of plugging in to a new form of energy; a working, wanting, creating sort of energy that seemed to be building on itself, and I wanted to just give it a bit of a push, a bit of myself, every now and then.

meanings and enriching meanings and that was special.

conversations and emailing them to the rest of the group.

We met again in January 2006 and discussed beginning to put together a meta-narrative about our methodology/approach. We explored the contradiction of being a collaborative writing group that writes mostly alone and then edits collaboratively. We recognized that, for us, the process of collaborative writing involves a lot of talking. We recognized the excitement and energy of sparking each other into a creative and connected space and developed a process that put all this together: we set aside 15 minutes for timed writing "decommissioning the editor" (Goldberg, 1990) and invited the "virtually absent" to contribute via email. One of us collated, or rather wove, these texts into one document to present to the group at the next meeting for collective editing.

When I left this meeting, I was in the same energized and questioning place that I had been in the previous meeting. I offered to type up my notes of our conversations and email them for everybody's reference. What a contrast this is to my relationship with technology at the start of this project.

At long last, we seem to be entering the arena of collaborative writing! I missed this meeting but wrote something on our process and emailed it on, for it to be joined up with everyone else's writing.

I offered to collate everybody's writing on our process perhaps using NVivo, the qualitative data analysis software I used for my research. Trying to email the group, I got terribly frustrated, as my message kept bouncing back undelivered. In the end I wrote: "Here it is again, as according to the system none of you received this. Q:

Oh, where would we
be without
technology? A: With
our children half an
hour ago."

In February, we critically explored the pros and cons of one person creating a new document out of everybody's writing and chose to explore an alternative: we ended our meeting with a 15-minute timed writing and agreed to put these texts on Blackboard for any of us to have a go at collating (or weaving, or braiding, or cobbling, or quilting together) and seeing how that may enrich the process. (They are still there, sitting on virtual shelves gathering virtual dust.)

In March, we began to explore our sense of identity and practices as a collaborative writing group and how this may compare with other groups with similar remits. During the 15 minutes allocated for timed writing, two of our members chose to reflect silently and without writing. This had never happened before, and we noticed how that meditative technology affected the dynamics of the group.

Once again, I came away feeling pleased that I've written something, pleased that I've said what I've said, heard what I've heard. I think there is something iterative in this for me; the so-called creativity in my writing outside of here feeds the creativity in here and vice versa.

These meetings where first we discuss, then we write, have been the most powerful and moving for me. Technology is never more than a shadow away, in that we always keep a record of our meetings and share it with the rest of the group electronically.

I had my laptop with me today, expecting to write and wanting to avoid having to type it up later. In the event it proved a very different experience: inserting or deleting without any trace of changes made, having less of a sense of flow. So much for "decommissioning the editor."

In June, we decided to submit an article to 'Qualitative Inquiry's special issue on 'technology within a collaborative writing group'. We wrote about our relationship with technology and one of us volunteered to weave all writings together for collective editing at the next meeting.

These days our meetings tend to follow the same pattern. At the beginning, it feels like we are all too busy; that none of us really has the time for it. But gradually something seems to grow that none of us really wants to pin down. It remains elusive, delicate—maybe pinning it would destroy it. It seems to thrive in a place of mutuality and creativity—in a place of meeting together, of being with each other. We all feel it and can talk about it. It seems to need real people in real time, holding a space for it, a space that rests in the trust of uncertainty, of letting it be. Would it have been different if we had agreed to meet in cyber space in real time? If we had all agreed to sit in front of our computers at a specified time and communicate with each other for two-and-a-half hours? It may have been worth a try, people apparently fall in love over the Internet. But I wouldn't put any

I am glad I came today. As usual, I did consider giving this meeting a miss. There are always other things that need to be done, deadlines to be met, commitments that feel more pressing. And a 300-mile round trip is never to be underestimated. And yet, as usual, I decided to come and once again it feels such a treat to have been here. There is something quite special about the conversations generated at these meetings; never about mundane things such as traffic or the weather. Most important, here there is mutuality in our contributions. Not like Blackboard, where I felt I would be intruding if I logged in, by knowing more personal or intimate information about others than they had about me. I soon forgot how to access those folders anyway, and it just seemed too much trouble to ask to be reminded of codes, pseudonyms, and such like.

I really look forward to weaving all these writings together and am already thinking about writing in parallel strands (enabled, of course, by technology). I came today determined not to volunteer for anything else; I really must focus on my thesis… Yet there is something about the work of this group that, important and demanding though it is, does not come with the feeling of work attached to it. In our face-to-face meetings, we have nurtured something quite special that goes well beyond our joint interests in identity construction and collaborative writing; we have carved a way of connecting with each other that generates a space for setting both intellect and creativity loose. I positively crave the opportunity to represent our experience, using columns as if presenting three distinct perspectives, although all 12 of us know that these are corridors in which we all keep wandering in and out of.

money on it
generating such a
strong feeling of
connectedness and
belonging.
Discussing digital
and face-to-face
identities has inspired
me to read a bit on
cyber cultures.
Turkle's (1999)
cyberspace
communities were
constructing
themselves in a
virtual version of
real, social time. It
may be that in some
online communities
they have a sense of
real social connection
in time, meeting
online, creating
different selves. I
would have to say our
real meetings are no
less virtual. I perform
myself and find
myself performed by
others differently
every time we meet.

A fortnight later, we caught a first glimpse of how our writings all fit together in one document. Intriguingly, there were our words, set in columns, side by side on the paper. And here were we, having more of our conversations, sitting side by side round a table: our way of 'doing' collaboration— through conversation for an hour or two of being together, then writing, with each of us separate for a while, and then coming together again. Now our writings are re-creating new conversations on a landscape of paper. Using Word would not have allowed us such flexibility to shift or interrupt column shape. Using Publisher has disrupted linearity and created space for multiple, contradictory, simultaneous stories.

Face-to-face conversation is richer in meaning for me, and it is what I remember best. But I do believe the technology helps me keep engaged in an ongoing, intermittent communication and sharing. I can (but often don't) meet at a deeper level when I am with someone or part of a group, but technology has enabled me to keep communicating— even after a long break— and that feels good. Maybe it was even worth the struggle with my ageing brain.

I was playing with my new laptop last night, beginning to feel more confident as I pressed more buttons and started to feel that I wasn't going to break it. I don't want to feel stupid and beaten by some of this technology. I'm excited by a lot of it but I'm still wary— and here in this group that's held me back or perhaps I should say I've allowed it to hold me back. It may be to do with age or gender—but I cannot change that.

In this imaginary, collective space there is still a chance of bumping into you, bumping up against your ideas. This space is constructed by all the stories we have told and still have to tell. It is busy with characters, people, plots, places, masks, locked rooms, and identities shared, hidden, buried, constraining, constituting, and bursting forth.

As we have begun experimenting with talking together, writing, weaving, re-presenting, scrutinizing, re-reading, and then re-writing, it is exciting to see how the text on the page seems to capture a sense of movement... of live conversations happening, of nomads travelling, always questioning, always on the move, camping for a while, but never settling.

The writing, in and out of voice columns, expresses the connections, the beginnings and ends overlapping as in dinner table conversation. Sometimes we all talk or write at once, sometimes there are

The task is no longer about which writing is whose, because nobody knows, but rather about stripping the writing back to its bones and then finding where it fits and why. Questions about individualized

When I'm at the keyboard in front of the screen my movement is slow, deliberate, and conscious. If I'm tired and my spatial difficulties become more pronounced, I cannot find the letters I need. Things have little groups in corners, sometimes we take big turns, the others hanging on our every word... sometimes the group takes a turn, and we swirl around together, all part of the turn in different ways, some nodding, some talking, some interrupting, some furiously tapping keys, and some quietly sitting, still part of the momentum.

ideas of authorship (Davies, 2000; Foucault, 1977) have extended for us into an embodied, discursive writing practice. The writing on the Blackboard archive, stored in themes, might one day be woven into a delicately retraced layered account in the manner of Ronai (1999).

greatly improved over the past few years as I have learnt to use my right hand more, but there is no fluidity or melody to it; it is simply functional (in contrast to dancing, which still flows irrespective of tiredness.)

This has all taken time. We could so easily have unravelled. We could have been overrun by the hurry so many of us were in at the beginning. There was a hurry to publish, market the book, write the chapter. We nearly derailed ourselves. Up against deadlines, commitments, assessment exercises, projects, applications, bids, doctorates, timetables, teaching loads, personal issues, technological turbulence. It all took time. Our writing technologies have been elusive, and we have perhaps happened on them by accident even though at least some of us were looking intensely for them. They have taken us by surprise. This writing, our current writing, is happening with urgency. It is a live flowing conversation in the continuous present (see Bird, 2004).

Most online collaborative writing technologies seemed to comprise different editing tools. They supported quilting processes that patched and sewed together clearly defined and individually authored layers, chapters, and

I feel an intense exhilarated ownership of these texts; not as mine, but rather as a hard-won expression of the collective. Looking at the recently woven script, I find I have no idea which piece I wrote. Stranger

We inhabit virtual, social, historical, narrative, and imaginary writing times and spaces. Imaginary time is quite other, it is neither social nor virtual. I am not in the group now, sitting in this café, yet here, tapping into my silver sections. There was no disruption to autonomous boundaried selves in there, no opportunity for extending collective biography practices, and no place for witnesses to stand and reflect or contribute silently. We are not quilters, but weavers: weavers of many threads of different textures at once.

still, I recognize all the writing, although I never saw most of it before it was collated. These are the various, contradictory voices of our community.

machine, I can stay in the living space generated by our mutual possibilities. I am not extending your moment of course, but I am extending your part in mine. "Not only can plot time be out of order… (arranged in a non-chronological sequence) but also it can slow itself down to an unworldly crawl, or accelerate to a frantic blur, or even skip years altogether without a word" (Murphet, 2005, p.65).

So, it seems technology has been somewhat divisive for us, at times leaving some feeling apprehensive or excluded. Much electronic technology seems to come from a different world, and perhaps it cannot be tamed or harnessed for our meanderings. It seems to have threatened to impose its own values of speed, competence, structure and anonymity, within the goal-focused climate of an academic context. Instead, we have thrived on collaboratively setting our own pace and boundaries and on our joint sense of connectedness; not to mention the commitment to a journey where both route and destination seemed unclear.

Well, who would have known, that in the end it was our frustration with electronic technologies that called for more frequent face-to-face meetings...

… that it is our meetings which seem to have facilitated our

collective sense of
identity and feeling
of belonging...

... but that it is
thanks to technology
that this has now
found an expression
and can be
communicated to
others.

PART VI

WRITING'S AGENCY

CHAPTER TWENTY-ONE

PROLOGUE TO PART VI

TESSA WYATT, DAVINA KIRKPATRICK, SUE PORTER, ARTEMI SAKELLARIADIS, JANE SPEEDY AND JONATHAN WYATT

This section of the book considers, in a sense, what writing does. The two chapters, 'After Writes' (Chapter 22) and 'Inquiring into Red' (Chapter 23), invite the reader to be "an insider-guest" and to stumble into the "clumsy and surprising language of collaborative and writing group rituals", to 'faff', eat, talk and read the last writing, writing into and under and over that writing and then reading and perhaps writing again.

The chapters are multi-layered; the authors respond to each other's stories by tentatively offering their own resonance and writing into spaces using reflections/similarities and differences. The text is littered with recensions and palimpsests. (openings through which later scribes take the text in different directions and/or the remains and residual or 'ghost' traces of older manuscripts)

These memories and visits are entangled; in 'After Writes' the theme is the (possible) ending of a collaboration. The 'Red' inquiry uses a more multi-modal approach, images and text both being produced during a collective biography workshop where red arose as a blush or a stain seeping amongst them that became referenced obliquely by material objects, metaphors and fairy tales." (p. XX). In the 'Red' chapter art and words riff off each other. People play; for example one person wonders at the specific hue for a red beret: blood, blush, cadmium, cardinal, carmine, crimson, hunting pink, magenta, maroon, rose, ruby, pillar box, scarlet, terracotta, Windsor. Then, a woman in a glass dress appears and runs riot through an autumn forest, a ribbon unfurling in italics through the text There is humour here and a willingness to let the writer's ego be subsumed into a collective spirit.

Throughout these writings there is a playful agility of spirit that is something of a rarity within the contemporary academy. Old subversive scholars sitting together on the kerbs of the academic highway, plotting to decolonise and even de-rail mainstream research (Diversi & Moreira, 2009) and then lead us into fairy-tale, magical realist spaces that the modern academy rarely inhabits (leaving aside the position of literary critic).

In terms of the history of the academy, these papers are not written by the equivalent of the scholars doing the work of translation of the bible, or the tales of Ovid, but rather, of the scholars illustrating those manuscripts with magical, colourful and sometimes downright bawdy images. In medieval times, the parchments from ancient, often more religious illuminated manuscripts were frequently re-used, with traces from older texts, or palimpsests showing through newer, more secular texts (de Hamel, 1992) and our chapter 'Inquiry into Red' has this kind of feel, with both written texts and images leaking and slipping out from underneath others.

In the words of Patti Lather, this last group of papers in the book demonstrates that just as we thought we had got the measure of 'doing' the collaborative writing 'the writing wrote us' so to speak (Lather, 1997, p.67) and poking around in the poetic interludes in 'after writes', in particular, 'sometimes you find poetry in the space between the words (Lahman et al., 2010, p.44). In most of the other sections of this book we have considered the humans, the writers, as those with agency, but in these two chapters, we end with questions about the agency and potency of the writing itself and of a poetics not only of human experiences, but of the spaces we leave between us and what we write and say, and of the myriad residual traces left behind and ahead of us as a map towards the collaborative methodologies of the future.

CHAPTER TWENTY-TWO

AFTER WRITES:
SOME LOOSELY THREADED TOGETHER
WRITING ABOUT ENDING/NOT ENDING OUR
TIME TOGETHER IN A COLLABORATIVE
WRITING GROUP[1]

BRISTOL COLLABORATIVE WRITING GROUP

I arrived late because I ran out of petrol and had to veer off to Shepton Mallet[2] for supplies.

"I'm not sure where they are", he volunteered when I arrived to collect my keys.

"Oh, don't worry", I replied, "They'll all be faffing about somewhere until supper... that's what we do", I told him, "when we arrive, we faff, we eat, we talk, and then, only then, do we begin to write".

"And how will you know when you've finished?", he asked astutely.

"Oh, we already have", I said. "We've already finished. This is a post-postscript kind of a writing retreat", and he smiled weakly and sort of glazed over.

The Bristol Collaborative Writing Group ("the Group") was formed to explore issues of 'identity' through collaborative writing—that is the official version of our beginning during early 2004. In fact, we had several beginnings and those of us who are the final members of the Group would

---

[1] This chapter was originally published in the journal 'International Review of Qualitative Research' as Bristol Collaborative Writing Group, 2012.

[2] The writing retreats of the Bristol Collaborative Writing Group have been held over the last several years at Ammerdown, which is not far from a little town called Shepton Mallet.

give differing accounts of how we began. We did not define either 'identity' or 'collaborative', and it is probably true to say that we also wondered at times about whether 'Writing' and 'Group' could be appropriately claimed by us.

Ours has been a journey of discovery, in that our community and processes have emerged from an odyssey where, in Moustakas's terms, "I know little of the territory through which I must travel" (1990, p.13). This landscape has been one of discovery, surprise and creative uncertainty, rather like Keats's concept of 'Negative Capabilities': of being willing and "capable of being in uncertainties, mysteries, doubts, without any irritable reaching after fact and reason" (Forman, 1952, p.71). The processes that have evolved have both created, and emerged from, relationships and community—experiences of discovery and surprise, of finding connections, interconnections, and constellations of ideas from a diverse range of academic disciplines and research interests.

Even during our first year our numbers began to dwindle from the initial 20 members. Some leavings were unavoidable, through job, location or death. Some were a loss of interest or time, or occasionally something more troubled. However, in October 2010 our Group found itself coming to an end. This is a story of our ending, drawn from writings of our 'final' one-day gathering in December 2010 and some 10 months later when we held one of our two-day writing retreats specifically to write about who it was that we had been, and to reflect on the reality of ending. The ending of writing was something we had each experienced before, in thesis, article or book, but what happens when ending 'collaborative writing'? One weekend in October 2011, we set out to reflect on coming together no more. However, in coming together again, the inevitable happened. It seems a little naive that we simply hadn't anticipated the inevitable, but you will see that we encountered more than we expected as we wrote together.

Our story of who we were points to a counter-intuitive, risky endeavor, requiring high degrees of trust in person and process—an endeavour that took us beyond comfort zones into an unfamiliar relationality that has seemed to us to be more than the sum of its parts. It is a form of learning and being, research and writing that was new to some of us. We will tell our story, from our writings (in italics), using spacing to indicate a different author or piece of writing.

From the Inside Out

Arriving, faffing chatting, eating drinking talking laughing singing, reading writing, attending and writing again.

There are other writing groups but this one has had a particularly meandering history, a particular blend of not even starting as a collaborative writing group, but ambling sideways into a faith commitment and practice and we have been about both turning up and much more than turning up.

... I carried on turning up. Each time I hesitated and part of me knew that I shouldn't really be coming—too many important things to do. And so I ignored my important things, a careful ignoring, and I came.

We have created a space where we know what to do—we write—often in the same room and, after writing, we read what we have written and, sometimes, write into the space created by that writing. In earlier versions of this group, there would be apologies, throat-clearing, as the absent Dick would say, before the reading—here we often read and there is little comment—the readings are followed by some space and a conversation starts—after the conversation there is a decision about writing or not writing.

Our collaboration has always resisted the factual, the analytical, the world of outcomes, tidy method or good behaviour. We cannot therefore present ourselves in the form of an artificially sequenced, tidy chronology. We have, to varying degrees, each mastered the tongue of research and academia. But when we come together, we discover another language—one that several of us are quite unfamiliar with outside of our collaboration.

One of the dilemmas of this chapter, and of our very existence, is the question of whose world we should live in, and what language we should speak. After much wrestling throughout most of our 8-year existence, we gradually allowed ourselves to loosen our moorings and glide away from the allegedly objective (etic) perspective that was our norm. Instead of a continual mindfulness on the outsider, be it individual or institution or even the reader, we realised that the heart of our collaboration was in simply allowing ourselves to be insiders together. It has been a sometimes-guilty indulgence to prioritize the self-referenced (emic) world that lived amongst us.

The independence of the etic continues to be widely valued in much of western society—the scientific findings that should not be 'contaminated' by insider perspectives. However, Zetterberg (2006) proposed that a promising approach for social science would be to accept the position of the emic: the insider account. More controversially, he went further to suggest exploring "the possibility that the emic language actually contains a deep structure that is the appropriate etic language" (p.246).

When we met together for our final writing weekend to share the journey of our ending in our own insider-language, we did indeed explore the 'deep structure' that is our own collaboration—something more than our writing itself—which has grown up in our midst. Yet how does such a deeply lived reality get communicated to an 'outside' world? Can we as insiders speak with integrity and relevance to an audience beyond? Whose interests and meanings 'should' prevail? Rather than trying to 'tidy ourselves up' for 'others', we prefer to simply invite you as the reader to be an insider-guest in our bewildering yet deeply comfortable world. And hope that the journey of our ending will create connections with stories beyond our world, stirring resonances with your own.

Telling our stories

In the Jewish faith, when somebody dies the mourners greet each other with Loachaim... to life! And then you tell stories of the person who has died. I understand this happens in Ireland too, at the wake.

Well, we did turn up again, didn't we? We turned up with our heads full of 'The Sense of an Ending' (Barnes, 2011), and our laptops full of stories of the group that have now become objects for us to write to...

We had ended—if we had not ended before there would not be that sense of commenting on something that had passed out of existence and suddenly was there again. Endings—that's what it's like, partly. Someone dies and the live interconnections with them that keep things alive and changing become reified in stories that become static—a one-sided interpretation and set of stories that don't come into contact any more with the object that could bring into questions those assumptions.

The story of our ending can best be told from excerpts from our ending-stories. It is the language that we speak. It has been claimed across many disciplines that it is fundamentally through narrative means that we make sense of our lives: that stories are not peripheral, but are central and fundamental to our ways of making meaning and creating identity. Stories have been at the heart of our Group's ways of being and discovering. In the words of Clarissa Pinkola Estes (1993, p.i),

> "Among my people, questions are often answered with stories. The first story almost always evokes another, which summons another, until the answer to the question has become several stories long. A sequence of tales is thought to offer broader and deeper insight than a single story alone."

Those of us less accustomed to it found our collaborative story-making to be a clumsy and surprising language to learn. It can certainly appear inefficient, often taking a circuitous route and frequently arriving at an unanticipated destination. When we laid out the boundaries or focus for our writing, it was weakened. Instead of being free to respond to each other in a collaborative way, the task itself began to become pre-eminent. Indeed, when we tried to impose a structure with regard to our use of technology, our attempts were continually thwarted (Sakellariadis et al., Chapter 20). Only when we had learned to hold the starting place, the topic and the outcome lightly, and trust the process of our writing, could we then begin, as a Group, to let the stories emerge.

We also had to find an appropriate way of holding ourselves and our views lightly, for to discover collaborative writing in our midst meant discovering the degree of difference amongst us. Most groups function on the basis of homogeneity (Rossol, 2001). It is what they share in common that creates the group dynamic. However, we have often been aware of the value of the uniqueness we each bring. The surprises in our story-sharing created responses that crossed boundaries of academic discipline, religion, continents, emotional health, and numerous personally policed taboos. This has been central to who we are—so much so that we can now trust the deeply treasured collaboration that will materialise in our midst when new facets of our diversity find their way into transparency.

We write bringing interconnecting voices from the past—writing linked and illustrated so that the images arise—some image of multiple connectedness—our links in to each other's thoughts and writing do not lead to a single point but spread out and shift and grow—it's that interconnectedness that we need to build again to write fluently as a group.

We have shared this becoming[3] us in relation to difference, divergence, janglements and tanglements and have benefitted perhaps from lacking a surface unity—we are not all Christians, or feminists, or lesbians or therapists or educators or..., or..., but maybe over the course of time, we have all become something of the qualities of those communities without stepping into them. There are other practices that border on ours, many of them fine, perhaps some of them finer, and the serendipity and resilience that brought us here together, sitting shiva, which cannot be replicated, can still be nurtured and sustained in others.

I went off to choir and we sang from Fleetwood Mac. I have issues when not present with giving and taking. There's a couple of lines from 'Go your Own Way' from Fleetwood Mac's 'Rumours': "If I could, I would give you my world. How can I, when you won't take it from me?"... The pain of this rejection of offer is part of who I am—it's about giving, needing a particular response and being at the same time so open that when rejection follows the pain is unbearable. When I was young, I learnt that asking my parents for things was hard for them—they wanted to give but if money was involved or time it simply was not possible. So, what I carry with me as a script from childhood is that I must not ask—so, if I do ask then in my psyche I am already emotionally heavily committed (need) and it is under those circumstances that the other, who assumes that I ask lightly, can reject—maybe to suggest another time—I don't get that far and I don't ask again. I have made progress with this one over my lifetime(s). In the collaborative writing group we have found a way of being that collaboratively transcends the space of individual psyches. I was aware those few hours that the mechanism was not kicking in.

This process of giving and taking in the writing—hearing, listening and writing, articulating—is a dance that allows our various positions and perspectives and actual spoken words to move in figures through our

---

[3] Our shared perspective on 'becoming' was rarely discussed explicitly but was present in much of our writing. It fits with the following: "As Deleuze and Guattari explain, the process of 'becoming' is not one of imitation or analogy, it is generative of a new way of being that is a function of influences rather than resemblances. The process is one of removing the element from its original functions and bringing about new ones" (Heckman, 2002). As well as the personal, we were also experiencing Group becomings. Through ever-changing processes of becoming we embraced multiplicity, continually transforming itself into a string of other multiplicities (Deleuze & Guattari, 1988, p.275).

crafted and not-so-crafted stream of consciousness emergings. I resisted the term therapeutic group—the energy that is present with Gerald[4] is healing—this is a space where we can write and articulate without that writing being judged.

I knew when I arrived here it would be OK to be exhausted, to simply be, I wouldn't have to perform, in the midst of our 'We' I could recover gently.

Exploring our ending

The nature of our ending has been just as much a surprise to us as the rest of our journey together. From our initial membership, we faffed and jangled our way through to become a group of 9 irregular members, participating variously as priorities would allow and often spurning priorities in order to indulge in being together. One weekend, we realised that two of us had slipped into invisibility, and we had become 'seven of nine'.

This reduced number brought no premonition of ending. Instead, we settled into a new rhythm for a number of gatherings, growing in our exploration of who we were with each encounter. However, later one of us confessed to an increasing 'forgettory' that was coming upon her as a result of illness. We met again, to write into that place of remembering and forgetting, discovering many more shared meanings than we realized (Martin et al., 2011; Chapter 15). One of us decided that now was the time for her to also step out, and we began to face the prospect of our own ending as a Group.

Ours has always been a group that was intimately aware of the surroundings in which it was located, whether feeling surreptitious and below the radar of institutional expectations, or in a place of peace, welcomed and at ease in the restored Dovecote at Ammerdown that was our regular writing and being space for our last several years. As well as our own voice, our environment always made its contribution to our story. Its symbolism adds richness for us to our own experience of the Group (Hewitt, 2000, p.44), and you will find it throughout our stories. Although it runs the risk of being an obstacle to an insider-guest (Katovich & Weitling, 2000), it is as much a part of our voice as any other.

---

[4] 'Gerald' refers to one of the names we have given to what emerges in our experience of being together and is explained in more detail later.

It was really no surprise therefore that in gathering to celebrate our ending in December 2010, the restaurant we shared lunch in spontaneously played the very song we had been singing several moments before—Julie Andrews coming alive in the hills to the 'Sound of Music'. Likewise, that when we returned to the University for our afternoon gathering, we found ourselves having to meet in a recently renovated, green-furnitured public space rather than our usual meeting room, so that several of us no longer felt we recognized our institutional home. The world had moved on. We parked unceremoniously outside the mens' toilets, not even seeking to become one with the attempt at greenness, aware of the irony of a final homelessness, even whilst one of us was summoned by disgruntled students into a premature departure from our final gathering. Sue gathered our parting thoughts together into our Requiem. We laughed. And ended.

Nowhere to be
Laurinda gone
There's nowhere to go
We have nowhere to go
We have all gone
Only voyeurs

Intangible news
Requiem for our productivity

Disbanded now
Intangible
And Roars of laughter
It's not within our power
Beyond us

We don't need to perpetuate us.
Who are we to perpetuate it?
Step back
This becoming is coming to an end
It's not us making it happen
What we've done is turn up and now we are not turning up anymore. It
takes you off.

A final reflection?

... now we have had our requiem, I feel we ought to have a last gig...

For some of us, our requiem was clearly experienced as an end. For others a gently hovering hope kept alive the possibility that we might find another excuse to write together. We even recognized that we had some unfinished writings and one or two were exploring how these might be taken further. Nonetheless, when we came together for our 'post-postscript kind of a writing retreat' to accept an invitation to write about our ending, it was, we thought, to consider the ending we had already experienced some ten months earlier.

Sincerely, we believed that this is what we were doing. Throughout our years together we had grown a tradition of reflecting on the puzzling journey we were part of, being simultaneously both observer and observed. Many times we realized that we were the learners in a process that had its own momentum and would do much better when we gave up trying to drive it, be responsible for it or even achieve any goals or targets. There is an irresponsibility in this position which members of the Group often battled with, but if we had surrendered to the important, we would have ended long before. Our methodology unfolded itself in our midst, prospering when we gave it less attention. Hindsight has been our friend and given us insight into our ways of being and writing, and writing and being. Ending, we admitted, needed to be just as much a part of our reflection as any other aspect of this journey that had written itself into our being.

And so yet again we arrive at our Dovecote bringing ourselves and the fragments of our various experiences and expectations, each one honored and valued for its unique contribution to the 'We' that becomes when we are together. Our journeying has allowed us to trust the process of simply bringing who we are. Through the offering of our difference, interspersed with laughter, song and tears, a shared understanding grows, a tangible multi-faceted oneness that we have variously named during the years as Gerald (female), Raspberry or simply It, and We (Speedy et al., 2010) in the "narrative cartography" (Pollner & Stein, 1996, p.204) of our Group.

We seem to carry a healthy curiosity about each other that thrives in an atmosphere of non-judgement. It is indeed a place of acceptance, but more than that, the tangible lack of judgement is part of our We that proclaims a 'welcome' that refreshes us on every encounter. It is an embrace that we are able to presume upon and even occasionally feel we begin to understand.

And so it was that we arrived, with stories to tell of endings and death—except this was our own death that we were so deeply engaged with, our Writing Group having already died. Even as we did, one of us was slipping gently into such increased forgettory and another was struggling with battles so significant that they were unable to join us.

Hello
We must be going
We cannot stay
We came to say
We must be going

Though we are gone
We still are coming
And we're going

Yes we are here
And we are going

We are not all here
We are dwindling
We have dwindled

Our friends are missing
And we miss them
Yet they are here
In some sense
Some sense of ending
Not some fictional construct
But some sense
Some intangible sense
Of ending, not dwindling

When we finished our writing group, that midwinter day with the basket of my mobility buggy filled with mistletoe and the stream of men passing, pushing back and forth through the tight space next to us to get to their lavatory, we didn't expect to be doing an encore. We thought that was it; over, done, finished. It had been a little unexpected for some of us maybe, but it was also like some of us had already started to shuffle along the row, focused on their next obligation, or opportunity.

I left this group about a year ago and I haven't been back except to say goodbye in December, since the group ended then and in some ways I see that it has ended, for the moment, in that it almost no longer needs to be a group that does, so much as one that reflects on what it has done... Or at least I think we are, but maybe we are composting.

We talk about and sing from the 'Sound of Music', but the end has happened for this group so we are remembering times past... now I have no expectations that I will write with these people again and, although I feel connections with them all and am open to the energy that connects us, my stance is other, outer.

Have you ever been to a gig where, when the band come back onstage for the encore, and start to pick their instruments up again, there are one or two of them missing? That really annoys me. It spoils the encore. I find myself wondering, worrying over it, trying to find possible explanations for, what I see as, their impolite behavior. When I first witnessed this, I thought that something must be wrong, that perhaps they had been taken ill. Then I worried that they might be taking advantage of their colleagues, leaving them to do the extra work. And then it occurred to me that it might be an act of generosity to their colleagues, allowing them extra performance space whilst starting to pack the van.

So, we begin to rise, to gather ourselves and our instruments (pens, MacBooks, iPads, Vaios) for one last effort. But I won't be there. It's not that I've left the band, it's just that I'm hanging around backstage. I'm not copping out on my obligations and I'm not sacrificing my space for others to use, nor am I packing the van for a quick getaway. I am just too unwell, too weak, in too much pain and a bit too worn down by the routine unkindness I now experience as a disabled person, to get there today. But, as I say, I will be hanging around backstage, maybe even noodling out a tune, or harmonising with a song or two.

I came having read Julian Barnes's 'The Sense of an Ending' (2011)— up for a Booker prize and I've been living with that sense for a while— Steve Jobs there on my laptop as I open the web—1955 to 2011—he's younger than me—will I go gentle into that night? I don't think so. I don't think that the shades that were around me as I arrived have quite dissipated into the light of connection—hard to write about endings after the endings—

Today I saw an ending, tragic and full of pain, broken and heart-rending, lost dreams and broken promises. I still carry the pain of that ending as it rippled through a community...

I think of my friend Stuart—whom we both knew was never really my friend—and the strange feeling that I knew his ending was close while he lived in the gentle self-deceit of calling it flu... It felt alarming, to have recognised what hadn't been spoken yet, and to know something as intimate as his ending. It was his ending and yet I held it in my hands. "See you next week"... and next week never came... and now I sit in his chair at the band. Or is it my chair now?

... rituals of faffing, eating talking, reading the last writing, writing into and under and over that writing and then reading and perhaps writing again.

And writing
Space to write
Writing generating writing
Writing into discovery
Writing as a way of being
Writing as relating
Writing as becoming

Writing slowly dwindling
Writing... running... out... of words

Writing curled up in a ball
Writing going to sleep

Insider short-hand

Foucault (1986, p.24) uses the concept of "heterotopic space" to refer to a space where we might see reflection as well as difference. Likewise, our practice has become to respond to each other's stories by tentatively offering our own resonance or stories and writing into that space with those reflections/similarities/differences. We had required of ourselves no particular form for these offerings—a word or phrase, story, song, or poem, laughter or tears, or even some well-referenced piece, or indeed nothing at all—all are given equal worth.

The myriad meanings of those stories shift and change, reflect and refract in diffuse ways in different interactions. Therefore, as audience, each person will read or hear stories differently, through the filter of her/his own consciousness, particular frame of reference, ways of construing the world, thus reflecting heterotopia. Our collaborative story-telling practices are intended as narrative invitations, for each other and any who would allow themselves to connect with their own stories in our story.

"It is the connection, the shared exchange that activates the story: interactivity that creates meaning that is more than the self" (Leach, 2004, p.19). Our stories of endings emerged from our interaction as a group. When we started speaking of endings, we already knew not to limit ourselves and our process to 'the ending' that we 'should' be talking about. Immediately, we transgressed any sense of boundary and brought the fullness of our experience of ending to each other. And from the blending of stories came Our Story.

Tonight there has been much talk of death; many of us, including me, have been ill since last we met. We are perhaps just getting older and in the natural course of things, bits and pieces are just dropping off us all here and there, but nonetheless, there has been talk of death and I find myself imagining the Dovecote as our shared tomb. The Chinese emperors took slaves, the Pharaohs living slaves and dogs and food for the journey... But if thousands of years later, they were to dig us out of this Dovecote they would find many of us lying on the floor, despite the ample seating provided, probably at least one of us with our legs in the air and head on the floor. They would find five women and traces of two more, several laptops and an abundance of other writing equipment, several bottles of wine, some half empty, piles of books and photographs and, mysteriously, tape after tape of silent digital video recordings.

I stop writing and look around the room at this group of women I love and realise that although I know and love them all individually and have friendships and workships with them all outside this room, we are as a community of writers something other and beyond ourselves. I am not talking here about the sense of Gerald we have referred to before. I am talking about almost a guild of craftspeople who conjointly practice a trade together... We are master craftspeople in the collaborative writing trade and when we get together there's a very ordinary workaday atmosphere that we wear lightly.

We are sitting now typing and writing into and under Sue's 'Requiem' for our group. The room has traces of laughter and song. Viv, who is currently right side up, was a short while ago, singing upside down, feet in the air, head on the floor. We remember writings past that contain traces of writings present that support our writings into the future and beyond.

We have tamed each other, after St Exupery's fox[5] but we don't need to tend our rose in person—yet it is something to do with the time that we have spent honing our practices that means that after a long break we could simply write together, read what we had written and write again into the space created by that speaking/reading.

We speak to each other in the forked and mysterious tongues of a group with a shared history... the evening in the snow, the large group workshop, the Chinese take-away moment, the seven of nine weekend, the evolution of It to Raspberry to Gerald to the dynamic relational sustenance that exists in the space between us, the It and Susan's 'We'.

In the moment, in the shorthand of old friends, our writing speaks with the voices of others over our time together in the last 24 hours and before that over our time as a group. Those shorthand allusions can be expanded to include writing from earlier about those times. They are the "torchbeams criss-crossed" from the end of Barnes's book (2011, p.150). These stories have a knot of meaning we might call "relevance" (Bateson, 1979) and the relevance can pass other readers, outside the group, by.

What I am struck by is how well we know how to write together... and I think of this later when Susan is talking about her Royal Marines band who just know how to play music together because, after so long, they know why they play together. We know how and why we write together.

'We' springs its surprise

As Leach notes, in a challenge to the linear model of life, "experience may be outside narrative... what surrounds, what threatens the path of the life, is fearful, chaotic, confusing" (2004, p.18). The linearity of narrative with its dominant tropes of life as a journey may have limitations as a metaphor of experience, for, as Heather Leach writes, "[s]tories can go in many directions. They circle and backtrack, they double back on

---

[5] This is a reference to the fox in the fable by de Saint-Exupery (1995).

themselves like hypertexts, they wander down side paths, one story is passed on from person to person" (2004, p.19). In addition, some experiences may not be readily storied; they may exceed our vocabulary or understanding; they may be chaotic or contradictory, for as Edward Bruner puts it, "life experience is richer than discourse" (1986, p.143).

In spite of our best commitments to end, as the weekend progressed, we came to a gradual realisation:

The trouble with us not turning up anymore, is that no one has told 'It'. It, and the We that becomes when 'It' is around, doesn't seem to know the meaning of an ending.

Moments like the toilets and the green furniture, the hills coming alive even in places where they shouldn't... even our attempts at an ending ooze more becoming and life than we can bear and somehow seem to reaffirm our becoming. Such moments give me the gentlest of hints that It and We are teasing...

According to Derrida, in calling a friend's name in his life, we are anticipating his name surviving his death... he writes in the mourning book that Barthes's name "already survives him" before he is dead... (2003, p.48). In remembering the dead, their names survive them but also part of the politics of mourning is our own infidelity, which we anticipate also by having more than one friend... we are already unfaithful to our friends in anticipation of their deaths before they die.

Just like the unfaithful musicians, we have maybe anticipated the death of our writing group, by ending it before it ended... but maybe this didn't work out because... we can be in as many writing groups/friendships as we like but this writing group is still in us however unfaithful we are...

Although we did not keep faith, or at least I didn't... the writing group... the 'We' if you like, kept faith commitment with me and kept embodied practice safe in my memory... as soon as we take up with each other we take up that practice...

I think this group's purpose, the one it didn't know it had, to discover the relationship between the I, the We and the It and work in those spaces, is now done. In that sense, the group has died and we are now tomb raiders, discovering how we did what we did and how we know what we know... That's what I think we think we are doing here... But what I don't know, by definition, is what is the purpose we have that we don't know about. Susan talked of being teased, but I do not feel teased, I feel brought back again and again to this space between the I and the We and the It.

'It' was there this weekend in the Dovecote, a special sort of silence, holding and full of listening—as Merton would say, "when all their silence is on fire" (1977, p.281). We/It is not ended since We/It is part of each of us and is freely given and taken (my image here is the energetic taking of Artemi's shoulder).

And yet I know that who we are will never cease to be... a smile when the inbox chimes with a hello from part of our 'We', that smile will never end...

Will 'It' ever end? I have visions of 'We' in our 80s and 90s, meeting together over supper, dribbling our gravy and admiring each others' walking sticks... and 'We' will be alive and well and much younger than us.

She had been eyeing it up ever since she got here, "That's a beautiful walking stick dear, where did it come from?"
"It's good, isn't it? I got it from this little shop in Shepton Mallet. You know, that place you go through if you take the long route to Ammerdown."
"Ammerdown... that rings a bell... do remind me dear."
"I always have this with me", she said, rubbing her fingers together, and as she turned her hand over, a beautiful pouch woven out of fine gossamer thread came into being. "It has Susan's 'We'—spelt 'w', 'e'—inside". For the next few moments they all pulled out Susan's 'We'—spelt 'w', 'e'—from their pockets, their hair, their handbags. To the young member of staff it looked as though one of them pulled something out of her nose, but she couldn't be sure.
"And do you remember this?", another one said, and reaching into the plug-in behind her left ear pulled out a sheaf of papers and laid out on the table a delicious Chinese takeaway.
"My favourite memory is right here", said another, as she morphed into a bird and gently placed herself, among other similar birds, high up on the wall overlooking the lake and filled the room with madrigal singing.
When the music subsided, snowflakes were lightly falling from the ceiling. They all reached out to catch them, each of their hands shaped like a triangular piece of wood. They gently stroked the snow in their

hands, easing it into shape—a camera appeared here, a laptop there, seven hens perched on a bench, a placard with no words. "And what have you got there?"—in one hand the leaf of snow was keeping on moving, changing shape and moving on to something else before it became the thing that it wasn't. "Me?", she said. "Oh, I always carry with me the possibilities that were, the writings we didn't write." They all looked at each other knowingly and smiled subversively. One of them said, "Shall we do some writing then?"

What was stunning in the moment of our weekend was the unexpected yet shared recognition, when we each added our part to the story in our beautifully divergent ways, that maybe we hadn't quite ended. So it felt a bit like ffffp, ffffp, ffffp, a little candle was lit with each reading, and by putting them all together we realized that in the midst of our ending, something simply wasn't dying.

And so to begin...

We have reflected elsewhere on 'Gerald' (Speedy et al., 2010) and the realisation of a deeper 'something' in our midst. True to form we have resisted any attempt to understand, define, pin down or interpret what for each of us has been a very real experience. But it seems entirely appropriate that we discovered It continued after our ending, and concluded that this We was indeed what we were really about, even though we did not know it.

Hindsight can easily deceive. How simple it would be to rationalise our faffing and meanderings and write ourselves into a story that feels purposeful with a comfortable consistent continuity. Yet the reality is that this Group that was convened to explore issues of identity has been grappling with issues of its own identity throughout its existence. Only in passing through a process of our ending have we really appreciated the meaning of who we still are and therefore we discover that we continue to be, in some as yet inexplicable fashion. And even now our experience of this is far from unified.

In a world where the individual is pre-eminent and the empirical is exalted, Gerald, We and It are invisible. They live in the gaps created by our bilateral relational trust (Bond, 2007) thriving on the "inherent human dignity" (O'Mathúna, 2006) that undergirds who our Group have had the privilege to become together. They come to us, consistently and reliably now, yet never at our bidding. As we reignite the connections of being together, so they appear again.

Is it possible to take some of the mystery out of this sense of We? Is it something reproducible by any Group who would choose to walk this path? Or did we experience something remarkably serendipitous that cannot be cultivated? Time will tell, perhaps. We are certainly not alone in this experience and much of what we have written here will resonate with feminist researchers and activists who have also claimed different "ways of knowing" (Belenky et al., 1997) to those referred to within mainstream propositional social research paradigms.

But there are those who would recognise We. Gilbert would perhaps begin by pointing out that we are creating a "plural subject" (1989, 2000), albeit perhaps in an irresponsibly simple form. We are naming a dynamic that occurs in our midst that does not belong to any one of us. Its presence is a combination of the blending of several and yet it is just as real a subject as any other that is present. Even the invisible and non-human subjects that are the language of myths, fable and perhaps religion are (mostly) presumed to be singular. Yet we were aware of a dynamic that arose because of our plurality.

Others would focus on process rather than We, exploring the dynamics in our midst. Complexity theory would look at the non-linear emergence of something (We) that cannot be directly attributed to its core elements (us as individuals) (Byrne, 1998; Stacey, 2002). If it was treated as a 'deep structure' located beyond the empirical and observable, critical realism may interpret 'We' as part of a wider "causal power" in the domain of the "real" (Bhaskar, 1975, 1991; Sayer, 2000). Even neuroscience might contribute, perhaps locating our capacity to recognize We in the insightful connection-building right hemisphere of the brain, rather than the detailed, factual and literal capacity of the left hemisphere (Lehrer, 2012).

Human geography can also lend its voice to this exploration. If We, It and Gerald are treated as a name for an intangible kind of 'place', it would be primarily social rather than physical, created from our relationality (Gustafson, 2001), rather than from bricks and mortar. Perhaps 'We' as a place is an outcome of our story-making, just as the car boot sale (Gregson & Rose, 2000, p.434) or the demolition derby (Haller, 2003) result from other kinds of performance. It's just that We emerges from a performance that is a ceasing from activity.

Perhaps we have created a non-material place through the meaning we have given to our Group (Smith et al., 1998, p.7)? Certainly We has benefitted from the "collective effect" (Pettit & Schweikard 2006, p.19) of being together. It is an "emotional space" (Moroni et al., 2000, p.192), with a "social energy" (Almond 1974, p.329) and at times a clear "spiritual essence" (Scharmer et al., 2001, pp.8-9). We are moving into the realms of the philosophy of space and place.

But perhaps at its simplest, We is the name for the "spirit of community" (Etzioni, 1992) that we found in our midst when we dared to abandon our attachment to function and goal. It is a community that comes to us when we are together and that is held in deep optimistic affection even when we are away and absorbed in our varied and separate worlds. After our ending, we now know that even when performance ceases, We, Gerald, and It will remain.

And where does such a community fit in a world of qualitative inquiry?

I think it's something profound about love... that in such deep hanging out, something more is created than was originally there... And now that we have created It and It has created We and We has created each of our mes... Now there is more love in my life... And somehow there is more love that I have to give... I find love in me because of the We.

This amazing group of women
Whom I love
A quality of relatingship that is unique to being we
A love within, between and among us

The Hebrew word for cemetery is beit chaim... the house of life... so death and life what a tangle... and not just in writing groups...

There seems to be an indomitable spirit about It and We. Who do we think we are, to even aspire to an ending?

Love is one of those four letter words, like God and other such unmentionables. But love is what It and We are really, don't you think...? A love that has been given birth to, a love that smiles when there is even a hint of us coming together, but remains unperturbed by the suggestion that we won't.

And in the end the love you take is equal to the love you make...[6]

---

[6] This was the last line on the last album recorded by the Beatles, 'The End', on 'Abbey Road', John Lennon, Paul McCartney, 1969.

I have this uncomfortable, disconcerting feeling that there may be life after the death of this group. So, L'chaim.

The only thing we have successfully ended is our beginning...

CHAPTER TWENTY-THREE

INQUIRING INTO RED/RED INQUIRING[1]

KEN GALE, MIKE GALLANT, SUSANNE GANNON, DAVINA KIRKPATRICK, MARINA MALTHOUSE, MCCLAIN PERCY, MAUD PERRIER, SUE PORTER, ANN RIPPIN, ARTEMI SAKELLARIADIS, JANE SPEEDY, JONATHAN WYATT AND TESSA WYATT

Introduction

In this chapter we take up the challenge of folding art and words together to conduct a multi-authored, multi-modal experiment in writing through red. With thirteen authors, the orchestration of the writing without a single authoritative 'conductor' was often complex and always surprising. Rather, we endeavoured to create a textual space where individual subjectivities and authorial voices emerge, merge, and disappear, to emerge again in different configurations and rhythms. So too, art and words intersect and infect each other. This space of collaborative writing and communal inquiry interrupts many of the norms of scholarly writing and the audit practices of our institutions that require academic authorship to be counted by our individual contributions[2]. Instead, this

---

[1] This chapter was first published in the journal 'Humanities', as Gale et al., 2013. See that online version for a sense of this chapter's colours and textures; and see Fig. 2.
[2] See special issue of 'International Review of Qualitative Research' (Vol. 5, No. 4, 2012) on collaborative writing, edited by Ken Gale and Jonathan Wyatt, for detailed discussions on the ethics and practices of collaborative writing in the academy.

project became a 'wondering' and a 'wandering' around how we might write and work otherwise, collaboratively.

Likewise, we desired a way to write stylistically and rhetorically disentangled from the norms of authorship when following our shared interests in narrative as a method of inquiry. The methodology of collective biography provided us with strategies for collaboratively investigating subjectivities, discourse and materiality in lived experience through memory (Davies & Gannon, 2006). A weekend in October 2012, spent together in Ammerdown, served as our starting point, although our inquiries—and our processes of writing and art-making—took us to new spaces and opened new possibilities. The narratives in this chapter are composed of memories and fictions and, rather than reifying the individual subject and the separateness of these texts, they bump against, inform and interrupt each other, as they did in our workshop. Our process and our writing seeks a mode of production that opens to the elusive movements of affect and matter, and that enables us to begin to map the "thicket of connections" between things (Stewart, 2008, p.72). The chapter's structure follows some tropes of narrative time and space with a loosely chronological organisation (a 'beginning', a 'middle' and an 'end') that is populated with distinct narrative voices and 'characters' rather than an abstract voice from nowhere. The chapter is infused with details of the everyday matter of our lives, the settings within which each of us grappled with the text, and with thought and theory that might assist our thinking. The colour red became our rhetorical thread and, throughout the text, literary strategies including recurring motifs, poetry and elements of magical realism link our textual fragments together.

Images are central to our method, as it was through image-making that our inquiries turned to materiality, to the very matter of red. We collaborated in one session to produce a long, red collage with paint and glue and ink and text where fragments, motifs, and both found and sculptured objects, cross across and through each other. We began in our own corners, but as in other phases of our process, we gained confidence and began to move along, between and across, to create and intensify reverberations and resonances. This was "a doubling", where art and words "complement, extend, refute, and/or subvert one another" (Springgay et al., 2005, p.900). We pushed method and writing towards the sort of productive failure that might mark their limits, and the possibilities of working otherwise.

Seeing Red

We were obsessed with red for weeks afterwards, texting and emailing each other about our encounters and entanglements with red in our everyday lives. After the workshop, our lives reddened— between reading and recommending texts to each other; conducting everyday tasks; experiencing technological breakdowns and undergoing international journeys:

Last week I had to have a particular red hat. I wanted a wool beret and was shocked and horrified at the prices. Now I'm stuck in traffic on the way home from Ammerdown and feeling the need to add a list of reds and choose the right colour for my hat. Where to start with red? It feels like it has caught me unawares and hijacked my senses. Where before it had been blue for years, searching out and collecting photos, beads, and accessories trying to capture a particular shade, now red looms large.

I find myself sorting through bowls of marbles and buttons, standing in shops chatting to friends with red-felted scraps in my hand. You send this to a woman who is spending her half-term making red buttons. I find myself unable to stop niggling notions of red; those images are my hauntings from meeting and sharing space with you…

Closing my eyes to the many leaves (red-red, purple-red, yellow-red, orange-red, brown-red, pink-red) that have fallen in the garden that I know will need raking!

When mulling over the red/ness writing from the weekend at Ammerdown, I was left with a feeling of layering, like the overlapping and positioning of many sheets of filo pastry when making baklava. I find myself mildly obsessed with red, layering, and thresholds. Would be lovely to constructively channel it instead of just craving baklava after reading our email exchanges.

I'm brain-dead and in mid-transit (one night in Paris), sneezing and suffering with a whole-hearted first London chill head cold. Red-nosed. The red lights of Montmartre as my friend walks me back to the hotel. I no longer remember my way home (to any home).

Colours for a red beret: blood, blush, cadmium, cardinal, carmine, crimson, hunting pink, magenta, maroon, rose, ruby, pillar box, scarlet, terracotta, Windsor.

Last week was my birthday and I got lots of red presents, including a red book from Sue and a red necklace. You keep reminding me of the protagonist in 'The Ice Queen' by Alice Hoffman. She loses the ability to see red: "Whatever had once been red was now cloudy and pale" (Hoffman, 2006, p.20). But it is not merely sight that is afflicted: "I never mentioned the lack of the colour red, the buzzing under my skin, the clicking in my head" (ibid., p.20). How would it be to lose the colour red? Did we ever ask if anyone was colour blind? What is buzzing beneath our collective skins? Your writing too, the red writing that I intervened in[3], reminds me of 'The Girl with Glass Feet' by Ali Shaw (Gannon et al., 2012).

Yes, fairytale-esque, magical realism and death... my favourite combinations.

Red Runs Riot

And so our connections around the globe, increasingly fuelled by metaphor, fairy tales and material things, went on and on and on... At our workshop, together, we had each written into red, or red had written into us and then we had intervened in each other's red-writings. A woman in a glass dress appeared and ran riot through an autumn forest and through this text that we were creating together. She intervened in our text, became a motif that unfurled like a ribbon in italics through our text. We began wondering and wandering with her, through our own and each other's memories, through the fragments of theory that interceded in our texts. We were implicit in, and witness to, an unravelling that might bring us all undone:

A moment in red. She sits sifting, letting the most immediate conversation settle, slips sideways, focuses on the dark red darning on pink gloves, the cross hatching and patching, the reforming of a hole, covering over but still being present, and the found object at her feet: metal with a hole not perfectly spherical, a little off kilter; the need to hold, press sharp edges into flesh, leave marks; she tries to let go. She wonders/wanders about, walking the paths of the glory wood in the glass dress spilling red ribbon and ash, an unravelling. She let herself drift back from the woods to the words, to the ribbons of paths, overlaid now with red enamel lines on

---

[3] A process we used during the Ammerdown weekend where we each 'intervened' in another's writing, e.g., by changing the form or writing the story from a different point of view. See Gannon, Walsh, Byers & Rajiva (2012) for extended discussion of textual interventions as a strategy for "deterritorializing" collective biography.

vistral re-imaginings, but also being pulled sideways to a memory of red blotching under the skin as the blood settled and mottled, patterned still, not rushing and fluid. Still she couldn't believe, comprehend, lack of movement and her mind kept putting it back in a flicker of eyelid, a breath, because then it wasn't end. It wasn't this, it wasn't cold, clammy mottled flesh of deadweight, of death... It was rosy-hued, it was rose-tinted, blush and bloom of coy seduction, pulse of blood through veins of movement, of life. But the memory of weight brings her back, the memory of blood on her gloved fingertips from behind the skull. She wonders/wanders about walking the paths of the glory wood in the glass dress spilling red ribbon and ash, an unravelling. Kneehigh's[4] representation of severed feet, stumps of legs with red ribbons falling beautiful and profane, poetic, visceral, to cover, re-cover, uncover, weave and knot, interleave-leave. Red-lining of an unworn jacket with red stitching detail on the sleeve and red buttons, softest, inky dark blue needlecord. It had to be that jacket, the one as yet unpaid for, unworn and kept for the right occasion, coffin attire and red socks, soft climbing socks with horizon embroidered across the toe and red darning markers of love and care. She wonders/wanders about walking the paths of the glory wood in the glass dress spilling red ribbon and ash, an unravelling.

There were three red riding hoods in the room when it all started. The red oozed out of Tessa's button and trickled down across the floor and over to Davina in her red coat, walking through the woods to her grandmother's house. A darker red, a congealed-blood-on-the-fingertips red, poured out from Davina's hands and across the floor. Scarlet, blood, maroon, pillarbox, cadmium, cochineal, plum, cranberry, beetroot, crimson, cardinal and rose. The reds ran riot and intermingled around us. I closed my eyes and caught bright, fleshy-red splodges of yellow-tinged light against the window. When I opened them, we were sitting in a pool of red. Entangled. Contaminated. *She wonders/wanders about walking the paths of the glory wood in the glass dress spilling red ribbon and ash, an unravelling.*

"Perhaps we should be writing about red this weekend", said Jonathan. Red is already writing all over me.
Here I sit, inscribed in red.
And, "Perhaps we should be writing about red this weekend," said Jonathan. Perhaps we should.

---

[4] Kneehigh Theatre Company, http://www.kneehigh.co.uk/, described by the poet Charles Causley as the "national theatre of Cornwall".

So much of this red is about threads, ribbons, wool, string, hair, ravellings, unravellings, arteries, veins, flows, lines. I'm reminded of the 'red thread', a metaphor for a line of argument that I understood as a sort of counter logic, a way of pulling through a disparate collection of thoughts or things. Although I heard it first in Germany, it's a version of an oriental metaphor—originally a Chinese but also a Japanese/Korean figure from folktales—representing an invisible red string that the gods tie around "the ankles of those that are destined to meet each other in a certain situation or help each other in a certain way"[5]. They might be lovers but, if they are not, I wonder if they might be us.

I am increasingly interested in how objects can have agency, but since that weekend at Ammerdown, colour also seems to have this quality. Latour's 'Actor Network Theory' (ANT) provides one kind of vocabulary for speaking about the politics of the material world, considering objects/colours and humans as actants or agents (Johnson, 2008). The theory, first developed by Latour, Callon and Law, is often now referred to as "later ANT inspired analysis" (ibid., p.107) or "ANT and after" (Johnson, 2008; Law & Singleton, 2005). Most recently, Barad develops a theory of "agential realism" where "human and non-human, material and discursive, and natural and cultural factors" are indivisible, where our perceptions of identity, separateness, or distinctiveness result from the particular lines or interpretive "cuts" we make rather than any essential or inherent properties of things, including human subjects (Barad, 2007, p.26). We are entangled in the matter of the world, and it is in this entanglement, in the volatile spaces of these "intra-actions" that agency and identity emerge (Barad, 2001, 2007; Davies & Gannon, 2012).

If we turn to materiality, and consider colour as matter, and as therefore already in and of the matter of the world, then its agency is integral to its materiality. The carmine red in Turner's paintbox, which faded almost as soon as he used it, "is really made of blood" (Finlay, 2009, p.126). This is not a metaphor. Would Turner be a painter if not for the blood squeezed from the cochineal bug, after its short life gorging on prickly pear on the other side of the world? Red was treasured by the Incas, the Aztecs, the Spaniards; was used for...

"... the robes of kings and cardinals, on the lips of screen goddesses, on the camel bags of nomads and on the canvases of great artists. And if it disappeared the next day many of its users didn't care, because on the day

---

[5] Wikipedia. "Red string of fate." Available online: http://en.wikipedia.org/wiki/Red_string_of_fate (accessed on 16 November 2012).

it is fresh, carmine—cochineal or crimson; it has many names—is one of the reddest dyes that the natural world has produced." (ibid., p.126)

Turner's paintbox also contained many natural red ochres from earth, and at least twelve types of madder, a red derived from the roots of the rubia tree; red lead, a colour made from heating white lead popular with Persian miniaturists; and cinnabar or vermilion, a red made by combining mercury and burnt sulphur (or the merging of the blood of an elephant and a dragon according to Pliny) (Finlay, 2009, pp.148-49). Turner emerges as a painter in the entanglements of this matter of the earth, of imagination, of tools, of arm and eye, assembled in the social economy that recognises art in the blood of a beetle smeared on canvas.

Another language of the agency of objects is magical realism, whereby the malevolent pins and needles fly out of the sewing box and embroider all the people in the room together, weaving red threads through their eyes and feet. In the literatures of magical realities, objects, humans and the living world alike all have agencies and the borderlines between different kinds of reality are routinely blurred and crossed (Bowers, 2004). *She wonders/wanders about walking the paths of the glory wood in the glass dress spilling red ribbon and ash, an unravelling…*

A sewing box and a red button: Thinking objects through mutable mobiles and agential reality (Barad, 2007): As Johnson points out, the nature of objects is to change, they "do not necessarily remain the same as they move across contexts and through time, rather objects can be 'mutable mobiles'" (Johnson, 2008 p.106). She elaborates how objects "resist closure, oscillating between various understandings and definitions even within the same context and time" (ibid., p.106). Then there is "thing-power", in Bennett's words, signalling "the strange ability of ordinary, man-made items to exceed their status as objects and to manifest traces of independence or aliveness" (Bennett, 2010, p.xvi). The locus of agency in thing-power, she says, is always in a "human-nonhuman working group", in vitality as a "function of the tendency of matter to conglomerate or form heterogenous groupings" where agency emerges and moves through assemblage rather than separation (Bennett, 2010, p.xvii). Objects gather together with each other and with other matter and bodies that become new things together in their movements.

Thinking about the sewing boxes, the objects and artefacts inside the box will have different meanings and uses for different people. They will bring those people into new relations. While physicists, like Barad (2001, 2007) will meet the universe halfway, novelists, like Shaw (2010), will entangle us all in multiple universes of the imagination.

Every object is inherently inconsistent and subject to change. This almost sounds like the physics of magical realism. If I ran out of pins hemming a dress, I could substitute a needle and then use the same needle later to remove a splinter. What if that splinter turned to gold? She wonders/wanders about walking the paths of the glory wood in the glass dress spilling red ribbon and ash, an unravelling... Is it the same needle when I hem a dress as when I mend a curtain? Was the steel recycled in an earlier life as part of a car? The objects in my sewing boxes will have different narratives and uses depending upon who opens the box. Will a wind blowing from the west make a difference to what we find when we open the box I wonder? She wonders/wanders about walking the paths of the glory wood in the glass dress spilling red ribbon and ash, an unravelling...

In the button box in our French house in Montjaux, there is a red button similar to the one that I have at home. I identified my button as coming from Mum's original button box. Now I think about it, it used to be on a red wool coat. I forgot that the buttons came in two sizes until I opened the button box at Montjaux. There were the larger ones down the front, and a smaller version on the pockets and cuffs. Dad always liked Mum's coat. The French buttons are in an old Turkish delight box. I don't remember there being any buttons in the Montjaux sewing box last time I looked. I can see Dad picking out the red buttons and handling them, thinking about Mum's red coat and then bringing the box to France. I have been wearing the button around my neck.

According to the principles of agential realism, agency is a matter of intra-acting; it is an enactment, not something someone or something has. Agency cannot be selected as an attribute of subjects or objects (as they do not pre-exist as such). Thing-power emerges and moves through human-nonhuman assemblages (Bennett, 2010). Magical realism, however, is dependent upon a seamless shifting between different realities, whereby magical tales and actual stories inhabit the same texts, cheek by jowl (Carpentier, 1995). She wonders/wanders about walking the paths of the glory wood in the glass dress spilling red ribbon and ash, an unravelling...

I tie the button around my neck. It will be a different colour back in the box; it is bright and reflective when I wear it. Someone could sew it onto a cushion, a dress, or I could make it into a ring. Where will it go next? Is it oscillating between different understandings as I write? Or is it an actant that is intra-acting within all these ideas, with me, with future possibilities I cannot see, and more? I had thought it was a red button that used to belong to my Mum. By holding the buttons I feel very close to Mum and her red coat. The button has an impact on me, it influences me, and it creates me as part of a mother-daughter assemblage with the object.

It all started with a button. *She wonders/wanders about walking the paths of the glory wood in the glass dress spilling red ribbon and ash, an unravelling...* There was an agential realism to the amount that matter mattered and colour counted and a magical realism to the fairy tale atmosphere of our weekend together, in a country estate shaded by a tree grown from a thorn brought to Glastonbury by Joseph of Arimathea, surrounded by a glory wood, the reciprocity born of our writing into a materiality that was writing, colouring and, indeed, obsessing us.

I have been tormented by buttons
My fingers played with the ridges and holes
I longed to play with polymer clay
Forming, manipulating, creating
My own representation
Clumsy, rough things
Finger prints, imperfect, my own representation
Totems to Mum and her red coat.
She wonders/wanders about walking
the paths of the glory wood in the glass dress
spilling red ribbon and ash, an unravelling...
Stories of memories, tinged with tones of red,
A spectrum of red from pink to maroon.
These stories weave degrees of redness
on, in, around and through objects
(both inert and living) and subjects.
A coming to life, through the colour red.
A remembering of life with the colour red.
Memories in life hinged on this colour.
Reflecting boyhood around the colour of red.
She wonders/wanders about walking
the paths of the glory wood in the glass dress
spilling red ribbon and ash, an unravelling...

I roamed around my iPad searching out red. Red was under scrutiny. I started, as is often the case, in the British Library and clicked on illustrated manuscripts... Surely there would be something red? Coral, crimson, cardinal, carmine? And there, first page, from sixth century Spain, was Silos Apocalypse[6], introduced by a seven-headed bright red serpent,

---

[6] Beatus of Liebana. 776. 'Silos apocalypse.' British Library, Illustrated Manuscripts, Spain, Available online: http://www.bl.uk/learning/cult/sacredbooks/religiousbooks/christian/silasapocaly pse1/silosapocalypse.html (accessed on 16 November 2012).

accompanied by angels of death with blackened wings, all on an orange background. The fires of hell perhaps? I made my own serpent with 'brushes' on my iPad. There was no room for any angels of death... only an angel from Mars on a separate page. Red and orange. The colours of blood and fruit, the colour of fires and Mars, the colours of hell. This was colour-full research.

I have just misread our keywords: I read 'genital and magical realisms'. It was almost as if, like Cixous (Cixous & Calle-Bruber, 1997, p.67), we could hear the writing writing us…

Gathering up the three red riding hoods, the ice queen, the girl with the glass feet and the angel from Mars they wondered and wandered about, walking the paths of the glory wood that surrounded them. Although ecumenical, Ammerdown was a Roman Catholic retreat centre in origin, riven with biblical intertextualities and evoking dreams and images of saints and sacred hearts. All this talk of angels, albeit from Mars, not to mention that the walls of the workshop were by now running with the colour red, was somehow in keeping with their surroundings. Collective biography groups often come together in unfamiliar, or at least not their usual surroundings (Davies & Gannon, 2006) to meet and write and this weekend workshop, dominated as it was by red writing, had been no exception. Gradually the surroundings crept into the writing and the writing crept, like the deep red ivy on the stone walls, into the surroundings.

She wonders/wanders about walking the paths of the glory wood in the glass dress spilling red ribbon and ash, an unravelling…

Interrupting Red

In this section of our chapter we turn to our childhood memories of red and the textual interruptions that were part of our workshop processes. If a text begins as 'mine', if the memory is mine alone, how can we find the points of connection that 'matter' amongst us, between us, across us? How can we push from a sense of ourselves as discrete and wilful individuals separate from each other and the world towards entanglements of being where childhood memories might be understood as affectively potent "blocks of becoming" that open "lines of flight" and demand inventiveness, and where our writing together and into each other's texts "strives to capture a shift in thought that is happening to the writer and which the writer is inviting" (Clough, 2007, p.14). There are at least two writers for most of the texts of childhood memories of red in this section, an original author and an intervening author who worked the text in a different direction—bringing in what they know of language and childhood, importing details from their own contiguous memories to write poetry, or to write from a different point of view, or to bring the body in, or to change the voice. In this textual intervention, they might thus begin to open up the narrative of memory to more than this and more than me, and move towards a sense of self as an assemblage. Beyond any particular authors were the particular assemblage of writers, readers and listeners in a particular place and time who also shaped each text and further worked through the assembling of this chapter. The process notes that begin this section hint at the affective potency and ambivalence of our strategies of textual intervention in red:

Mike took my writing about the rosette and cut it back to form it into a poem. I enjoyed the element of not knowing: the awareness that he had spent time with my writing, giving it attention, but not knowing what he was up to over my left shoulder; before, opposite me across the room, beginning to speak. I thought about it as a kind of witnessing. Hearing 'my' story emerge in Mike's voice as something else, someone else, was both tricky and a pleasure. I didn't 'like' some of the re-framing, wanted to change it back; but have since liked the poem's new sharpness. I amended Jane's, writing more of the body and affects into it. At first I felt stuck because Jane had already brought the reader into the affects and sensations of the scene, but I found moments where I asked 'what might be happening there? What might she be looking at, noticing of Wendy or in herself?' And then it became fun, seeing the zit on Wendy's face. A part of me had the sense of being Jane at that point—Jane as adult, now, with her sense of mischief—and what she might enjoy; I thought I could hear her voice:

Wendy ran up behind her in the playground and pushed her roughly into the wall of the wooden hut. She was a big girl Wendy Mott. Huge. Bigger than the others. She felt the urge to pee. "Your Mum's a red innit?"

"Wor you mean?"

"Standin fer the council, your Mum is, she's a red, intshe?" Wendy leant her face close to hers, so close she could see her spit.

"Bloody outsiders, comin down from London, standin fer the council. My dad says she's a Jew an all, but I put him right on that I 'splained she can't be a Jew, cos you're in the Brownies…"

"My mother is standing as an independent councillor and we moved here from London when I was five", Jane explained, pulling herself up to her

full height. She came up to Wendy's chin, her eyes level with the buds of Wendy's newly erupting breasts...

"My dad's on the council, he's a Tory. Tory born and bred Sussex born and bred... never even been ta London..."

"Garn, wodja mean ee's never been ta London, it's only up the road!"

She saw that Wendy had a zit just below the corner of her mouth, about to pop. A red zit, a pox, a bloody bursting.

"Bloody long road tho innit... and what's at the end of it... bunch of Jews and reds... and all sorts; bunch of drugtaking villains that's wo my dad finks... he really knows this area my dad, knows all the people, he's a local... everybody knows im... everybody knows Mott's is the best butchers... Wots your dad do anyway? S'your dad a red 'n all?"

She could, if she'd wanted, reach up and squeeze the zit between her fingers; and felt, just then, like she could do it. Or punch her. Or grab her tits. Wendy would yelp. But she didn't. Couldn't.

"My dad, well my dad, my dad works in London, in an office, goes up every day on the train..."

"London, eh, an office in London. What's wrong with the offices in Chichester then, eh? S'he a red an' all is ee, your dad?"

Wendy's voice rose with her excitement, her voice piercing her, hurting her ears.

"Wot's wrong with local, if he likes London so much why doesn't your dad live there, along with all them other reds and Jews?... Course Jews can't be in the Brownies...think of yer Brownie promise girl... 'I promise to do my best, to do my duty to God an' the Queen, to help other people every day, especially those at home...'Jews don't believe in Jesus, or the Queen, my dad says, so Jews can't be in the Brownies... can they?"

Jane opened her mouth to argue, but no words came out, her mouth had suddenly filled up with gobules of fear and spit, one of which dribbled down her chin...

In bed
white metallic blinds
cut the posters with morning light. Navy blue lines of Cardiff City, then
Orient, Arsenal, Liverpool, Sunderland and more
cut from the magazine.

His head
tilted at the cork pin board cut through
team colours, rosettes and Paddington (he didn't tell his friends).
The rosette
red pillar box Georgie Best.

His name –
Georgie (for girls)—never a real favourite. City Blues,
now there's a thing, secretly preferring, with black and white clarity, the
sliding goal that won
the cup
from Gornik Zabre.

His hand supporting him,
he leaned and pulled the red
genius George from his drawing pin. Lying back for a moment,
Looked at handsome George for the last time and took his place in the new
day.

Reader, close your eyes. Can you smell gardenia soap on your
mother's skin, or the Maja perfume that she dabs at her wrist, in the fold of
her elbow and on your arm if you are hovering close at the right time? Can
you still see the little red and black box with the Spanish dancer on her
dressing table, by the cut glass bottles that you are sometimes allowed to
touch? Can you feel the talc drifting up your nose when you are bathed
and clean and dressed and snuggling as close as you can to her? Do you
feel her hands on your still damp hair, the brisk line the comb makes on
your scalp, her hands on your shoulders holding you back so she can see if
it is straight, and her fingers pressing down the wayward drifts ready for
the photo? Do you remember pushing your face into her neck, your little
animal snuffles as you burrow into her smell and into her skin, just above
the thick seams of her bodice? And do you remember how she pulls you
away, slightly, puts her hand on your shoulder to turn you to the front?
Probably you would press your head back into her but she would hold you
away a little, fix you in place with her right hand, ready for the photo. Do
you remember the new baby on her knee, taking most of the space? His
fingers wrap around hers, his eyes are on hers, and hers are on him. You
know he can't see her properly yet. He can't see the colour of her frock,
that it is red, a particular exact dark red, that you later learn to call
crimson. A colour that is more often for other ladies, a Spanish dancer on a
perfume box, a black-haired aunt on the other side, and for you, in the
frock that she has made for your doll from the offcuts. Close your eyes as
you press your face into the doll. Her frock feels like your mother's on

your skin. You know, don't you, that there must have been a photo with you in it too, but the one you have has just your mother and the baby. You can't see them properly now in this little black and white photograph, and her dress is grey, her dressing table a monochrome collection of shadows. But, with your eyes closed, you know that colour, that exact deep crimson of the particular shape she makes amongst the greys, and you remember its velvety feel against your cheek as you wrap your arms around her waist and press your body into hers.

Hearing Susanne read her version of my text opened up memories, history was rewritten. I was forced to expand my version. Were you there? How could you know? How could I have forgotten so much? It was like viewing what happened by gazing at it reflected in my mother's dressing table mirror. Another and parallel reality.

She strutted across the flagstone backyard to throw the scraps to the geese. "Keep back", she told him, "they could break your leg!" A little scared he sheltered in her lee as she brushed past the drying undies pegged with the gypsy-whittled wood. Nana always bought something when they came, even if she swore at them for coming alone with just the lucky heather—of course it held no luck, and she bought it nevertheless.

The red geraniums on the scullery windowsill glowed behind him when he turned to the noise of the cat spilling an outdoor plant pot. "Nana", he said, "why can't we go in the cellar?" It'd been playing on his mind for a while, with overheard strands of confusing worlds. The words were mixed like a summer pudding—the dark oozing maroon seeping tantalisingly through the white bread, all unseen until the brick weight was removed and the basin turned onto the waiting plate. And then the juices, bitter tastes of late summer berries against the chipped crockery. The words whispered of the dangerous unknown. "Hanging", "spiked", "scrubbing down", "the slab", "hooked". The bucket and the sharp-spiked brush, the sleeves rolled to the shoulders and the washing down with carbolic. The smell, never quite quelled by the pink soap. What was it all about, he wondered? How did it fit into this wonderful "Nana-world"?

She threw the bucket contents over the gate and turned on him. "Why can't we?" he asked again. "You don't want to see that", she said, "not for little ones."
"Where's the pigs?", he asked, remembering the squeals and a sneaked peak around the shed door.

He recalled the splashing sounds against the bucket—the drumming on enamel. "Black pudding", she said.

And then he remembered how mum had told him how she'd hid in the cellar when the planes had come up the valley shooting their guns, and Beryl had been hit, the red blood seeping through her white blouse.

We were provoked into a space of writing otherwise and beyond the thresholds of ourselves and of the present moment, into a productive liminality, "a fractal chaos, a storehouse of possibilities" where "new forms and structures" might emerge (Turner, 1986, p.39).

A large home exhibition, they stand agitated and fidgeting, trying too nonchalantly not to be caught into the game of ultimate class and power, hierarchy and celebrity beyond measure. They are primed, told how to behave, what to say. Will anyone transgress, speak before being spoken to or make an utterance that is unexpected, unplanned? Bodyguards, black-suited men ripple outwards. She doesn't want to be affected, wants not to care if he speaks to her or not, wants it not to matter but in knowing how much she wants it not to matter she knows that it does; that centuries of serfdom and fiefdom cannot be ignored, rewritten in this moment—even by an artist.

Filled with a crowd. Big bodies and voices crammed into narrow alleys and stands. She feels herself slipping, growing translucent, transparent, wraith-like, slipping between the bodies, slipping into the bodies, inhabiting the voices.

Unnoticed amidst the adults' pursuits, unnoticed the subtle changes occurring between conversations and pauses. Bodies suddenly pressing against another or letting a touch linger or tracing a finger down the curve of a spine, the arc of a well-developed calf muscle; looks of shock, amusement, anger, disgust.

She honed in to a model of a house, encased in a glass box. The miniature doors, synthetic trees, draw her in, enraptured by this protected world. She melts through the glass into the house, running between the rooms, up and down the stairs and constantly finding new rooms and doors, staircases that change, configurations that shift and it is huge and endless and a joy getting lost.

Her glance moves sideways to the tallest wall amongst the ivy, an out of proportion ladybird has been planted in the décor. It stretches, flexing its wings and then whirring them so they sound like the sound of 'r's rolling in the mouth, the sound of Rumpelstiltskin's spinning wheel as he worked all night spinning flax into gold—endless tasks of impossibility; a rhythmic whirring. This eccentric detail calls to her, reminding her of cold nights tucked up in woollen blankets having stories rewoven, re-enlivened with sounds and colour and red. The red dressing gown with a hood hanging on the back of the bedroom door—"hush, hush whisper who dares, Christopher Robin is saying his prayers…"

Seeing and hearing the unexpected insect brings out the strangest desire in her; the only childlike thing in a grown up place. Through her, back through layers of time and place, skittering through her mind threads and threads—some loose, some joined, some tangled and knotted. First she barely allows herself the fantasy; to have it and hold it clasped in her hand—this skein of wool, thread, flax, gold, blood, guts, smooth, rough, fibrous, sleek, "to say it is mine, it is me".

She was a bright girl. The stories swirled around the playground, dancing and playing as they escaped from her lips. They ebbed and flowed, pop stars tangled in the skeins, threads tied themselves around the audience, plucking at their heart strings. The words swelled and absorbed energy and time sometimes exploding, a Norse God helped them on their way.

The energy for stories changed and developed over time, hidden between paper sheets and mathematical formulae. It seeped and crept into tubes of paint, washed in thin layers across the paper.
It clung to brushes, a painting kit. It escaped swirling round the girl, as she played with new art equipment and paper.

One of its favourite places was the art department in Sissons and Parker. It danced up the wooden staircase, cast shadows on the slabs of colour, roaring with laughter at the sheer size and volume of the materials available to play with.

The girl seemed to become blind; she ignored the call of the colours. Her mother's power overwhelmed the need of the stories, which became drained as the girl recited the names of different white paints in her mind.

The mother's energy grappled with its own stories of red, fallen women, red shoes, ankle bracelets, danger. The girl inhibited by fear that emanated from her mother chose blue, it calmed and soothed and restrained the energy, which might overwhelm her if given loose rein.

Finally the energy broke through, the stories swirled and danced again, vivacious and energetic. They represented the girl's life force, Estée Lauder red lipstick became her new badge of choice.

Conclusions

What are we doing here? We have created a voluptuousness of writing as our inquiry into red. Between us, scouring our memories, we have written ourselves into a saturation of red buttons, ribbons, dresses, politics, footballers and lipsticks, layered with photographs and other images of angels, trees, leaves, buildings and statues, in what Geertz (1973) might call a thickening of our description, or, dare we say, a "reddening" of our description. This work represents what Springgay and her colleagues (2005) in their advocacy for a/r/tography as method would call a "reverberation and excess" of obsessive red writings and image making. There is congruence of method with our madness. Like Deleuze (1995, p.14) we have a fascination with the ways that writing (and other expressive art forms, like image-making) "flies off in all directions and at the same time closes right up on itself like an egg". Like Pink (2009, 2011) we crave academic language that speaks in both discursive and visual forms and acknowledges the space, and lack of translation, between modalities. Like Roswell (2011), we are interested in the sensory loadings of objects and of matter and how these provoke new relations with ourselves and with each other. We are interested in the agency of objects and of art, in "thinglyness" and in creative (and political) processes of writing and of making (Kollectiv & Kollectiv, 2010).

We set down layer after layer of our work: writings engorged by our memories of red, photographs and other visual images suffused in different red shades, layering them all into each other.

This "doubling" of words and art "resists transparent rereadings and rewritings of experience, preferring complexities and the process of appreciating complex meaning making" (Springgay et al., 2005, p.900); in qualitative research, it generates new methodologies that acknowledge processes as well as products of research. But our text is not merely a doubling of text and word, combining or trebling as it also does all manner of material things, and then there is the matter of red that came to infuse our inquiry. Perhaps like Hoffman's ice queen we are "just more sensitive to colour than most people" (2006, p.210). And, through this process, perhaps each of us can now say that, "in our house every room is red, each a different shade: ruby, scarlet, cherry. Some people think it's all the same, but the tones couldn't be more different, so much so as black from white" (ibid., pp.210-11).

Indeed, when we began to paint together in reds, the tone(s) of our voices were radically different, despite painting into and out of each other's drawing spaces, just as we had intervened in each other's red writings. Unexpected figures emerged, like the woman who wonders and wanders about walking the paths of the glory wood in the glass dress spilling red ribbon and ash, an unravelling... We followed her red ribbons of glory and of ash through the forests of Ammerdown in autumn, through our imaginations and memories inside that room in the country estate, and afterwards, when we too had dispersed—or perhaps fallen away like the autumn leaves—to our own home places.

This chapter embodies more than an arts-informed method of research, whilst equally it is not art-as-research: it is more research text as artefact. It encompasses a/r/t/ography's "loss, shift and rupture" (Springgay et al. 2005, p.898) as criteria and all of the difference that practice-based work makes to this text, the difference made in the doing: that is to say, the making as well as the writing of our work (Barratt & Bolt, 2009). Yet our work is not just about methodology, but also about epistemologies and ontologies. In working our layers of red writing and image-making, we have accumulated a body of knowledge: a way of seeing red. This text embodies obsessive, excessive and passionate ways of knowing and understanding alongside congruent methods of researching our world(s). Both a poetics and physics of agency have been brought to bear here, sharing, as they do, a life at the borders of current post-colonial literary (Bennett, 2010), post-structural and scientific theory (Barad, 2001, 2007), where matter matters and human and non-human agencies co-exist in both the same, and multiple realities. Barad (2007) warns against an uncritical transfer of theories across disciplines, but we are not advocating an undisciplined purloining of theoretical positions, or suggesting quantum physics and magic as analogies or mirrors of each other; rather we are offering layered literary (arts-informed, aesthetic) and physical (environment-based, scientific) realisms as converging refractions of the new material turn.

We conclude with two final texts, our final textual disruptions of our red method. One is a poem, one a narrative; one is an embrace of red, the other, an apparent refusal. This rhythm too, was part of the affective labour entailed in our collaborative work together:

Seeing red, she came up the ramp on Sunday morning
after her good night's sleep
and there it was, unfurled boldly across the room...

The long red banner
emblazoned with icons in red and gold and sticky-lipped kisses,
dripping with stick-ons and stand-ups, some
hanging off and others loitering at the joins,

She had slept through the silence whilst
in the chamber beneath her the world had caught fire.

There were flying red pigs or were they cows and crocodiles, Lacoste
perhaps? And pages torn from ancient books,
Of spells and kells, with hanging Babylonian pages, falling at angles off
the edges,
And all manner of texts within texts without texts...
When all of life's a text, and all the texts are red,
what's next?

They sat opposite each other; the kitchen was suffused with warmth and light from the stove. There was a bottle of wine on the table between them. They shared a mood of shadow and latent intensity.

"I don't do red."

The stark finality of that assertive, performative utterance; disclosing an obtuseness, a finality that didn't seem to sit with how she understood his normally generous, compliant and fluent way with the world.

"Red is so crude, so obvious, I can't live with its pervasiveness and the way in which it infects the world with its dominant and dominating aspirations."

She was taken aback by his directness; to assert such a strong denial and rejection of what she felt was the obvious warmth and geniality of that colour simply seemed to heighten this suddenly apparent and revealed contrariness, his stubborn refusal to accept and his increasingly frequent inclinations to thinly veiled anger and a growing tendency to awkwardness.

They sat silent for long minutes. He seemed glazed and uncommunicative. She found herself basking in barely dreamed landscapes of warmth, in which the indistinctness of objects were further blurred by their glowing auras of red.

"Red; it's so fuckin' atonal."

She reeled with shock at his directness as he spat his words across the table and was surprised by the venomous passion with which he blurted them out.

They continued sitting, obliquely facing each other: their quietness returned.

The bottle of red wine that sat between them on the worn wood of the kitchen table seemed to become more inviting to her. Her feeling of dis-ease, which seemed to grow, prompted, at least in part, by the fierceness of his outbursts, seemed to make her thirsty. Without looking at him, she leaned across the space between them; she sensed an electricity in her arm, cutting through the shimmering intensity of the force field humming between them; feeling suddenly energised she re-filled their glasses and eased back in her chair and looked across at him.

"I hate the imperialism of red and I hate the discursive force of the way in which it colonises senses of colour, reducing, blunting and actually dis-colouring through the very processes which lead to its existence."

EPILOGUE

CHAPTER TWENTY-FOUR

WHAT NEXT FOR COLLABORATIVE WRITING?

DAVINA KIRKPATRICK, SUE PORTER, ARTEMI SAKELLARIADIS, JANE SPEEDY, JONATHAN WYATT AND TESSA WYATT

This being the epilogue, and us being determined to show our workings out alongside our answers, we wrote it first before the prologues to each section or the introduction on our weekend's writing retreat for collating this book. "What next?", was the question we asked ourselves (although Artemi changed the question to 'Whatever Next?', the title of a children's book about mother bear snoring so that father bear, who couldn't sleep, was forced to go out of the bear's house for a middle of the night wander about.) Quite what Artemi was doing wandering about intertextually (Allen, p.2000) in amongst the children's books in the back archives of her mind's eyes we don't know, although we were all ready to keep our narrative inquiry space as wide open as possible, and include all the simultaneities of slippages, leakages and sediments of books, stories, life and writing events, images, ghosts and dreams that were accumulating rapidly in our writing retreat space.

One of our practices of beginning in collaborative writing groups (that we failed to put in the beginnings section of this book) is our shared practice of social dreaming, borrowed from the Bion groups held at the Tavistock Institute (see Lawrence, 1998, 2003): sharing and looking for mutualities and interdependencies, amongst the dreams we have on our writing retreats together. We often end the days we spend together by deciding and agreeing what to dream about that night ('what next?' was our agreed dreamscape last night) and we then begin our days by remembering and re-telling the stories of our dreams. This sense of psychical dreamscape and inner-world collaboration is surely one of the greatest challenges that our practices can put to established concepts of individualised, boundaried, selves and subjectivities?

Sue dreamt last night in the present tense:

"I found myself in an office, maybe in a local authority planning department? I was trying to influence a bureaucrat, and to find evidence to influence him/an outcome.

At first I was on my own, arguing my corner, searching through papers, citing case law, taking a position (or two).
Then I found another woman who was doing the same thing, and I could add her researches to mine, my voice to hers, we could join forces. Not that we just had one aim/or campaign, but that we could have a sense of common cause together.
I felt less alone, less stressed, less frightened, much heartened."

The dream had several cycles (like the cycles of action research and other collaborative processes).

That night, after she got home, Jane dreamt (in the past tense) that one of us had died. Remembering the funeral, she realised it had been held at Ammerdown in the little chapel beside the new labyrinth. Davina (an artist whose PhD explored rituals of death, dying and mourning) had designed all our costumes for the funeral, which she'd had made out of purple parachute silk. There had been a procession through the meadows full of bee orchids with us all following the coffin in our flowing purple robes. But who was in the coffin? This was definitely the funeral of one of us, yet we were all there in the procession behind the coffin. Perhaps we would decide when we got to the chapel?

We are weaving together the layers of this epilogue the day after we sat together in the same room constructing them: spatial/geographical proximity being one of the contingent, intimate elements in our way of collaboratively collating/editing this book together. We are sitting in Ammerdown. Ammerdown exists in both our physical and virtual realities simultaneously. Ammerdown is a newly-formed Dropbox folder that Jane has just made, with chairs of various kinds and a flecked browny carpet and a load of electronic gadgets and six bodies, all of which are now inside a rectangular golden electronic folder thing.

We're immersing ourselves in a book, with chapters and parts and titles and thousands of words, which I don't feel I know yet. Though what does it mean to know? We're feeling our way in together, fingers on keys, after talking about it for 20 minutes. It feels—I (Jonathan) feel—a responsibility, being in this folder within a folder of a book, surrounded by other folders of others' work, waiting to know how and what to write in order to stitch some together and then it all.

Maybe not stitch it together; maybe it's waving at each text, or flying between them with thread; or word baristas sprinkling chocolate powder on some and cinnamon on others.

Conclusion as Launch-pad.
Exploring the ending.
Welcoming another beginning.
Imagining a prospect.
Explosion of modalities.
Words, images, sounds.
New lines of flight.
Richer collective encounters.
Expanding loving communities.
Inquiring, probing, exploring.
Remaining forever curious.
Selves and stories.
Embodied and imagined.
Examined, explored, shared.
Walking unchartered territory.
Seeking alternative pathways.
Exploring novel routes.
Diving in possibility.
Engaging raw energy.
Riding innovative breezes.
Floating, flying, soaring.
Naked explorations.
Enthralling, beguiling experiences.
Original, unpredictable outcomes.
More loving communities.
Celebrating shared humanity.

Rituals of starting… rituals of ending. How one begins or if one begins at all…Putting the places in pieces or the pieces in place in order to inhale, dive in, begin.

Drawing my way in, making marks, making decisions, responding to what comes or what my hands and eyes and the materials to hand create together.

Marks resonating echoes of spoken metaphors of working together collaboratively writing—fabric and cloth, stitching and weaving—and then the texts that are already formed, waiting like un-tasted puddings to be savoured and tasted, sucked from the spoon or hurriedly swallowed so the feeling of overfull-ness can inhabit this body.

Now I've lost the plot, don't know what the rule is… what are we writing, for what purpose, for what ending? Maybe there isn't an ending, maybe just a circular process of beginning again a bit like singing a round that goes on for ever, or the end of 'Hey Jude'; interminable choruses of "la, la la la la la, la la la, hey Jude…" (Lennon & McCartney, 1968) Does everything "lead back to this: the fires/and the black river of loss whose other side/is forgetting". (Oliver, 1983) Sensitivity monitor attuned to loss and grief and death as ever…

So what are we doing… take it back to the spontaneous marks on card with red ink and black ink, graphite and collage… mud flats, tree stumps, reflections in water and crosshatched pattern of net or cage or space between.

For all our writing, there is so much more to knowing and expressing that we can collaborate in and through.

This book is primarily about collaboration through the medium of writing, but also beyond it, as is evident from the 'Red' writing paper. For why restrict ourselves to writing? Or possibly the question is, "What is it that so often restricts us to writing?"

The academy values writing above other presentational forms, regardless of the type of knowledge we are attempting to explore and impart. Even arts scholars are expected to write about images, to en-word that which is better presented through a different sort of line expressed through other parts of the brain and body.

As I struggle now to write about my making-self, I'm reminded of how easy it is for me to slip from a grounded 'This next' feeling through making. How my hands-led, embodied practices of assembling and my eyes-led image making and image taking can feel unserious, frivolous, unworthy of a place in 'serious' company. I notice a shyness about sharing, not the objects, the films, the images, but the knowing that the making takes me to.

So this is by way of a plea, to myself as much as anyone, to remember the value of the multi-layered, interwoven inquiry. The one that might start from reading and thinking, develop through walking and sensing and re-membering in place, and emerge into an accessible narrative through mapping and making. To be written or sung or hung on a wall, shared through a blog, revealed in a podcast, worn on a body, on its way to shared meaning making, the next stage of collaboration.

All narratives carry spectral traces of their own futures, just as this book carries us forward into a hypermodal collaborative future wherein the future stories we live by, embedded as they are in the texts of our pasts and presents, bring hauntings and fragments of the texts to come.

Davina has brought a bottle of black Indian ink: indelible, thick, black Indian ink... It is as if she knows about my recent love affair with this ink in Esme's art class... I have been obsessed with it for the last three weeks. The other students are coy with it: gentle watered down washes with soft squirrel brushes, but I am boldly going with it where no woman has gone before, (except Elizabeth Frink that is: see Frink & Lucie-Smith, 1993): thick black inkscapes, undercut with wax resist and chalky white paper... intense black patinaed black surfaces...

We go out into the courtyard and my handmaidens: Davina, Tessa and Artemi fix me up with black ink in a plastic mug, balanced precariously in a round-bottomed watering can. I sit and, armed with a thick twig, a toothbrush and a green wax crayon, make marks on leftover 'redwriting' paper. Bold marks and brush strokes and shooting dribbles of splashy ink: layer on layer of green resisting black, all schmoozing into white...

What next? This is what's next for me alright, bold marks and splashes... and then it begins to rain... and I call for Artemi, who replies "that's tough Jane..." and I begin to cry before I can see that she is only joking and is coming, followed by Tessa, to help me bring things in...

I wipe my nose on Chris's old black shirt (he is dead so he will not mind. I do not think he would have minded anyway, alive or dead.) And now I am back inside, surrounded by the other five, writing and making, in the beige room with the Flotex carpet: I have a strong urge to pee on this carpet... which is after all, what Flotex is for...

Layers of ink, wax crayon, writing and images, still and moving: collaborative texts, spliced with music and installation; texts you can climb inside like the sculptures in Barbara Hepworth's garden (www.tate.org.uk/stives/hepworth/): texts to wrap around you and take on a journey; texts that slide between object and subject between people and things. Hybrid texts that are neither one thing or the other: that are neither chairs nor legs but, rather, wheels at the ends of bionic bodies that move us around. I am waiting until they make fleshy wheels that they weld on to hips... and now that Daleks can go upstairs, I believe we are almost there...

Jane's writing on "ethical know-how" (Chapter 6), in part two of this book, ends in many ways with how we would like the whole book to end: she says,

"This book [Gale et al., 2012] is about collaborative writing, and yet all writing is collaborative, insofar as all writing is an embodied and imagined accumulation of selves and stories. All writing, to quote Gale & Wyatt (2009) is about love. All explicitly collaborative writing is about bringing what Weems (2005) describes as the imagination-intellect into play and extending the social imaginary of the academy; collaborative writing is about engaging with the highly subversive activity, much neglected amongst scholars, of building loving communities within and across groups of writers, across disciplines and themes and across continents. To write collaboratively is to engage with reconsiderations of scholarship and of what it means to be a human being living amongst other human beings and other species and elements on this planet." (p.52-3)

But how would you like this book to end? What's next?

Whatever it is that is next for you, our collaborative readers and co-inquirers. It is up to you to take, amend and extend these practices now.

REFERENCES

Acker, S., Hill, T., Black, E. (1994). Thesis supervision in the social sciences: managed or negotiated? *Higher Education*, 28, 483-498

Almond, R. (1974). *The healing community: Dynamics of therapeutic milieu.* New York: Jason Aronson.

Althusser, L. (1990). *For Marx.* London: Verso.

Anderson, R. (2001). Embodied writing and reflections on embodiment. *Journal of Transpersonal Psychology*, 33 (2), 83-98

Augé, M. (1995). *Non-places: Introduction to an anthropology of supermodernity.* (Transl. J. Howe). London: Verso.

Bachelard, G. (1964). *The poetics of space.* New York, Beacon Books.

Badiou, A. (2007). *Being and event.* London: Continuum.

Baldwin, E., Longhurst, B., McCracken, S., Ogborn, M., & Smith, G. (2004). *Introducing cultural studies.* Essex: Pearson Education Ltd.

Barker, C., & Galasinski, D. (2001). *Cultural studies and discourse analysis – a dialogue on language and identity.* London: Sage.

Barnes, J. (2011). *The sense of an ending.* Croydon: Vintage.

Barad, K. (2001). Re(con)figuring space, time and matter. In M. DeKoven (Ed.). *Feminist locations: global and local, theory and practice*, pp. 75–109. New Brunswick: Rutgers University Press

—. (2007). *Meeting the universe halfway: Quantum physics and the entanglement of matter and meaning.* Durham, N.C.:Duke University Press.

Barratt, E. & Bolt, B. (Eds.). (2009). *Practice as research: Approaches to creative arts enquiry.* London: Tauris.

Bateson, G. (1979). *Mind and nature: A necessary unity (Advances in systems theory, complexity, and the human sciences).* New York: Hampton Press.

Baumlin, J., Jensen, G., & Massey, L. (1999). Ethos, ethical argument, and ad hominem in contemporary theory. In F. G. Gale, J. L. Kinneavy, & P. Sipiora (Eds.). *Ethical issues in college writing*, pp. 183-219. New York: Peter Lang.

Belenky, M.F., Clinchy B., Goldberger N. & J.M. Tarule (1997). *Women's ways of knowing: The development of self, voice and mind.* New York: Basic Books.

Bennett, J. (2010). *Vibrant matter: A political ecology of things*. Durham: Duke University Press.

Berman, J. (2001). *Risky writing: Self disclosure and self transformation in the classroom*. Amherst: University of Massachusetts Press.

Bhaskar, R. (1975). *A realist theory of science*. Leeds: Leeds Books.

Bhaskar, R. (Ed.) (1991). *A meeting of minds —Socialists discuss philosophy—towards a new symposium?* London: The Socialist Society.

Bond, T. (2004). Ethical guidelines for researching counselling and psychotherapy. *Counselling and Psychotherapy Research*, 4(2), 10-19.

—. (2007). Ethics and psychotherapy: An issue of trust. In R. Ashcroft, A. Dawson, & H. Draper (Eds.). *Principles of health care ethics*. (2nd Edition) pp. 435-442. Chichester: John Wiley & Sons.

Bowers, M. (2004). *Magical realism: The new critical idiom*. London: Routledge.

Bowles, P. (2006). *The sheltering sky*. (Original publication 1949.) London: Penguin.

Bristol Collaborative Writing Group. (2010). Encountering "Gerald": Experiments with meandering methodologies and experiences beyond our "selves" in a collaborative writing group. *Qualitative Inquiry*, 16(10), 894-901.

—. (2012). After writes: Some loosely threaded together writing about ending/not ending our time together in a collaborative writing group. *International Review of Qualitative Research*, 5(4), 427-447.

Brann, E. (1991). *The world of the imagination: Sum and substance*. Savage, Md.: Rowman and Littlefield.

Bruner, E. (1986). Ethnography as narrative. In V. Turner and E. Bruner (Eds) *The anthropology of experience*. Chicago: University of Illinois Press.

Buber, M. (1970). *I and thou*. (Trans.W. Kaufmann). Original publication 1937. New York: Charles Scribners Sons.

Butler, J. (1990). *Gender trouble: Feminism and the subversion of identity*. London: Routledge.

—. (2005). *Giving an account of oneself.* New York: Fordham University Press.

Byrne, D. (1998). *Complexity theory and the social sciences*. London: Routledge.

Carey, M., Walther, S. & Russell, S. (2009). The absent but implicit: A map to support therapeutic enquiry. *Family Process*, 48 (3), 319 – 331.

Carpentier, A. (1995). On the marvellous real in America. In W. Faris & L.P. Zamora (Eds.). *Magical realism, theory, history, community,* pp.75-88. Durham: Duke University Press.

Cavarero, A. (2000). *Relating narratives: Storytelling and selfhood.* Abingdon: Routledge.

Chesnais, J. (1981). *Histoire de la violence.* Paris: Robert Laffont.

Cixous, H. (1986). *The newly born woman* (B. Wing, Trans.). Minneapolis: University of Minnesota Press.

—. (1991). Coming to writing. In D. Jenson (Ed.), *Coming to writing and other essays.* Cambridge, MS: Harvard University Press.

Cixous, H., & Calle-Gruber, M. (1997). *Rootprints: memory and lifewriting.* London: Routledge, 1997.

Clandinin, J., Huber, J., Huber, M., Murphy, S., Orr, A., Pearce, M. & Steeves, P. (2007). *Composing diverse identities: Narrative inquiries into the interwoven lives of children and teachers.* Abingdon: Routledge.

Clough, P.T. (2007). Introduction. In. P.T. Clough with J. Halley (Eds.). *The affective turn: Theorizing the social,* pp.1–33. Durham: Duke University Press, 2007.

Crawford, J., Kippax, S., Onyx, J., Gault, U., & Benton, P. (1992). *Emotion and gender – constructing meaning from memory.* London: Sage.

Csikszentmihalyi, M. (1992). *Flow: the psychology of happiness.* New York: Harper and Row.

Davies, B. (2000). *(In)scribing body/landscape relations.* Walnut Creek, Oxford, Lanham: AltaMira Press.

—. (2010). *The problem of agency.* Guest lecture within the University of Bristol's research theme ' Identities', March 23rd.

Davies, B. & Gannon, S. (2006). *Doing collective biography.* Maidenhead: Open University Press

Davies, B. & Gannon, S. (2012). Collective biography and the entangled enlivening of being. *International Review of Qualitative Research* 5(5), 357–76.

De Botton, A. (2003). *The art of travel.* London, Penguin.

De Hamel, C. (1992). *A history of illuminated manuscripts.* London: British Museum Press.

Deleuze, G. (1990). *The logic of sense.* (M. Lester, Trans.). New York: Columbia University Press.

—. (1995). *Negotiations, 1972–1990.* New York: Columbia University Press.

—. (2004). *Difference and repetition*. (P. Patton, Trans.). London: Continuum.

Deleuze, G. & Guattari, F. (1988) *A thousand plateaus: capitalism and schizophrenia*. (B. Massumi, Trans.). London: Athlone

Deleuze, G. & Parnet, C. (2002). *Dialogues II*. (H. Tomlinson and Barbara Habberjam, Trans.) London: Continuum.

Denzin, N. K., & Lincoln, Y. S. (2000). The policies and practices of interpretation. In N. K. Denzin & Y. S. Lincoln (Eds.). *Handbook of qualitative research (2nd ed.)*, pp. 897-992. Thousand Oaks, CA: Sage.

Derrida, J. (1992). *Acts of literature.* London: Routledge.

—. (1994). *Specters of Marx*. New York: Routledge.

—. (2003). *The work of mourning*. Chicago: University of Chicago Press.

Didion, J. (2006). *The year of magical thinking*. New York: Harper Perennial.

Diversi, M. & Moreira, C. (2009). *Betweener talk: Decolonizing knowledge production, pedagogy and praxis*. Left Coast Press.

Eliot, T. S. (2009). *The waste land*. London: Faber and Faber.

Ellis, C. (1999). Heartful autoethnography. *Qualitative Health Research*, 9(5), 669-683.

Epston, D. (1994). Extending the conversation. *Family Therapy Networker.* 18(6), 31-37.

Estes, C.P. (1993). *The gift of story*. New York: Rider.

Etherington, K. (2004). *Becoming a reflexive researcher: Using our selves in research.* London: Jessica Kingsley Publishers.

Etkind, M. (1997). *... or not to be: A collection of suicide notes.* London: G. P. Putnam's Sons.

Etzioni, A. (1992). *The spirit of community: The reinvention of American society*. New York: Touchstone.

Finlay, V. (2009). *Colour: Travels through the paintbox*. London: The Folio Society.

Forman, M. B. (Ed.). (1952). *The letters of Keats*. London: Oxford University Press.

Foucault, M. (1977). *Language, counter-memory, practice*. Ithaca, New York: Cornell University Press.

—. (1986). *Of other spaces.* Diacritics, 16(1), 22-27.

Fox, H. (2003). *A review of therapeutic documents*. http://www.narrativepractice.com/Articles.htm#therapeutic%20docum ents. Retrieved from the world wide web on 18 October 2013.

Fox, N. (2003). Is dementia hereditary? In N. Fox, *Living with dementia*, (accessed June, 2010) http://alzheimers.org.uk/site/scripts/documents

Freeman, M. (1998). Mythical time, historical time, and the narrative fabric of the self. *Narrative Inquiry*, 8, 27-50.

—. (2006). Autobiographical understanding and narrative inquiry. In Clandinin, J. (Ed.). *Narrative Inquiry: mapping a methodology.* Thousand Oaks: Sage.

Frink, E. & Lucie-smith , E. (1994). *Frink: a portrait.* London: Bloomsbury

Fryer, D.R. (2004). *The intervention of the other: Ethical subjectivity in Levinas and Lacan.* New York: Other Press.

Gale K. (2009). Cyberculture and poststructural approaches. S. Wheeler S (Ed.). *Connected minds, emerging cultures: Cybercultures in online learning,* pp.159-167. Charlotte N.C: Information Age Publishing.

Gale, K. & Pineau, E. (2012). Flows, tides and transatlantic drifts: an emergent methodology of collaborative performative writing, *International Review of Qualitative Research*, 4(4), 317-335.

Gale. K. & Wyatt J. (2007). Writing the incalculable: a second interactive inquiry. *Qualitative Inquiry*, 13(6), 787-808.

Gale, K. & Wyatt, J. (2008). Two men talking: A nomadic inquiry into collaborative writing. *International Review of Qualitative Research*, 1(3), 361-380.

Gale, K. & Wyatt, J. (2009). *Between the two: a nomadic inquiry into the collaborative writing and subjectivity.* Newcastle-upon-Tyne, Cambridge Scholars.

Gale, K., Pelias, R., Russell, L., Spry, T. & Wyatt, J. (2012). *How writing touches: An intimate scholarly collaboration.* Newcastle-upon-Tyne: Cambridge Scholars.

Gale, K., Speedy, J. & Wyatt, J. (2010) Gatecrashing the oasis? A joint doctoral dissertation play. *Qualitative Inquiry*, 16(1), 21-28.

Gannon, S. (2001). (Re)presenting the collective girl: A poetic approach to a methodological dilemma. *Qualitative Inquiry*, 7(6), 787-800.

—. (2004). Crossing 'boundaries' with the collective girl: a poetic intervention into sex education. *Sex Education*, 4(1), 81-99.

Gannon, S., Walsh, S., Byers, M. & Rajiva, M. (2012). Deterritorializing collective biography. *International Journal of Qualitative Studies in Education,* online first, doi:10.1080/09518398.2012.737044.

Gardner, H. (1983). *Frames of mind: The theory of multiple intelligences.* New York: Basic Books.

Geertz, C. (1973). *The interpretation of cultures.* New York: Basic Books.

Geller, S. (2012). Therapeutic presence as a foundation for relational depth. In R. Knox et al. (Eds.). *Relational depth: new perspectives and developments.* Houndmills: Palgrave Macmillan.

Gendlin, E.T. (1997). *Experiencing and the creation of meaning.* Evanston, IL: Northwestern University Press.

Gilbert, M. (1989). *On social facts.* London: Routledge.

—. (2000). *Sociality and responsibility: New essays in plural subject theory.* New York: Rowman and Littlefield Publishers.

Gone, J. P., Miller, P. J., & Rappaport, J. (1999). Conceptual self as normatively oriented: The suitability of past personal narrative for the study of cultural identity. *Culture & Psychology*, 5(4), 371-398.

Gregson, N. & Rose, G. (2000). Taking Butler elsewhere: Performativities, spatialities and subjectivities. *Society and Space*, 18, 433-452.

Gustafson, P. (2001). Meanings of place: Everyday experience and theoretical conceptualizations. *Journal of Environmental Psychology*, 21, March, 5-16.

Guttorm, H. E., Hilton, K., Jonsdottir, G.U., Löytönen, T., McKenzie, L., Gale, K., & Wyatt, J. (2012). Encountering Deleuze: Collaborative writing and the politics of stuttering in emergent language. *International Review of Qualitative Research*, 5(4), 377-398.

Halberstam, Judith (1998). *Female masculinity. Durham and London:* Duke University Press.

Hall, S. (1990). Cultural identity and diaspora. In J. Rutherford (Ed.). *Identity: Community, culture, difference.* London: Lawrence & Wishart

Haller, A. (2003). Art of the demolition derby: Gender, space and antiproduction. *Society and Space*, 21,761-780.

Hannerz, U. (1973). The second language: An anthropological view. *TESOL Quarterly*, 7(3), 235-248.

Haraway, D. (1988). Situated knowledges: The science question in feminism and the privilege of partial perspective. *Feminist Studies* 14(3) 575-99.

Haug, F. (1987). *Female sexualisation: A collective work of memory.* (Transl. E. Carter.). London: Verso.

Hawton, K. & van Heeringen, K. (2002). (Eds.) *The international handbook of suicide and attempted suicide.* New York: Wiley.

Heckman, D. (2002) "Gotta catch 'em all": Capitalism, the war machine, and the Pokémon trainer. *Rhizomes*, 5, Fall, Retrieved from http://www.rhizomes.net/issue5/poke/glossary.html on 21 October 2013.

Hedtke, L. & Winslade, J. (2004). *Re-membering lives: Conversations with the dying and the bereaved.* Baywood Publishing: New York

Hertz, R. (Ed.). (1997). *Reflexivity & voice.* London: Sage.

Hewitt, J.P. (2000). *Self and society: A symbolic interactionist social psychology.* (8th Edition). Needham Heights, MA: Allyn & Backon.

Hoffman, A. (2006). *The ice queen.* London: Vintage.

hooks, b., (1999). *Remembered rapture: The writer at work.* New York: Henry Holt Ltd.

—. (2000). *Feminism is for everybody: Passionate politics.* New York: South End Press.

—. (2009). *Belonging: a culture of place.* New York: Routledge.

Hsiung, G. & Sadovnik, J. (2007). Genetics and dementia: Risk factors, diagnosis, and management. *Alzeimers and Dementia,* 3(4), 418-427.

Ingold, T. (2007). *Being alive: essays on movement, knowledge and description.* Abingdon: Routledge.

—. (2008). Bindings against boundaries: entanglements of life in an open world. *Environment and Planning,* 40(8), 1796–1810.

Jackson, A., & Mazzei, L. (2008). Experience and "I" in autoethnography: A deconstruction. *International Review of Qualitative Research,* 1(3), 299-318.

Jackson, A. & Mazzei, L. (Eds.) (2009). *Voice in qualitative research.* Abingdon: Routledge.

Jackson, C. & Tinkler, P. (2000). The PhD examination: an exercise in community building and gatekeeping? In I. McNay. (Ed.). *Higher education and its communities.* Buckingham: Society for Research into Higher Education and Open University Press.

James, H. (1888). *The art of fiction in partial portraits.* New York: MacMillan.

Jamie, K. (2012). *The overhaul.* London: Picador Poetry.

Jenkins, R. (1996). *Social identity.* London: Routledge.

Johnson, E. (2008). Simulating medical patients and practices: Bodies and the construction of valid medical simulators. *Body & Society,* 14(3), 105–28.

Jones, O. & Cloke, C. (2002). *Tree cultures: The place of trees and trees in their place.* Oxford: Berg.

Katovich, M.A. & Wieting, S.G. (2000). Evil as indexical: The implicit objective status of guns and illegal drugs. *Symbolic Interaction,* 23(2), 161-182.

Kiely, R. (Ed.). (2006). *Language, culture and identity in applied linguistics.* Selected papers from the Annual Meeting of the British Association for Applied Linguistics. London: British Association for Applied Linguistics.

King, N (2000). *Memory, narrative, identity: Remembering the self.* Edinburgh: Edinburgh University Press.

Kingsolver, B. (2009). *The lacuna*. London: Faber and Faber.

Klein, M. (1984). Notes on some schizoid mechanisms. In R. Money-Kyrle, B. Joseph, E. O'Shaughnessy and H. Segal (Eds.). *The writings of Melanie Klein.Vol III.* (Original work published 1946.) London: The Hogarth Press.

Kollectiv, P. & Kollectiv, G. (2010). *Can objects perform? Agency and thingliness in contemporary sculpture and installation.* Sculpture and Performance Conference, Henry Moore Institute and TATE Liverpool, Liverpool, UK, March.

Kristeva, Julia (1984). *Powers of horror: An essay on abjection*. New York: Columbia University Press.

Lahman, M., Geist, M., Rodriguez, K., Graglia, P., Richard, V. & Schendel, R. (2010). Poking around poetically; research; poetry and trustworthiness. *Qualitative Inquiry*, 16(1), 39-48.

Laqueur, Thomas (1992). *Making sex: Body and gender from the Greeks to Freud.* Cambridge, Mass: Harvard University Press.

Lather, P. (2000). Against empathy, voice and authenticity, in: Jackson, A and Mazzei, L. (Eds.) (2009).*Voice in qualitative research.* Abingdon: Routledge.

—. (2007). *Getting lost: Feminist efforts towards a double(d) science.* Albany: State University of New York.

Law, J. & Singleton, V. (2005). Object lessons. *Organization*, 12(3), 331–55.

Le Blanc, G. (2003). *Grieving the unexpected*. BelleVille, Ontario: Essence Publishing.

Leach. H (2004). Crossing the line: stories on mapping the maze. *Times Higher Education Supplement,* (Nov 5th 2004, pp. 18-19).

Lee, K. V. (2005). Neuroticism: end of a doctoral dissertation. *Qualitative Inquiry.* 11(6), 933-938.

Leenaars, A. (1988). *Suicide notes.* New York: Human Sciences Press.

Lefebvre, H. (1991). *A critique of everyday life*. London: Verso.

Lehrer, J. (2012). *Imagine: how creativity works*. New York: Canongate Books.

Leslie, A.M. (1987). Pretense and representation: The origins of "Theory of Mind". *Psychological Review*, 94 (4), 412-426.

Lester, D. (2004). *Katie's diary: Unlocking the mystery of a suicide*. New York: Brunner-Routledge.

Levitas, R. (2007). Looking for the blue: the necessity of utopia. *Journal of Political Ideologies,* 12(3) 289-306.

Levin, D.M., Ed. (1997). *Language beyond postmodernism: Saying and thinking in Gendlin's philosophy.* Evanston, IL: Northwestern University Press.

Levitin, D. J. (2006). *This is your brain on music.* New York: Dutton.

Linnell, S., Bansel, P., Ellwood, C., & Gannon, S. (2008). Precarious listening. *Qualitative Inquiry,* 14(2), 285-306.

Lukacs, C. & Seiden, H. (2007). *Silent grief: Living in the wake of suicide.* London: Jessica Kingsley.

Luzio-Lockett, A. (1998). The squeezing effect: the cross-cultural experience of international students. *British Journal of Guidance & Counselling,* 26(2), 209-223.

MacCurdy, M. (2000). From trauma to writing'. In C. Anderson & M. MacCurdy, (Eds.) *Writing and healing: Toward an informed practice,* pp.158 - 200. Urbana, Ill: National Council of Teachers of English.

MacLure, M (2008) Broken Voices, dirty words: on the productive insufficiency of voice. In A. Jackson & L. Mazzei (Eds.). *Voice in qualitative research,* pp. 97-103. Abingdon: Routledge.

Macy, J. & Brown, M.Y.(1998). *Coming back to life: Practices to reconnect our lives, our world.* Gabriola Island, B.C.: New Society Publishers.

Mair, M. (2012). Enchanting psychology: the poetry of personal inquiry. *Journal of Constructivist Psychology,* 25(3), pp.184-209.

Marshall, J., & Reason, P. (2007). Quality in research as "taking an attitude of inquiry". *Management Research News,* 30(5), 368-380.

Martin, V., Bridges, N., Brown, L., Williams, S., Wilson, S., Speedy, J., & Sakellariadis, A. (2011). Remembering and forgetting with Sue: some stories of hanging on in there. *Emotion, Space and Society,* 4, 121-125.

Massey, D. (2000). *For space.* London: Sage.

—. (2006) Landscape as a provocation: Reflections on moving mountains. *Journal of Material Culture,* 11(1-2), 33-48.

Mazzei L.A. (2007). *Inhabited silence in qualitative research: Putting poststructural theory to work.* New York: Peter Lang.

Mazzei L.A. & Jackson A. (Eds.) (2009). *Voice in qualitative inquiry: Challenging conventional, interpretive, and critical conceptions in qualitative research.* London: Routledge.

Mearns, D. & Cooper, M. (2005). *Working at relational depth in counselling and psychotherapy.* London: Sage.

Merton,T. (1977). *The collected poems of Thomas Merton.* (Original publication 1946). New York: New Directions Paperback.

Mills, J. (2001). Being bilingual: Perspectives of third generation Asian children on language, culture and identity. *International Journal of Bilingual Education and Bilingualism,* 4(6), 383-402.

Morley, L., Leonard, D. and Miriam, D. (2002). Variations in vivas: quality and equality in British PhD assessments. *Studies in Higher Education,* 27(3), 263-273.

Moroni, A., Boienti, C., D'Arrigo, L., & Forresti, G. (2000). Getting out of the institutional maze: Transformation of a psychiatric ward into a therapeutic community. *Therapeutic Communities,* 21(3), 185-196.

Morrison, T. (2005). *Beloved.* (Original publication 1987). London: Vintage.

Myerhoff, B. (1980). *Number our days.* New York: Simon and Schuster.

—. (1982). 'Life history among the elderly: Performance, visibility and re-membering'. In J. Ruby (Ed.). *A crack in the mirror: reflexive perspectives in anthropology.* Philadelphia: University of Pennsylvania Press.

—. (1986). Life not death in Venice. In V. W. Turner and E. M. Bruner (Eds.). *The anthropology of experience.* Chicago: University of Chicago Press.

Nancy, J-L. (2007). *Listening.* (Trans. C. Mandell). New York: Fordham University Press.

Norton, B. (1997). Language, identity and the ownership of English. *TESOL Quarterly,* 31(3), 409-429.

—. (2000). *Identity and language learning: Gender, ethnicity and educational change.* Essex: Pearson Education Ltd.

Norton, W. (2009). *Everyday sociology blog*: http://nortonbooks.typepad.com/everydaysociology. Accessed April 15th, 2010.

Oliver, M. (1983). *American primitive.* New York: Black Bay Books.

O'Mathúna, D.P. (2006). Human dignity in the Nazi era: Implications for contemporary bioethics. *BMC Medical Ethics,* 7(2).

Onyx, J. & Small J. (2001). Memory work: the method. *Qualitative Inquiry,* 7(6), 733-786.

Palmer, S. (2008). *Suicide: Strategies and interventions for reduction and prevention.* London: Routledge.

Park, J (2005). *Writing at the edge: narrative and writing process theory.* New York: Peter Lang.

Park-Fuller, L. (2000). Performing absence: The staged personal narrative as testimony. *Text and Performance Quarterly,* 20, 20-24.

Pease, B. (2000a). Beyond the father wound: Memory-work and the deconstruction of the father-son relationship. *Australian and New Zealand Journal of Family Therapy.* 21(1) 9-15.

—. (2000b). Reconstructing heterosexual subjectivities and practices with white, middle-class men. *Race, Gender and Class.* 7(1), 133-145.

Pelias, R. (2004). *A methodology of the heart: evoking academic and daily life.* Walnut Creek: Alta Mira Press.

—. (2007). *Performative writing workshop.* Third International Congress of Qualitative Inquiry, Urbana-Champaign, May 2007.

Pettit, P. & Schweikard, D. (2006). Joint actions and group agents. *Philosophy of the Social Sciences,* 36(1), 18-39.

Pink, S. (2009). *Doing sensory ethnography.* London: Sage.

—. (2011). Multimodality, multisensoriality and ethnographic knowing: social semiotics and the phenomenology of perception. *Qualitative Research* 11(3), 261–76.

Pitt, A. & Britzman, D. (2003). Speculations on qualities of difficult knowledge in teaching and learning: an experiment in psychoanalytic research. *International Journal of Qualitative Studies in Education.* 16 (6) 755-76.

Pollner, M. & Stein, J. (1996). Narrative mapping of social worlds: The voice of experience in Alcoholics Anonymous. *Symbolic Interaction,* 19(3), 203-223.

Pryke, M., Rose, G. & Whatmore, S. (Eds.). (2003). *Using social theory: Thinking through research.* London: Sage/Open University Press.

Pullman, P. (2003). *Lyra's Oxford.* Oxford: Knopf.

Rambo Ronai, C. (2005). Multiple reflections of child sex abuse: Argument for a layered account. *Journal of Contemporary Ethnography.* 34(5), 560-585.

—. (1998). Sketching with Derrida: An ethnography of a researcher/erotic dancer. *Qualitative Inquiry,* 4(3), 405-420.

—. (1999). The next night sous rature: Wrestling With Derrida's mimesis. *Qualitative Inquiry,* 5(1), 114-129.

Reed, M. & Speedy, J. (2011). Scrapbooks and messy texts: Notes towards sustaining critical and artful narrative inquiry. In S. Trahar (Ed.). *Learning and teaching narrative inquiry: Travelling in the borderlands.* Amsterdam: John Benjamins.

Reinharz, S. (1997). Who am I? The need for a variety of selves in the field. In R. Hertz (Ed.). *Reflexivity & voice.* London: Sage.

Reyes, A., & Lo, A. (Eds.). (2009). *Beyond yellow English :toward a linguistic anthropology of Asian Pacific America.* Oxford: Oxford University Press.

Richardson, L. (1997). *Fields of play: Constructing an academic life.* New Brunswick: Rutgers University Press.

—. (2000) Writing: A method of inquiry. In N.K. Denzin & Y.S. Lincoln (Eds.). *Sage handbook of qualitative research.* (2nd ed.). Thousand Oaks, CA: Sage.

—. (2001). Getting personal: Writing-stories. *International Journal of Qualitative Studies in Education,* 14(1), 33-38.

Richardson, L. & St. Pierre, E. (2005). Writing: A method of inquiry. In N.K. Denzin & Y.S. Lincoln (Eds.). *Sage handbook of qualitative research,* pp.959-978. Thousand Oaks, CA: Sage.

Ricoeur, P. (2004). *Memory, history, forgetting.* Chicago: University of Chicago Press.

Riley, P. (2007). *Language, culture and identity: an ethnolinguistic perspective.* London: Continuum.

Rilke, R. M. (2004). *Letters to a young poet.* (Trans. M. D. H. Norton.). London: Norton.

Rippin, A. (2006). Refusing the therapeutic: Marion Milner and me. *Culture and Organisation,* 12(1), 25-36.

Rippin, A. & Porter, S. (2010). *Nomads, twitters, uncertain negotiations and women in love: Explorations in collaborative, performative writing from the University of Bristol.* Paper presented at the Sixth International Congress of Qualitative Inquiry, Urbana-Champaign, USA, May 2010.

Roberts, M. (1995). *All the selves I was.* Virago: London.

Rogers, A. G., Casey, M. E., Ekert, J., Holland, J., Nakkula, V. and Sheinberg, N. (1999). An interpretive poetics of languages of the unsayable. In R. Josseloson & A. Lieblich (Eds.). *Making meaning of narratives: The narrative study of lives, Vol. 6,* pp. 77-106. London: Sage.

Rosen, H. (1998). *Speaking from memory: The study of autobiographical discourse.* Stoke on Trent: Trentham Books.

Rossol, J. (2001). The medicalisation of deviance as an interactive achievement: The construction of compulsive gambling. *Symbolic Interaction,* 24(3), 315-341.

Roswell, J. (2011). Carrying my family with me: artifacts as emic perspectives. *Qualitative Research,* 11(3), 331–46.

Sacks, O. (1995). An anthropologist on Mars. London: Picador.

—. (2007). Musicophilia. London: Picador.

Sakellariadis, A., Chromy, S., Martin, V., Speedy, J., Trahar, S., Williams, S., & Wilson, S. (2008). Friend and foe? Technology in a collaborative writing group. Qualitative Inquiry, 14(7), 1205 -1222.

de Saint-Exupery, A. (1995). The little prince. New York: Wordsworth.

Salih, S. (2002). Judith Butler. London: Routledge.

Sarbin, T. R. (2005). If these walls could talk: places as stages for human drama. Journal of Constructivist Psychology, 18, 203-214.

Sarup, M. (1996). Identity, culture and the postmodern world. Edinburgh: Edinburgh University Press.

Sayer, A. (2000), Realism and social science. London: Sage Publications.

Scharmer, C.O., Arthur, W.B., Day, J., Jaworksi, J., Jung, M., Nonaka, I., Senger, P.M. (2001). Illuminating the blind spot: leadership in the context of emerging worlds. Retrieved 26th March 2006 from http://www.dialogonleadership.org/indexPaper.html.

Sealey, A. (2004). Applied linguistics as social science. London: Continuum.

Seeba, H. C. (1996). Cultural versus linguistic competence? Bilingualism, language in exile, and the future of German Studies. The German Quarterly, 69(4), 401-413.

Sedgwick, E. (1997). Novel -gazing: Queer readings in fiction. Durham NC: Duke University Press

Shange, N. (1975). For colored girls who have considered suicide when the rainbow is enuf, New York: Scribner. Zetterberg, H. L. (2006). The grammar of social science. Acta Sociologica, 49(3), 245-256.

Shaw, A. (2010). The girl with the glass feet. New York: Henry Holt.

Sheringham, M. (1993). French autobiography: Rousseau to Perec. Oxford: Oxford University Press.

Shildrick, M. (1997). Leaky bodies and boundaries: feminism, postmodernism and (bio)ethics. London: Routledge.

Smith, S. (1975). Selected poems. Harmondsworth: Penguin.

Smith, J.M., Light, A. & Roberts, D. (1998). Philosophies and geographies of place. In A. Light & J.M. Smith (Eds). Philosophies of place. pp. 1-20. Lanham, Maryland: Rowman & Littlefield.

Storr, A. (1992). Music and the mind. New York: Free Press.

Speedy, J. (2001). Unpublished personal e-mail communication.

—. (2004). Living a more peopled life: Definitional ceremony as inquiry into psychotherapy 'outcomes'. International Journal of Narrative Therapy and Community Work, 3, 43-54.

—. (2005). Collective biography practices: Collective writing with the unassuming geeks group. British Journal of Psychotherapy Integration, 2 (2), 29-38.

—. (2008). Narrative inquiry and psychotherapy. Hound Mills: Palgrave.

—. (2010). Continuing to become a collaborative writer.

www.writeinquiry.org. Retrieved from the World Wide Web, 24 October, 2013.

Speedy, J., Bainton, D., Bridges, N., Brown, T., Brown, L., Martin, V., Sakellariadis, A., Williams, S., & Wilson, S. (2010). Encountering "Gerald": Experiments with meandering methodologies and experiences beyond our "selves" in a collaborative writing group.' *Qualitative Inquiry*, 16(10), 894-901.

Speedy, J., Margie, Fay, Jack, Pauline & Jones, J. (2005). Failing to come to terms with things: A multi-storied conversation about poststructuralist ideas and narrative practices in response to some of life's failures. *Counselling and Psychotherapy Research*, 5(1), 65-74.

Speedy, J. & Worth, L. (2007, June). *Lateral responses: physical performance and dramatic text: performative responses to collective biography with the unassuming geeks.* Paper presented at Arts-based Educational Research Conference, University of Bristol.

Springgay, S., Irwin, R.L., & Kind, S.W. (2005). A/r/tography as living inquiry through art and text. *Qualitative Inquiry,* 11(6), 897–912.

Spry, T. (2001). Performing autoethnography: An embodied methodological praxis. *Qualitative Inquiry*, 7(6), 706-732.

St. Pierre, E. (1997). Methodology in the fold and the irruption of transgressive data. *International Journal of Qualitative Studies in Education.* 10(2), 175-189.

Stacey, R.D. (2002). *Complexity and group processes: A radically social understanding of individuals.* Hove, Sussex: Brunner-Routledge.

Sternheimer, K. (2010). *Everyday sociology reader.* New York: Norton.

Stewart, I. (2007). *Transactional Analysis counselling in action.* (3rd edition.) Thousand Oaks: Sage.

Stewart K. (2008). Weak theory in an unfinished world. *Journal Of Folklore Research*, 45(1), 71–82.

Stiegler, B. (2004). *Culture and technology.* Lecture delivered at Tate Modern Gallery, London. 13 May 2004.

Stuart, M. (1998). Writing, the self and the social process. In C. Hunt & F. Sampson (Eds.). *The self on the page: Theory and practice of creative writing in personal development.* London, Philadelphia: Jessica Kingsley.

Till, K. E. (2010). *Mapping spectral spaces.* In Mapping Spectral Traces. Symposium guide. http://eprints.nuim.ie/2733/ Retrieved from the world-wide web on 18 October 2013.

Tillman-Healey, L. M. (2003). Friendship as method. *Qualitative Inquiry*, 9(5), 729-749.

Tschacher, W. & Bergomi, C., Eds. (2011). *The implications of embodiment: Cognition and communication.* Exeter: Imprint Academic.

Turner, V. (1986). Dewey, Dilthey and drama: An essay in the anthropology of experience. In V.W. Turner & E. Bruner (Eds.). *The anthropology of experience*, pp.33–44. Chicago: University of Illinois Press

Varela, F. J. (1999). *Ethical know-how: Action, wisdom, and cognition.* Stanford University Press.

Voight, A. & Drury, N. (1997). *Wisdom from the earth.* Cammeray, Australia: Simon and Schuster.

Wackermann, J. (2011). In quest of human nature: Rediscovery of the body. In W. Tschacher & C. Bergomi (Eds.). *The implications of embodiment: Cognition and communication*, pp. 3-30. Exeter: Imprint Academic.

Weems, M. (2005) *Public education and the imagination-intellect: I speak from the wound in my mouth.* Farmington Mills: Thomson- Gale.

Wertheimer, A. (2001). *A special scar: The experiences of people bereaved by suicide.* London: Routledge.

Wheeler B., Metcalfe C., Martin R.M. & Gunnell, D. (2009). International impacts of regulatory action to limit antidepressant prescribing on rates of suicide in young people. *Pharmacoepidemiology and Drug Safety.* DOI: 10.1002/pds.1753. Retrieved from the world wide web on 18 October 2013.

White, M. (1995). *Re-authoring lives.* Adelaide SA : Dulwich Centre Publications.

—. (2000). *Reflections on narrative practice: Essays and interviews.* Adelaide, SA: Dulwich Centre Publications.

—. (2005). *Michael White: Workshop notes.* Retrieved from: www.dulwichcentre.com.au/michael-white-workshop-notes.pdf. Retrieved from the world wide web on 20 October 2013.

White, M. & Epston, D. (1990) *Narrative means to therapeutic ends.* New York: Norton.

World Health Organisation. (WHO). (2009). Suicide prevention statistics worldwide. Retrieved from: http://www.who.int/mental_health/prevention/suicide/suicideprevent/en/.

Wilson, E.A. (2004). Psychosomatic: Feminism and the neurological body. Durham, NC: Duke University Press.

Winterson, J. (2004). Lighthouse keeping. London: Fourth Estate.

Wood, W., Quinn, J. & Kashy, D. (2002). Habits in everyday life: Thought, emotion, and action. Journal of Personality and Social Psychology, 83(6),1281–1297.

Wordsworth, W. (2006). *Ode: Intimations of immortality from recollections of early childhood.* (Original publication 1884). Whitefish, MT: Kessinger.

Worth, L. & Royal Holloway College Postgraduate Physical Theatre Group. (2008). *A gaze that scours the landscape.* Invited performance for International Student Festival of Theatre in English. Debrecen: Hungary.

Wright Mills, C. (1959). *The sociological imagination.* Oxford: Oxford University Press.

Wyatt, J., Gale, K., Gannon, S. & Davies, B. (2010). Deleuzian thought and collaborative writing: A play in four acts. *Qualitative Inquiry,* 16(9), 730-741.

Wyatt J., Gale, K., Gannon, S., & Davies B. (2011). *Deleuze and collaborative writing: Writing on an immanent plane of composition.* New York: Peter Lang.

Zander, B. & Zander, R. (2000). *The art of possibility: Transforming professional and personal life.* Boston: Harvard Business School Press.

INDEX